D0191226

PUCCINI'S *TURANDOT*

PRINCETON STUDIES IN OPERA

Puccini's Turandot: *The End of the Great Tradition*
by William Ashbrook and Harold Powers (1991)

*Unsung Voices: Opera and Musical Narration in the
Nineteenth Century* by Carolyn Abbate (1991)

PUCCINI'S
TURANDOT

❖

THE END OF THE
GREAT
TRADITON

❖

WILLIAM ASHBROOK
AND
HAROLD POWERS

PRINCETON UNIVERSITY PRESS

PRINCETON, NEW JERSEY

Library of Congress Cataloging-in-Publication Data

Ashbrook, William, 1922–
Puccini's Turandot : the end of the great tradition / William Ashbrook
and Harold Powers.
p. cm. — (Princeton series in opera)
Includes bibliographical references and index.
ISBN 0-691-09137-4 (cloth : acid-free paper)
ISBN 0-691-02712-9 (paper : acid-free paper)
1. Puccini, Giacomo, 1858–1924. Turandot.   I. Powers, Harold.
II. Title.
ML410.P89A7   1991
782.1—dc20   90-8890

This book has been composed in Linotron Galliard

For our children
Cornelia Powers *and*
William Ashbrook III

CONTENTS

---------------- ❧ ----------------

PREFACE

❧

THE AUTHORS of this book were seduced early in life by the "Great Tradition" of Italian opera in the form it took in William Weaver's *Golden Century . . . from Rossini to Puccini*. For both of us the first encounter with Puccini's unfinished *Turandot* was the magnificent Cetra/Parlophone recording of 1937/38, with Gina Cigna, Francesco Merli, and Magda Olivero. In our writings and scholarship since World War II, Ashbrook has remained remarkably faithful to his first love, but Powers has returned to it only recently, after straying into strange paths. The occasion for our collaboration in a book on *Turandot* has given us both an opportunity to probe into our own hitherto unanalyzed special love for the work, and our feeling that it is more than merely a significant historical symbol, an epitaph for an artistic epoch. For each of us it is a beautiful, imaginative, powerful work of art as well, and we attempt here to find those things in the work and its life that make us feel that, and try to call attention to them in a way that makes our sense of the work plausible. We have done so first for the work as a whole, summarizing its culture-historical context in the Introduction and the work itself in outline, and its principal problems and symbols, in Chapter I. In Chapters IV and V much of the music of *Turandot* is discussed, taking off from two particularly significant aspects, Puccini's use of tonal coloration and his treatment of the two major dialogues for the Prince and Princess. But a work of musical art also exists in its prehistory and its posthistory: in the generic expectations, musical and dramatic suppositions, and creative ideas that gradually took firm shape in a blueprint for production, that is, the score; and in the continuance and the reception of the work, that is, in the congeries of representations and critical interpretations that followed the completion of the blueprint. The prehistory of Puccini's *Turandot* is discussed in Chapter II, a brief summarizing of its predecessors and its sources, and especially in Chapter III, in which its transformation over a four-year period from an exotic suggestion into "the last grand opera" is described with some care. Its posthistory from the first representation to the present is sampled in Chapter VI. And discussions of any one of these three phases of the work's life—its background and creation, its design and dynamic, its representations and reception—necessarily often look forward or backward in anticipation or recollection of aspects of the other two.

The book is collaborative in that each of us has contributed to every phase of the whole, has read, reread and edited every sentence, but the primary responsibilities of writing and research have been weighted according to our particular interests and experience. Chapter VI is largely Ashbrook's work, Chapters IV and V Powers's; Chapter II was drafted by Ashbrook, and the Introduction was written by Powers; Chapters I and III are fully collaborative.

Of our colleagues and friends we would particularly like to thank Roger Parker, who brought us together on this project; Kii-Ming Lo, who kept us regularly informed of the progress of her own researches on *Turandot*, above all for her provision of a copy of the original long Act I libretto—a crucial element in our analysis—in advance of its appearance in her 1988 Heidelberg dissertation; Jürgen Maehder, to whom we are indebted for his work on the Alfano endings; Michele Girardi, whose recent work on Puccini in general and *Turandot* in particular resonates so concordantly with our efforts here; Francesco Degrada for a copy of Forzano's *disposizione scenica*; and Bruno Zanolini for a copy of Gazzoletti's *Turanda* libretto. Special thanks are due to William Weaver for tracking down the Fassini music box and for playing his taped recording of some of its contents over the air; that tape has clarified several misconceptions about Puccini's sources for Chinese melodies. And very special thanks are owing to Casa Ricordi, for almost two centuries chief promoter and custodian of the Great Tradition: to Mimma Guastoni for authorizing our use of materials belonging to Casa Ricordi, including the measures from Puccini's autograph transcribed as Example 35, Puccini's sketch partially transcribed as Example 43, and the passages from Forzano's typescript *disposizione scenica* translated in Chapter VI; and as always, to Carlo Clausetti, archivist, adviser and friend to all scholars working on the Great Tradition in its Golden Century.

PUCCINI'S *TURANDOT*

THE CONTEXTS

ON THE FINAL page of William Weaver's *The Golden Century of Italian Opera*—actually a decade or so more than a century—appear the following words:

> as he reached the conclusion of Liù's death scene, Toscanini laid down his baton and said, in effect (he has been quoted variously): "The opera ends here, because at this point the Maestro died. Death was stronger than art."

The opera ends here. Toscanini might have been speaking not just of Puccini's last work but of Italian opera in general. Of course, other new Italian operas were composed and performed in the decades that followed, and some of them enjoyed a certain success, a certain theatrical life. But Puccini left no Crown Prince. With him, the glorious line, Rossini, Bellini, Donizetti, Verdi, came to a glorious conclusion.[1]

Weaver's "Golden Century" is of course only the last of several centuries of Italian opera, the culminating phase of a continuous Great Tradition that began in mid-seventeenth century. So if indeed it is "Italian opera in general" that "ends here," Puccini's *Turandot* holds a remarkable position in the history of artistic genres. It is not often that one can put so definite a *finis* to so long-standing a cultural manifestation, saying that with one last Work and the death of its Creator all was effectively over. In this spirit, at the end of Chapter V we asked ourselves rhetorically what might have happened to the Great Tradition if Puccini had lived to be eighty-eight, as did Verdi, instead of dying at sixty-six: "Where would our sense of the Great Tradition stand now? or would all have gone just as (perhaps inevitably) it has?" And at the end of our last chapter we answered the question, again rhetorically, beginning "it is aesthetically and culture-historically inconceivable that genuinely new works still mining that vein can be created." As Toscanini may or may not have said, "Death was stronger than art," or as Weaver put it, "Puccini left no Crown Prince," any more than did Richard Strauss: not among his once successful contemporaries who survived him through the fascist era, notably Mascagni and Giordano; not among the contemporaries of Berg, the so-called generation of the eighties, neither such as Zandonai who accepted the Puccinian stylistic nor such as Pizzetti who rejected it; and certainly not among the generations that followed, such as Hindemith's near contemporary Dallapiccola with his *Volo di notte* (1940) and *Il prigoniero* (1949/50), or Henze's and Reimann's contemporary Sylvano Bussotti with his *Lorenzaccio* (1972).

But in fact, neither Art nor the Great Tradition died. Rather, the public for "Art" and the public for "the Great Tradition" continued the divergence already well begun in Puccini's lifetime. Dallapiccola and Bussotti have continued the tradition of Art; the Great Tradition, including the operas of Puccini, has gone on in two other ways. The first and more obvious we mention in the continuation of our conclusion to Chapter VI, pointing out that

> if the operas in the Great Tradition are in one sense museum pieces, nonetheless they cannot be hung on walls; like other manifestations of the temporal arts, they must be produced. . . . Italian opera in the Great Tradition lives on in production—and in the affections of the opera-going public the tradition shows no signs of coming to an end.

Nor do we regard the expression "museum pieces" as derogatory: if Madonnas and altarpieces can survive out of cultural and historical context in a museum—if they can "live" for us even though they are no longer "living" in their original places for their original purpose—why not operas?

But if the Great Tradition has survived in that sense, with the great opera houses of the world as its museums, and with its notes and words (if not its production directions) reverently preserved, its latter-day socio-cultural role was absorbed by another medium. As Rubens Tedeschi has pointed out, it was no coincidence that the last decades of grasping after vital new work in the Great Tradition coincided with the first decades of the movies.

> While waiting for the film properly speaking . . . there existed already a horde of spectators looking for the same sensations and celebrities as the *melodramma*: the thrill of the future *Great Train Robbery*, the wonders of the yet to be born *Last Days of Pompeii*, the pathos of *Broken Blossom*. Before the spread of the film, the genres were ready—adventurous, spectacular, pathetic—and the recipes to cook them were in place, the principle—the doling out of effects—as well as the choice of plots. The *melodramma*, in short, opened the way for the film, which was to become, in the twenties and afterwards, the *melodramma* for everybody, reduced to its most elemental form and industrialized according to the rules of commerce and the needs of a society with universal suffrage.[2]

And as we have noted in Chapter VI, both the handling of crowds and the acting style called for in the typescript production book (*disposizione scenica*) for the *prima assoluta* of *Turandot* in April 1926 clearly reflect the experience of its stage director, Giovacchino Forzano, as a director of silent films.

Puccini's heirs, then, were D. L. Griffiths and Cecil B. De Mille—or in our day, Dino De Laurentiis and Franco Zeffirelli. Perhaps the emergence of Zeffirelli—like Forzano, director of films and director of operas, but also director of operas as films—may even be taken as symptomatic of a final convergence of these two modes of survival for the Great Tradition of Italian opera. From an *Aida* with Sophia Loren on the screen and Renata Tebaldi on the sound track, through Zeffirelli's own travesties of *La traviata* and *Otello* with the actual singers on screen, we may have reached an ultimate stage where videofilm and videodisc—such as the videotape of the Arena di Verona *Turandot* from 1983 to which we have referred in our book—freeze Great Productions that were first staged, as scores preserve words and notes, and recordings the interpretations of singers and conductors. At any rate, it is no longer of "Verdi's *La traviata*" that most of us talk as of this writing—his is taken for granted—or even of "Toscanini's *La traviata*": it is of Zeffirelli's.

Thus the Great Tradition of Italian opera has been preserved in its original medium as a museological phenomenon, or as a supplier of vehicles for régisseurs; if its ethos and pathos persisted into new works, those works were in a different medium. But if this is how the Great Tradition has ended up, when and how did it begin? Weaver's text starts with a discussion of Rossini's *Il barbiere di Siviglia* (Rome, 1816), which is the oldest opera of the Golden Century to have survived continuously, though as Weaver has noted, Rossini's first opera to go on to international success was *Tancredi* (Venice, 1813); in the light of the revival of Rossini's serious operas in the late twentieth century, as well as for the appeal of an alliteration, perhaps the Golden Century should run "from *Tancredi* to *Turandot*." But while it is true that, from the perspective of the Golden Century, "at the very beginning of the nineteenth century, Italian opera was in a period of decline" so that "Rossini exploded on the scene" (Weaver, pp. 8–9), the apparently fuelless vacuum from which Rossini appears to have exploded is historiographic, not historical. Little enough is known of Italian opera and opera in Italy during the Revolutionary and Napoleonic period, but it was from those operas, in that region, and at that time that the Rossinian explosion was lit. The Great Tradition certainly seems to have been renovated by Rossini, but he did not invent it.

Received music-historical doctrine attributes the invention of opera to theater and theory in Florence around 1600, or perhaps to such monuments as Monteverdi's preserved early and late ventures into musical theater, *Orfeo* in 1607, or *L'incoronazione di Poppaea* in 1642. To our way of thinking, however, these works—along with Renaissance court entertain-

5

ments, madrigal comedies, and the activities of traveling troupes—are fore-runners of the Great Tradition, not part of its essential continuity. The Great Tradition as we know it began only in the third quarter of the seventeenth century, when patterns of production, in both the public and the musical senses, assumed their familiar forms. This is the period, as Lorenzo Bianconi and Thomas Walker have demonstrated, in which

> travelling companies with their own (or hired) extremely minimal or-chestral apparatus declined and were replaced by great travelling so-loists (usually in the pay of a ruler, or at least formally under his pro-tection); at the same time regularly operating theatres (with more or less stable orchestras) became established throughout Italy.[3]

That has a familiar ring. It is that period, moreover, in which "the dramatic structure of the action is itself standardized to a considerable degree," and it is the period of "the establishment of the concerted aria (c. 1675) [as] the minimum significant entity . . . on which the attention and interest of the spectator/listener are focused."[4] That too sounds familiar. Or as Powers had put it some years earlier—in an essay showing the convergence, during this period, of various heterogeneous practices into the da capo aria prin-ciple—the musico-dramatic basis of the Great Tradition originated

> in the development of a specific technique for making traditional gen-res of theatrical music more integrally a part of the dramatic structure . . . [or] in a more familiar way . . . in the development of a specific technique for forcing the drama itself to provide occasion for formal music.[5]

Two Golden Centuries later—one Metastasian, one Verdian—came the beginning of the end, and Puccini's *Turandot* represents a retrogressive last flowering of an underlying musico-dramatic technique that was established not in Rossini's but in Cavalli's time. The most striking feature in the grad-ual shaping of *Turandot* from 1920 to 1924 was its gradual reversion to-wards this technique. After his experiment in *La fanciulla del West* with a whole evening of almost exclusively Pizzettian declamation against a col-orful instrumental background, after his attempt to strike into a more pop-ular vein with *La rondine*, after his retreat to pure vignettes with *Il tabarro*, *Suor Angelica* and *Gianni Schicchi*, Puccini began working back to the es-sence of the Great Tradition as he had known it towards the end of its heyday; that was the Italian Romantic *melodramma* in the slightly over-blown Frenchified form it took in *Aida* and *La gioconda*. Our Chapter III is an outline of how *Turandot* evolved retroactively into a fitting Finale for the Great Tradition, into a number opera in the grand manner of *Semira-*

mide and *Aida*, as though Puccini and his librettists had been step by step "forcing the drama itself to provide occasion for formal music."

This was only a momentary regression, however, in a process that had been developing steadily in Italian opera since the unification of the country in the 1860s, since the somewhat selfconscious entry of Italian intellectuals into the mainstream of later nineteenth-century European cultural developments; a process in which the littérateurs were winning the final battles in the age-old war of music and drama, succeeding at last in their struggles to convert opera from music engendered in drama to drama accompanied by music. Rubens Tedeschi characterized the new focus of post-Verdian Italian opera in his usual pungent way, drawing attention again to the concomitant socio-cultural anticipation of an immanent new medium.

> The only novelty, if one can so put it, was in the shift of the center of gravity of opera. In nineteenth-century *melodramma* it was for the music to provide the tragic events. The deepening of character, and then with Verdi, of emotional and political problematic, was achieved through the enrichment of musical events. It was for melody, timbre, harmony to give a tragic sense to the banal verses with which King Philip laments the inconsolable loneliness of the powerful ("Ella giammai m'amò / No, quel cor chiuso è a me / amor per me non ha!").
> From *Andrea Chénier* onward, the functions are reversed: the plot comes to the fore; the "story-telling" [*romanzesco*] seizes the attention, while the music declines to a subsidiary task, that of reinforcing the rhetorical act with rhetorical vocalism. . . . Comparison with the immanent stylistics of commercial cinema, which provoke tears and laughter using devices whose efficacy is proportional to their elementarity, proves once again opportune.[6]

The extreme cases of this reversal of roles in the opera house are what has been called *Literaturoper*, in which a stage play, rather than being transformed into a libretto (as had been the case with Verdi's and Puccini's operas), was set to music more or less as it stood, as in Debussy's setting of Maeterlinck's symbolist *Pelléas et Mélisande* or Strauss's setting of Oscar Wilde's "Decadent" *Salome* (somewhat abbreviated from Lachmann's German translation of Wilde's French original). Wagner's shift from rhymed verse in his earlier works culminating in *Lohengrin* to the non-metric quasi-prose Stabreim of *Das Rheingold*, or Mussorgsky's experiments with the musical declamation of actual prose in his setting of Gogol's *Svad'ba* that led to the prose portions of *Boris Godunov*, are forerunners of the move towards literary "Realism" and eventually *Literaturoper* in the opera house.

The first Italian manifestation of *Literaturoper* was Mascagni's *Guglielmo*

Ratcliff (1889–1895), a setting of Andrea Maffei's translation of Heine's early dramatic poem; better known are Montemezzi's setting of Sem Benelli's *L'amore dei tre re*, or Zandonai's setting of D'Annunzio's *Francesca da Rimini*.[7] All three of these plays are in verse, to be sure, but it is the verse of the spoken theater, the enjambed and unrhymed *endecasillabi sciolti* that are the Italian equivalent both metrically and functionally of Elizabethan blank verse. Heretofore in Italian opera this meter, in combination with unrhymed and enjambed *settenari sciolti*, had been used only for recitative, while the poetry for more musical moments had been cast in end-stopped and rhymed *versi lirici*. The libretto poetry for opera in the Great Tradition comprised "polymetric" mixtures of recitative verse and many kinds of lyric verse, culminating in Arrigo Boito's beautifully crafted polymetric poems for Verdi's *Otello* and *Falstaff*. Puccini himself always insisted on polymetric verse libretti, though in many instances once he got what he wanted he chopped and altered lines out of all metric recognition, to suit preconceived musical passages.[8]

In our discussions of Liù's Act III arias "Tanto amore segreto" and "Tu che di gel sei cinta" in Chapter IV we have called attention to Puccini's request for particular kinds of verse for music already composed, music that on the face of it would not seem to call for the kind of verse requested, and in the case of "Tanto amore segreto" we have proposed an ad hoc interpretation of the apparent anomaly. In Chapter V we have offered a similarly ad hoc interpretation of a place in Turandot's speech in the ensemble coda to the Enigma scene, where Puccini rode roughshod over an obvious musico-dramatic textual pattern given him by his librettists in order to accommodate his design for the musical climax. The general question of relationships—or lack of relationship—between verse and music in *Turandot*, however, seems to us to be only a facet of the larger problem, not just of versification in Puccini's operas, but of the general abandonment of the polymetric libretto in the Italian musical theater.[9]

Extending Weaver's "Golden Century of Italian opera" backward in time as well as forward, including it as the culminating phase of a "Great Tradition of Italian opera" makes historiographic sense, but it leads to a hidden contradiction, for the words "century" and "tradition" have different kinds of temporal implication. Weaver's word "century" includes by synecdoche what happened during that approximate time span. Our word "tradition," to the contrary, implies nothing regarding finite temporal span; rather, it implies continuity through time, continuity of practices partially remembered from the past, existing as part of the eternal present, and doing their part towards stabilizing an expected future. Only loosely can "tradition" usefully be conceived as having temporal boundaries as well as temporal continuity, in the way we have suggested for Italian opera from about 1675 to about 1925. Our expression "Great Tradition," used here in its sense as a social-science term (as opposed to the same expression used by F. R. Leavis writing about the English novel), implies not so much historical spread as cultural spread, and properly speaking it should be used with its correlate "Little Tradition"—though this is obviously not the place to develop the correlation. The Great Tradition/Little Tradition coupling was developed by Robert Redfield, to characterize within a whole civilization the relationship between practices and concepts of a widespread elite (usually urban) and local customs and beliefs (usually rural).[10] The concept provides a conceptual framework for the mutual feedback between high culture and folk or popular culture. As both extended and narrowed to opera, the notion brings under the same umbrella both the cyclic renewals of high-culture musical theater through popular elements and the vulgarization of elaborate operatic devices for use in popular musical theater: on the one hand, the simple reiterative melodic lines and accompaniment textures of much operatic music from the Golden Century, or the making of librettos from plays in the tradition of popular French melodrama; on the other hand, not only the parody but also the imitation of operatic effects in the operettas of Offenbach, Sullivan, or Lehàr—not to mention Gershwin, Kern, or Rodgers—or the use of orchestral textures invented by Debussy, Ravel, or Strauss in expert musical accompaniments to Tedeschi's modern melodramas, in the film scores of the mid-twentieth century by such as Alfred Newman, Bernard Herrmann, Miklos Rosza, or Dmitri Tiomkin.

As the basic unit for observing the Great Tradition/Little Tradition symbiosis, Redfield's disciple and colleague Milton Singer proposed what he termed "cultural performance," a notion that contributes a further dimension to the metaphor for the musical theater as well. As Singer pointed out,

> "cultural performances" . . . include what we in the West usually call by that name—for example plays, concerts, and lectures. But they include also prayers, ritual readings and recitations, rites and ceremonies, festivals, and all those things we usually classify under religion and ritual rather than with the cultural and artistic. . . . As I observed the range of cultural performances . . . it seemed to me that my Indian friends—and perhaps all peoples—thought of their culture as encapsulated in these discrete performances, which they could exhibit to visitors and to themselves.[11]

It is tempting to see Singer's "cultural performances . . . which they could exhibit to visitors and to themselves" as a general rubric covering, among other things, what Bianconi and Walker called the

political and civil functions of opera theatre . . . [which] once established as an institution that includes the possibility of impresarial initiative and subvention, functions as an *instrumentum regni*, a public
demonstration and representation of authority.[12]

This too will sound familiar to students of the Great Tradition during the
Golden Century. From the preferred subjects of nineteenth-century opera
to the manner in which new opera houses arose, opera continued to be
both a demonstration and a representation of what it meant to be among
the rich and powerful, whether represented by the State or its institutional
agents, as in Europe, or in their own persons, as was the case in seventeenth-century Venice and has been the case in the United States in the
nineteenth and twentieth centuries.[13]

But whatever the social and political status of the group from which the
necessary principal supporters of "public opera" may come, a substantial
portion of its audiences belongs, as it always has, to groups that could not
by themselves finance these spectacles of the Great Tradition, spectacles
that continue to enjoy a popularity comparable to the popularity of grand
sporting events in the fanaticism they can engender, if not quite in sheer
quantity of fans. It may well be that, as Bianconi and Walker have put it
for seventeenth-century Venice, "such 'popularity' is to be understood as
induced or imposed 'popularity,' in the sense of 'best-selling.' "[14] That
would be just as true of sporting events and cinema, though, and hardly
accounts for the continuing vitality of operas in the Great Tradition, where
so many of the plays on which they were based are dead, or for the depth
and intensity of private as well as public joy that Italian opera still brings
to so many ordinary persons all over the world, even in the late twentieth
century—including the authors of this book.

Turning to the social and political implications of *Turandot* in particular,
we have alluded in several contexts in our book to Puccini as a man of his
own time (1858–1924), a European living through the heyday of European
imperialism and heir to a tradition of orientalized exoticism, in music as in
literature and painting, that now seems at the very least patronizing. To
Puccini, of course, the Far East was not yet our East Asia of Sony and
Yamaha, let alone the East Asia of the surviving heirs of the Long March
or of Tiananmen Square. But neither was his China the China of the
Opium Wars and the Treaty Ports, a land of European mercantilist and
financial oppressors and Asian urban and rural oppressed. *Turandot* is easily seen as an unconscious manifestation of racial arrogance; the "authentic" Chinese melodies victimized by Puccini's monster orchestra are symbolic enough of that. But Puccini the composer was not aware of what his
work might imply about Puccini the European; for him the "chinoiserie"

was merely an artistic resource, like the equally victimized Stravinskyisms in his bitonal harmonizations, and we have seen no reason to advert to the obvious malapropisms of either.

In the same way, we have alluded more than once in our book to the interpretations by Adami, Simoni and Puccini of Gozzi's bloodthirsty bluestocking Princess, and to the contrast between their Turandot and Puccini's particular contribution, the humiliated and self-sacrificing fin-de-siècle Chinese mannequin of the European *decadenza*, Liù—as well as to Puccini's machismic solution to the dramatic problem posed by Turandot's ultimate conversion. Except for the all-American Minnie, the principal female characters in Puccini's operas, as in the majority of the operas in the Golden Century, come to a sad or at least a subordinated end at the hands of men, or through "female disabilities" (to use Anthony Trollope's term from *The American Senator*) consequent upon a culturally enforced dependence on men. This certainly touches most particularly on the more general question of female roles in the theatrical tradition from which most operatic subjects in the Golden Century were drawn, most typically manifested in the French *mélodrame* and its more pretentious compeers, from Anicet to Hugo and Dumas to Sardou. It touches also, however, on the social and artistic position of the *prima donna* from Colbran to Callas, and in that regard, on the need for dramatic situations that will provide for musically intense exploitation of the human voice in its highest registers, after the fading away of the castrati at the beginning of the Golden Century, and concomitant with the ever-increasing emphasis on large ensembles in its opera houses. That Puccini's *Turandot*—more than any of his other works—could play as relevant a role in feminist criticism as it could in social criticism is as obvious as it is irrelevant to our more limited concern with Puccini's use of such voices and such situations for musical ends. Our concern is not with *Turandot* as one among a number of socio-historical reflections of a phase or an aspect of Western culture, but simply as a work worthy of consideration in its own terms, as the last Monument in the last Golden Century of one of the world's Great Traditions of musical theater.

CHAPTER I

❧

THE OPERA

TURANDOT AND THE GREAT TRADITION

Opera is a compound, not an amalgam. For convenience, elements in the compound may be thought of as mined separately from the Aristotelian quarries of action, character, social and physical mise-en-scène, language, and music. When they co-occur in the theater, however, the elements do not retain all their separate and original properties; they become a new substance altogether, with properties all its own. Subatomic features in the several elements are electrically bonded in the chemistry of the genre. If those generic elements are dissociated from the compound analytically, alone they may appear impoverished or distorted. Libretto language stripped of its music may seem fustian; theatrical music torn from its context may seem bombastic or formless; a lavish mise-en-scène visualized apart from the highly stylized action, words and music that go with it may seem pointlessly sybaritic.

This being so, the conventional approach that "tells the story" of an opera act by act, in continuous narrative prose, mentioning an aria incipit or returning motive here, a concerted piece or instrumental interlude there, is usually unsatisfactory. It is not simply that opera plots are unrealistic or confusing; taken by themselves they often are. It is rather that they ought not to be taken by themselves. Opera plots have no significance away from the musical and scenographic events whose particular effects they have inspired, away from the musical articulations whose verbal and visual correlates they have become through the kind of creative process traced in Chapter III.[1]

To put it in terms of a particularly familiar kind of operatic compound: it is not really the case that a certain recurring figure, or harmony, or rhythm is a musical label for a character, or environment, or event in a drama. It starts that way, but in the compound as finally bonded it is the other way around: the character, or the environment, or the event has become a label for the musical phenomenon. What is said or seen is a representational embodiment of some melodic configuration, harmonic and/or timbral effect, rhythmic pattern, in short, of some music: music of a kind that would be able by itself to evoke a nonverbal and invisible generalized response—an affect—that is already predisposed by the musical-cultural

12

background of an attuned spectator. The music needs actions, words, and mise-en-scène only to provide a concrete focus of attention, a specific who, where, and what. Indeed, the great convenience of theatrical music for the musical analyst is the fact that musical phenomena can so often have real names—"the Scarpia motive" or "the Tristan chord"—rather than having to be designated abstractly and forgettably, "the opening motive" or "the half-diminished seventh chord."

In the earlier phases of Italian Romantic *melodramma*, long-range musical recurrences were tied to events or persons previously seen, or to previously-heard sung words or stage instruments. They are often called "reminiscence themes": Rossini's *Semiramide* has a couple, for instance, and Verdi's *Aida* has several, to mention two of *Turandot*'s predecessors also on exotic subjects. By Puccini's time the device of the "reminiscence theme" had been reinforced, even denatured, by quasi-Wagnerian and post-Wagnerian overuse of *Leitmotive*, but in *Turandot* recurring music is usually part of some larger musico-dramatic design, even where it functions as a "label" or as a "reminiscence theme" as well. Of the three themes with which the Princess Turandot herself has been associated, the only one used as an index to her person—the one we shall be calling "Mo-li-hua"— is also the one most used in a purely formal way; of the other two, one is embodied in a particular event (impending or achieved), while the other (which returns only once) is associated with a particular line of text. And there is nothing like a "theme" for the slave-girl Liù (the *seconda donna*), or for the unknown Prince (the principal tenor) or his aged father (the principal bass): the music they embody is marked rather by its general character. For the Chinese slave-girl a quasi-"Chinese pentatonic" is used, as in her two arias "Signore, ascolta" (Act I) and "Tanto amore segreto" (Act III). The Prince embodies a normal Puccinian Romantic-diatonic style, as in the famous tenor *romanza* "Nessun dorma" in Act III, or as in his aria "Non piangere, Liù" in Act I. The music for the Prince's father, the deposed king Timur, is also of this character, as in his *arietta* "Perduta la battaglia" near the beginning of Act I.

For all its occasionally fluid structure and sometimes decadently up-to-date texture, moreover, *Turandot* is a "number" opera in the Great Tradition of Italian Romantic *melodramma*—or rather, during the course of its long genesis it gradually became one. In the fantastic play by Carlo Gozzi that was the source of the libretto, as outlined in Chapter II, the dramatic nucleus was already a set piece, a confrontation laid out as three formal sequences of challenge and response. In the opera this became a highly formalized "dialogue duet" between the cruel Princess and her suitor the unknown Prince—the Enigma scene, analyzed in Chapter V—a "ritual scene," to use Frits Noske's term.[2] As shown in Chapter III, the Enigma scene originated as the climax of an originally very long Act I with two sets. At that early stage of its composition, however, the rest of the opera seems to have been headed toward the fluid musico-dramatic congeries of choruses and short genre pieces more characteristic of *Madama Butterfly*. Typical from the final form of the opera are the two tiny 2/4 *ariette* near the beginning of the present Act I in which the principal bass (Timur) and the *seconda donna* (Liù) introduce themselves; or the choral and ensemble episodes later in Act I during the confrontation of the three Ministers and the unknown Prince; or a passage near the end of the present Act II in which the ancient Emperor of China hopes the unknown Prince will become his son-in-law. But during the long course of the opera's genesis the original Act I was split in two, and three additional major set pieces found their way into what are now Acts I and II of the opera. First, the order of two arias before the change of set in the original Act I was reversed: what had been the first of the two, the Prince's aria "Non piangere, Liù," is now second, and it has become the lead-off solo for a grandiose *concertato* in the manner of the Act III Finale of *Manon Lescaut* or the Act I Finale of *Tosca*, a *concertato* added on to cap the now much shorter Act I. Second, a long scene for the three court Ministers alone, on an independent set, was introduced to open the new Act II—a scene that shows the traditional four-movement sequence of open-ended kinetic movements alternating with formally closed lyric movements typical of the Italian Romantic *melodramma*.[3] Later on, just before the Enigma scene itself, an entrance aria for the Princess Turandot was interpolated, an impressive *aria di sortita* for the *prima donna*. The torture and death of Liù (the *seconda donna*) is another succession of four movements alternately open-ended and closed, conceived still later for the third act.

Thus Puccini's *Turandot* became a "number" opera, like Verdi's *Aida* or Rossini's *Semiramide* before it. On the one hand, there are extended passages that are relatively homogeneous: oriented tonally around one or two keys; consistent in pacing and rhythmic character; limited to a small number of ideas worked over at some length; or characterized by a particular instrumental color and texture. On the other hand, there are passages that carry us from one relatively stable musico-dramatic phase to the next, shifting keys, themes, or instruments as they go, acting as musical introductions, interludes, or transitions while they accompany changes of action or discourse. To be sure, as in *Aida* Act III, the formal seams are often stitched over, sometimes to the point of covering up an applause point for an important solo: the end of the Prince's *romanza* "Nessun dorma" in Act III is a particularly awkward one for a conductor, but Turandot's *aria di sortita* "In questa reggia" in Act II also merges directly into the music that follows. The beginnings of these two arias, however, as of other big set pieces in the opera, are carefully prepared, as such pieces always had been.

TURANDOT AS A NUMBER OPERA

The overview of *Turandot* that follows below is set forth at three levels, differently marked in the headings. Each of the three acts is designated with an upper-case Roman numeral. Upper-case letters denote major musico-dramatic "numbers" (I.B, D / II.A, C, D, E / III.A, C, D), as well as expositions (I.A, C / II.B / III.B) and conclusions (II.F / III.E). Shifts in mise-en-scène—either of set and lighting together (in Acts II and III) or of lighting alone (in Act I)—take place at this level.

Individual "movements" within the larger numbers, be they static solos and choruses or kinetic action movements, are marked with Arabic numerals. At this level are found the "arias," for instance Liù's "Signore, ascolta" (I.D.2), Turandot's "In questa reggia" (II.D.3), and the Prince's "Nessun dorma" (III.A.2); choruses like the sequence of Moonlight chorus, Children's chorus, and funeral cortège for the Prince of Persia (I.B.1–3); dialogues like the Recognition scene for the unknown Prince, Timur his father, and the faithful slave-girl Liù (I.A.2), not to mention the individual challenge-and-response cycles in the Enigma scene itself (II.E.1–3); individual movements in ensemble scenes, as in the separate scene for the three Ministers (II.A.1–4); climax ensembles like those that cap the Enigma scene (II.E.4) or the scene of the torture and suicide of Liù (III.C.4), not to mention the *concertato* that ends Act I (I.D.4); introductions and interludes; and so on.

Precise locations of musico-dramatic moments are identified with the help of the rehearsal numbers found in Ricordi's available published scores; the rehearsal numbers are the same in the piano-vocal and orchestral scores, and are separately enumerated for each act. Act number and rehearsal number are preceded by "rh" (for "rehearsal"); these are sometimes followed by a plus sign and another number, which indicates a location so many measures after the rehearsal number (with the measure at the rehearsal number counted as "1"); the whole is enclosed in parentheses. For instance: at the magnificent climax to the funeral cortège for the Prince of Persia, Turandot appears on the palace balcony high above the crowd accompanied by the *fortissimo* appearance in E♭ major of the theme we shall refer to as "Mo-li-hua"; this moment would be located with the rehearsal-number *siglum* (rh I.23 + 5). The equally magnificent climax to the aftermath of the Enigma scene, the last exchange between Turandot and the unknown Prince in Act II, capped by "Mo-li-hua" now in C major, would be located with the rehearsal-number *siglum* (rh II.64 + 13).

An abbreviated outline of this overview is given as the Appendix, for cross-reference in connection with Chapters III, IV, and V.

ACT I

A. Sunset: awaiting the execution

> "The walls of the Imperial City enclose steps in a semi-circle. Stakes are affixed to the bastions and upon them are impaled the skulls of the beheaded suitors [of Turandot]. At the left and back three huge gates pierce the walls. It is the blood-red hour of sunset. The square is filled with a picturesque crowd of Chinese people."

1. Introduction (rh I.0). The "Execution" motive; the Mandarin's proclamation to the crowd: "Popolo di Pekino" (accompanied with "bicentric" harmonies). *Andante sostenuto*, 2/2, f♯ minor.

EXAMPLE 1. (rh I.0): The Execution motive and the first bicentric chord [I.A.1]

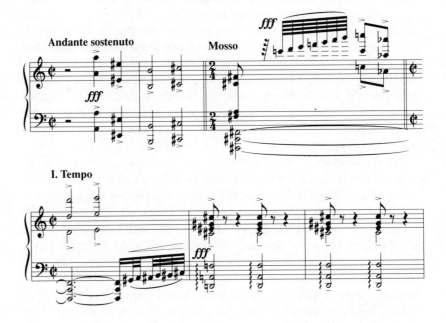

2. Recognition (rh I.4). The unknown Prince, his father Timur, the slave-girl Liù: "Indietro, cani!" // "Il mio vecchio è caduto." *Largo sostenuto*, 3/4 (Ex. 2). Sequence from f♯ minor through g minor and a♭ minor, to arrive at a minor for the entrance of the Executioner's servants.

3. Interlude (rh I.7). *Ariette* of Timur ("Perduta la battaglia") and Liù ("Nulla sono"). *Andante*, 2/4; G major and b♭ minor.

4. Executioners' chorus (rh I.9): "Ungi, arrota." *Allegro*, 2/4; f♯ minor (Ex. 3), contrasting section in d minor over a low B♭ pedal.

EXAMPLE 2. (rh I.4): The Recognition melody [I.A.2]

EXAMPLE 3. (rh I.10 + 1): The Executioners' chorus [I.A.4]

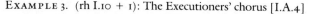

B. Moonrise: funeral cortège of the Prince of Persia and the first appearance of the Princess Turandot.

> "While the assistants depart to bring the Executioner his sharpened sword, the crowd watches the sky, which has gradually darkened."

1. The crowd awaits the moonrise (rh I.17): "Perchè tarda la luna?" *Andante molto sostenuto*, 4/4, D major. Sequence from D major through Eb major and E major to F major, to climax back in Eb major for the entrance of the Executioner: "Pu-Tin-Pao!"

2. Children's chorus (rh I.19): "Là sui monti dell'est." *Andantino*, 2/4, Eb major; "Mo-li-hua" harmonized (as usual) with lowered leading tone (Ex. 4).

> "The gold in the background has changed to silver. The cortège leading the young Prince of Persia to the block appears."

3. The funeral cortège for the Prince of Persia (rh I.21). Cortège ("O giovinetto!") (Exs. 5, 6); appearance of Turandot, and the unknown Prince is smitten ("O divina bellezza!"). *Andante triste*, 4/4, eb minor (with augmented seconds) and Eb major ("Mo-li-hua").

4. Interlude (rh I.25): Liù and Timur beg the Prince to leave with them ("Figlio, che fai?"); the Prince of Persia is beheaded offstage: ("Turandot!")—see Example 32 in Chapter V. *Andante*; 2/4, 4/4, 3/4;

EXAMPLE 4. (rh I.19): The Children's chorus: Mo-li-hua [I.B.2]

EXAMPLE 5. (rh I.21): The Prince of Persia's funeral cortège [I.B.3]

Andante triste

EXAMPLE 6. (rh I.22 + 8): Preparation for Turandot's first appearance (Mo-li-hua) [I.B.3]

Sostenendo con gravità

modulation and sequence, to "Mo-li-Hua" and "Execution" motives, then ostinato leading to

C. The three Ministers and the unknown Prince

   1. The Ministers try to dissuade the Prince from striking the fatal gong (rh I.28): "Fermo! che fai?" *Allegro giusto*, 2/4 + 3/4, A♭ major.

EXAMPLE 7. (rh I.28): Entrance of the three Ministers [I.C.1]

   2. Interludes (rh I.35)

     a) Chorus of Turandot's handmaidens: "Silenzio, olà!" *Andante lento*, 3/4; c♯ minor > f♯ minor.

     b) Ministerial warnings: "Guardalo, Pong." *Allegretto*; 2/4, 3/4, 5/8, 4/4; f♯ minor > b minor.

   3. The ghosts of Turandot's former suitors (rh I.38): "Non indugiare!" *Lento*, 3/4; a minor, atonally harmonized (Ex. 8).

   4. Conclusion (rh I.39)

     a) The Ministers try again: "L'ami? Che cosa? Chi?" *Allegro*; 2/4, 3/4 (Ex. 9); sequential modulation on the "Execution" motive. "Turandot! con tutti quei citrulli," E♭ major > B♭ major.

     b) The Chief Executioner shows the severed head of the Prince of Persia: "Stolto! Ecco l'amore"; d minor, "Execution" motive.

D. Finale

   1. Transition (rh I.41 + 3): "O figlio, vuoi dunque ch'io solo." *Pesante e sostenuto*, (3/4), modulation (but see Chapter IV, Example 35 and pp. 103–4).

   2. Aria of Liù (rh I.42): "Signore, ascolta." *Adagio*, 4/4, G♭ major (Ex. 10).

EXAMPLE 8. (rh I.38): The ghosts of Turandot's former suitors [I.C.3]

3. Aria of the unknown Prince (rh I.43): "Non piangere, Liù." *Andante lento sostenuto*; 2/2, 3/2; eb minor. Lead-off solo (Ex. 11) for the

4. Concluding *concertato* (rh I.46): "Ah! per l'ultima volta." (*Andante lento sostenuto*); 9/4 + 6/4 + 9/4; eb minor (ostinato); The Prince strikes the gong: "Turandot!" > D major ("Mo-li-hua") > eb minor (final orchestral ostinato and fivefold cadence).

EXAMPLE 9. (rh I.40): The Ministers, the Prince, and the Executioner [I.C.4, end]

the Prince: a   me il tri - on - fo, a me l'a- mo - re

(. . . il boja appare in alto . . .
colla testa mozza del
Principe di Persia.)

EXAMPLE 10. (rh I.42): Liù's first aria [I.D.2]

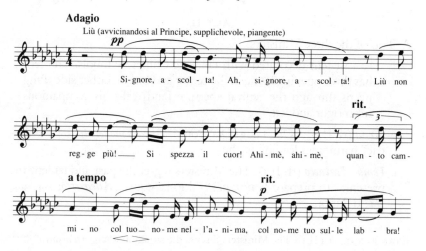

EXAMPLE 11. (rh I.44 + 10): The end of the Prince's first aria and the beginning of the *concertato* [I.D.3 > I.D.4]

ACT II

A. Trio of the three Ministers

> "a vast tent decorated with fantastic Chinese symbols. The tent has three openings, one in the center and one on either side. Ping peeps through the central aperture [and] calls his companions from right and left."

o. *Scena* (rh II.0): "Olà, Pang! Olà, Pong!" *Allegro moderato*, 3/4; "bicentric" harmonies leading to the

1. *Tempo d'attacco* (rh II.1). The Ministers regret the past and lament the present: "Io preparo le nozze," "Ed io l'esequie." *Allegretto*; 2/4, 3/4, 2/4; d minor.

EXAMPLE 12. (rh II.1): The Ministers discuss the situation (*"tempo d'attacco"*) [II.A.1]

2. *Andantino* (rh II.9). The Ministers nostalgically recollect their country retreats: "Ho una casa nell'Honan." *Andantino mosso*; 2/4, 3/4; D major.

EXAMPLE 13. (rh II.9): The Ministers' nostalgia [II.A.2]

3. *Tempo di mezzo* (rh II.13)

    a) The Ministers recall recent executions: "O mondo pieno di pazzi innamorati," *Andante mosso*, 3/4, B♭ major; "Vi ricordate il principe regal di Samarcanda," *Allegretto* (Executioners' chorus) 3/8, 2/8, e♭ minor. They bid farewell to ancient China: "Addio . . . stirpe divina," *Molto moderato*, 4/4, E♭ major.

    b) They hope this time to prepare a bridal chamber instead: "Il talamo le voglio preparare," *Poco più mosso*, 2/4; the "Guiding March" (see Chapter IV, Example 33 and p. 96) as dominant preparation for the

4. *Stretta* (rh II.21): "Non v'è in China." *Allegretto moderato*, 2/4, G major.

EXAMPLE 14. (rh II.21 + 2): The Ministers' hopes (*"stretta"*) [II.A.4]

Allegretto moderato

Nou v'è in Chi-na, per nos-tra for - tu-na, don-na— più che rin-ne-ghi L'a-

mor! _____

B. Change of set: the Court assembles

    1. Transition. The *stretta* is interrupted by an offstage march (rh II.25 + 2), heard first at a distance with stage instruments and later in full from the orchestra pit.

        "A vast piazza within the palace appears. An enormous marble staircase almost in the center is lost in the heights . . . There are three huge landings on the staircase."

    The march leads uninterruptedly through the change of set, functioning as a dominant harmonic preparation for the opening tonality (G♭ major) of the

    2. Processional (rh II.26). March tunes and entrance of the Court: *Moderatamente*; 2/4, 3/4; various tonalities in sequence, leading to the Imperial hymn (E♭ major) and choral Acclamation of the Emperor (A♭ major) (Exs. 15, 16).

C. The first confrontation

    1. The Emperor and the unknown Prince (rh II.34): "Un giuramento atroce mi costringe" / "Figlio del cielo, io chiedo d'affrontar la prova." *Andante energico e solenne*; 2/4, 3/4; C major (Exs. 17, 18).

EXAMPLE 15. (rh II.31 + 13): The Imperial hymn [II.B.2]

EXAMPLE 16. (rh II.33 + 2): The Acclamation of the Emperor [II.B.2]

Die - ci mi - la an - ni   al nos - tro Im - pera - to - re!

Glo - ria a   te!

EXAMPLE 17. (rh II.35): The Emperor's request [II.C.1]

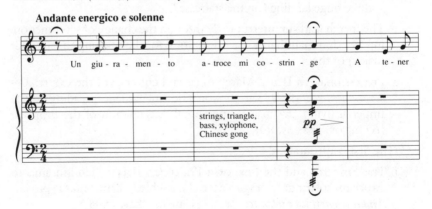

Andante energico e solenne

Un giu - ra - men - to   a - troce mi co - strin - ge   A te - ner

strings, triangle,
bass, xylophone,
Chinese gong

pp

EXAMPLE 17. *(cont.)*

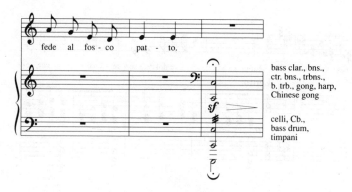

fede al fos-co pat-to.

bass clar., bns.,
ctr. bns., trbns.,
b. trb., gong, harp,
Chinese gong

celli, Cb.,
bass drum,
timpani

EXAMPLE 18. (rh II.36 + 6): The Prince's response [II.C.1]

[**Andante energico e solenne**]

Fig-lio del cie-lo, io chie-do d'af-fron-tar la pro-va! [orchestra]

2. Brief ceremonial conclusion (rh II.39): "Diecimila anni"; *Largo*; 4/4, 5/4; F major > Bb major.

D. Turandot

1. Reprise of the Mandarin's proclamation from Act I (rh II.40): "Po-polo di Pekino," *Andante sostenuto*, 4/4, f♯ minor.

2. Reprise of the Children's chorus from Act I (rh II.42): "Dal deserto al mar," *Andantino*, 4/4, D major.

3. *Aria di sortita* of Turandot (rh II.43): "In questa reggia," *Molto lento*, 2/4, D major, modulating to "Principessa Lou-Ling," *Lento*, 4/8, f♯ minor (Ex. 19).

The aria concludes with a *maggiore* peroration: "Mai nessun m'avrà," *Largamente*, 4/4, Gb (= F♯) major (Ex. 20).

An abrupt shift to Eb major brings a modulating coda with a new motive for the Princess, "Gli enigmi sono tre, la morte è una!" answered by the Prince singing the same motive in F♯ major, replacing "la morte è una" with "una è la vita" (Ex. 21).

27

EXAMPLE 19. (rh II.44): The principal subject (*minore*) of Turandot's *aria di sortita* [II.D.3]

They sing the motive a third time together in A♭ major, which contin- ues as the tonality for a choral conclusion on the "Mai nessun m'avrà" melody, followed by a modulation leading into

E. The second confrontation: the Enigma scene: "Signore, ascolta!" *An- dante sostenuto*, 4/4; d minor, d minor, e♭ minor; the "Enigma" motive (Ex. 22).

EXAMPLE 20. (rh II.27): "Mai nessun m'avrà!"—the *maggiore* conclusion to Turandot's *aria di sortita* [II.D.3]

EXAMPLE 21. (rh II.48): The Prince's confidence [II.D.3]

EXAMPLE 22. (rh II.50 + 2): The Enigma motive [II.E]

The "Enigma" motive is associated with two other motives yet briefer: one or more almost pitchless tritone thumps in bass instruments, scale degrees 2 and ♭6 of the key; and one or more unprepared 2–3 suspension-resolutions marked "come un lamento (Ex. 23)."

1. The first enigma and response (rh II.50 + 2): "Nella cupa notte" / "La speranza!"; d minor, "Enigma" motive.

> "In the dark of night an iridescent phantom flies . . . everyone invokes it . . . every night it is born, every day it dies" / "yes, born again in exultation . . . hope!"

2. The second enigma (rh II.54 + 3): "Guizza al pari di fiamma" / "Il sangue!"; d minor, "Enigma" motive.

> "It flickers like flame . . . sometimes it is delirium, a fever of longing . . . if you fail, it chills . . . if you dream of victory it flares up . . . it is crimson like the sunset."

The Prince hesitates; all encourage him: *Allegro moderato*, 3/4, a development of the "Execution" motive (its second appearance in Act II and its final appearance in the opera). The Prince responds:

> "Yes . . . it flares up and languishes in the veins . . . blood!"

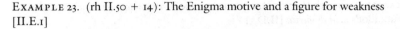

EXAMPLE 23. (rh II.50 + 14): The Enigma motive and a figure for weakness [II.E.1]

3. The third enigma (rh II.59 + 2): "Gelo che ti dà foco" / "Turandot!"; e♭ minor, "Enigma" motive.

> "Ice that sets you afire, and from your fire is chilled . . . in freeing you it enslaves you, but taking you as slave it makes you King."

The Prince hesitates again, and Turandot taunts him:

> "What is the ice that sets you afire?"

At last the Prince responds:

> "You have yourself given me my victory, and my fire will melt your ice: Turandot!"

The chorus echoes "Turandot!" triumphantly, with "Mo-li-hua" in E♭ major, and continues with a richly contrapuntal *pianissimo* harmonization of the "Acclamation" melody in A♭ major.

4. Coda and concerted piece (rh II.63). The Princess wants to renegue: "Figlio del cielo!" (*Sostenuto*, 4/4, A♭ major, and the "Acclamation" melody continue); "Non gettar tua figlia" (modulating sequence on a

transformation of the "Recognition" music from I.A.2); motive reduction and crescendo leading to "Mo-li-hua" (G major > C major, and see Chapter V, Example 41 and pp. 128–31).

F. The third confrontation

1. The Prince's enigma (rh II.65 + 9): "Tre enigmi m'hai proposto." The Prince offers to release Turandot if she can learn his name by dawn; she agrees. *Largo sostenuto, Moderato sostenuto*; 4/4; d minor (the "Enigma" theme) to D♭ major and the "theme of the Prince's name" (cf. Example 24 below).

2. The Emperor's reaction (rh II.67 + 3): "Il cielo voglia." *Molto sostenuto*, 4/4, d♭ minor: the "Guiding March" (see Chapter IV, pp. 96–97, and cf. Example 33).

3. Full ceremonial conclusion (rh II.68 + 3): "Ai tuoi piedi ci prostriam. . . . Dieci mila anni." *Andante maestoso e sostenuto*, (4/4), F major > B♭ major.

ACT III

"The very spacious garden of the palace, a rolling landscape studded with dark shapes of statues of the gods. To the right is a pavilion reached by five steps, upon one of which the Prince is reclining. It is night."

A. The Prince alone

1. Introduction and chorus of heralds offstage (rh III.0): "Così comanda Turandot." *Andante mosso, misterioso*, 6/8, a minor in "bicentric" harmonization.

2. *Romanza* of the unknown Prince (rh III.4): "Nessun dorma." *Andante sostenuto*, 4/4; G major > D major (two stanzas).

3. Extension and transition (rh III.6 + 5). Entrance of the three Ministers and the populace: "Tu che guardi le stelle." *Allegro*, 2/4; D major > G major.

B. The tempting of the Prince

1. The first temptation (women) (rh III.8 + 5): "Guarda, son belle." *Lento*, 2/4, g minor > d minor.

2. Two more temptations (wealth, glory): "Che vuoi? richezze?" (rh III.9). Threats; Liù and Timur forcibly brought in. *Allegro*; 2/4, 4/4, 2/4; d minor > E♭ major > dominant of G♭, for the

3. Entrance of Turandot (rh III.16 + 5): "Principessa divina," *Largo*, 4/4, G♭ major; "Mo-li-hua." "Sei pallido, straniero," *Meno largo*, 3/4: modulation to c minor and sequence of "Recognition" melody (I.A.2

EXAMPLE 24. (III.4 + 10): The theme of the Prince's name [III.A.2]

in its original form) from c minor through a♭ minor to arrive at e minor for

C. The slave-girl and the Princess

1. *Tempo d'attacco.* Torture of Liù (rh III.20): "Sia legata! Sia straziata!" *Allegro, Andante*; 2/4; e minor and G major, over low E pedal point, leading to

2. Aria of Liù (rh III.24): "Tanto amore segreto." *Lento*, 4/4, F major.

EXAMPLE 25. (rh III.24 + 5): The melody of Liù's second aria [III.C.2]

3. *Tempo di mezzo.* Further torture of Liù (rh III.25 + 6): "Sia messa alla tortura!" *Allegro moderato*, 2/4: Executioners' chorus from I.A.4 in f♯ minor, accompanied at the tritone (F♯ under c′).

EXAMPLE 26. (rh III.25 + 7): Liù's torments (continued) [III.C.3]

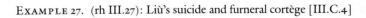

EXAMPLE 27. (rh III.27): Liù's suicide and furneral cortège [III.C.4]

4. Suicide and funeral cortège of Liù // Timur's grief (rh III.27): "Tu che di gel sei cinta" // "Ah! tu sei morta." *Andantino mosso*, 2/4 + 4/4.

D. The thawing of the Princess

1. The Prince's accusation and his wooing (rh III.35): "Principessa di morte!" *Andante sostenuto*, 2/2; a minor, modulations, C major, F major.

EXAMPLE 28. (rh III.35): The Prince's accusation [III.D.1]

2. The Princess weakens (rh III.39): "Oh, mio fiore mattutino" (Ex. 29). (*Andante sostenuto*); 6/4, 4/4; a minor > B major ("La mia gloria è finita") > C major.

3. Aria of Turandot (rh III.42). The Princess confesses that she both loved and hated him from the first moment, and now she begs him to leave her in peace: "Del primo pianto." *Con ansia ma non troppo mosso*; 2/4, 4/4; eb minor > Eb Major (Ex. 30).

EXAMPLE 29. (rh III.39): The Princess weakens [III.D.2]

EXAMPLE 29. (*cont.*)

EXAMPLE 30. (rh III.42): Turandot's confession [III.D.3]

4. The Prince tells his name (rh III.46): "Il mio mistero? Non ne ho più," (*non troppo mosso*), 4/4, > B♭ major (Ex. 31); "La mia gloria è il tuo amplesso" (modulations).

E. Change of set (as in Act II set 2): the final scene.

1. Fanfares: appearance of the Court (rh III.50): "Diecimila anni" *Larghissimo*, 4/4; E major > C♯ major > G♭ major.

2. The Princess tells the Prince's name (rh III.53): "Padre augusto, conosco il nome," *Lentissimo*, 4/4, modulation to

3. The final chorus (rh III.54): "O Sole! Vita! Eternità!" *Larghissimo*, 4/4, D major.

TURANDOT AND THE PRINCE

THE FINAL PROBLEM

In following the evolution of the libretto in Chapter III we shall see that at the time of Puccini's death a problem raised by the final duet coming hard upon Liù's sacrificial death and funeral cortège remained incompletely resolved. Given the closely-woven pattern of musico-dramatic cross-references in the opera as a whole, it is clear that the climax and dénouement was meant to be the second confrontation of Turandot and the unknown Prince. Yet as it has turned out, at first blush the closing passages of the opera seem unmotivated, perhaps even shocking, as though Butterfly's suicide had been vulgarly and anticlimactically followed by a final love duet for Pinkerton and Kate.

A couple of lines in a letter to Adami of 22 October 1924 may reflect some awareness on Puccini's part that the difficulty he had been experiencing with the "big duet" might have its roots in the preceding number, that the original dramatic purpose of Liù's renunciation and self-sacrifice might have got lost in sympathy generated by the figure of the slave-girl *in extremis*.[4] Turandot has little to say in the torture scene (III.C), and unless the transformation of the "Recognition" music to which she sings her plea to her father in II.E.4, after her defeat by the Prince, is meant to hint at an unrecognized softening towards the Prince on her part, the only indication that the Princess's character has been or could be softened in any way, is her question to Liù at the end of III.C.1, "Chi posa tanta forza nel tuo cuore?" and her questioning "Amore?" echoing Liù's answer. That "Amore?" of Turandot's, however, is not part of the libretto text; it was added very late to the score by Puccini himself. In the absence of any more

EXAMPLE 31. (rh III.46): Calàf tells his name [III.D.4]

EXAMPLE 31. (*cont.*)

overt musico-dramatic response on Turandot's part during Liù's farewell and suicide or Timur's grieving, that late addition of her one-word echoing question at the end of the first torture sequence is the only real suggestion that the icy Princess might be experiencing some unaccustomed, not yet understood emotion. However great the dramatic skill of the singer of Turandot may be at that single moment, it could never be enough to counteract the overwhelming effect of Liù's answering aria "Tanto amore segreto," not to mention the powerful ensemble of her death and funeral cortège. There occurs in this number (III.C) a fatal shift of focus away from Turandot, the principal character who must change and eventually does change, and on to Liù, a secondary character who does not change, who remains only ever more pathetically herself.

A psychological basis for Turandot's sudden and surprising conversion is finally provided, to be sure, in Turandot's aria "Del primo pianto" (III.D.3), in which the Princess explains that from the moment the unknown Prince appeared she had reacted to him as she had never done to any previous suitor. This thematic idea recurs several times in the later acts of Gozzi's play, so that there her reversal had been well prepared. As this same solution is used in the opera, however, it suffers from two disadvantages, one structural, one circumstantial. In the opera it is entirely retrospective and far too late, coming as it does only after Turandot's sudden sea-change has already been effected by the Prince's kiss; about that defect nothing can be done. But worse than that, it occurs in a piece that has sometimes been cut in performance, and that is a defect easily remedied. Thinking about this aria today, we can only reaffirm what Ashbrook wrote a number of years ago, that this aria should be retained in performance. Its relatively low *tessitura* provides necessary relief in a scene that is pretty much written at the top of the voice—in both senses. With some release of tension, the scene seems shorter, in fact, *with* the aria than without it. Furthermore, this aria is essential in making Turandot's conversion convincing. Those who reject this aria, who say what does it matter since Puccini did not write it anyway, are using an untenable argument. Puccini's sketches show that he *did* want the aria, and he left indications of how he wanted it to begin.[5]

Another way to see the problem is in terms of the Prince's relationship to Liù on the one hand and to Turandot on the other. Many find it difficult to accept that the Prince does not reciprocate the great, ultimately sacrificial love that Liù bears him. That the Prince does *not* love the slave-girl, however much gratitude and pity he may come to feel, has been made perfectly clear throughout Act I, above all in his aria "Non piangere, Liù" (I.D.3), leading off the final *concertato*; but that insight into the situation too easily vanishes in the intense poignancy of Liù's torture, renunciation, suicide, and funeral cortège. If the Prince's reaction is seen in the perspective of the whole, however, it is clear that his regard for Liù, whatever her feeling for him, is that of a nobleman for an extraordinarily loyal retainer. Her loyalty is worth defending, for when she is being manhandled he struggles to come to her defence; he is shocked and moved when she falls lifeless at his feet; but his heart is, as it has been, wholly engaged elsewhere. And it is that engagement of his heart—the confrontation of the fiery Prince, with all that he embodies musically and dramatically, and the icy Princess, with all that she embodies musically and dramatically—that is what this opera is about.

A STUDY IN SILVER AND GOLD

Puccini's *Turandot* unfolds almost without interruption from sunset at the beginning of Act I to sunrise at the end of Act III. This quasi-Aristotelian unity of time resonates in symbolic polarities of night and day throughout, most notably the opposition of moon and sun, of silver and icy white to fiery red and gold. Moonrise is death for the Prince of Persia: it is the moment of the cruel Princess's first appearance, but it is also the moment at which the unknown Prince first sees her and determines to win her. Sunrise is love: it is the moment of Calàf's triumph, but also the moment of Turandot's defeat. At Turandot's first appearance, at the $E\flat$-major climax of the Prince of Persia's $e\flat$-minor cortège in Act I, the cold, white light of the moon falls upon the merciless Princess—"encased in ice" as Liù puts it

41

in the e♭-minor suicide scene and cortège in Act III—but in the final scene her silvery robe becomes only the outer cover for the warm body awakened by the Prince's fiery kiss. The golden warmth of the sun apostrophized by the D-major chorus on the "theme of the Prince's name" at the end of Act III echoes its appearance in "Nessun dorma" tonally as well as thematically; it is in similarly striking contrast to the invocation to the moon in Act I, which also begins in D major, but a D major reached from the opening tonality of f♯ minor associated with sunset and the Executioners' fire. That earlier D Major is then expunged during the choral sequence finishing in E♭ major with the call for Pu-Tin-Pao at moonrise and the appearance of "Mo-li-hua" and the Princess herself.

These contrasts—gold and silver, light and dark, fire and ice, life and death, "the Prince's name" and "Mo-li-hua," D and E♭—find their apical expression in the text and music of the Enigma scene. The posing and the solution of Turandot's enigmas, which replace the purely satiric ones of Gozzi's original, and their setting as prolonged cadences in d minor ("Hope" and "Blood") and e♭ minor ("Turandot"), cement the coherence of the work on the level of musico-dramatic symbolism. And above and apart from all these associations, in the immobile pure white C-major center of music and drama alike, sits the hieratic figure of the Emperor Altoum, the Son of Heaven—"Figlio del cielo"—that heaven in which both sun and moon reside.

CHAPTER II

THE SOURCES

TURANDOT AS A
SPOKEN PLAY

CARLO GOZZI'S *TURANDOT*

Carlo Gozzi (1720–1808) is chiefly remembered today as the original author of fantastic plays made into operas: *Turandot*; *La donna serpente* (Wagner's *Die Feen*); *L'amore delle tre melarancie* (Prokofiev's *Lyubov k trem apel'sinam*), and *Il re cervo* (Henze's *König Hirsch*). Like Carlo Goldoni (1707–1793), Gozzi incorporated aspects of traditional *commedia dell'arte* into written plays, but where Goldoni took a decisive step toward realism, Gozzi felt that the old form lent itself better to fantasy, to myth, to fairytale, to pantomime, and indeed to opera, so far as opera is conceived as fundamentally anti-realist. The operatic cognates of Goldoni's comedy of manners are not only *opere buffe* or *semiserie* composed on his influential libretti, such as Haydn's *Lo speziale* or Piccinni's *La buona figliuola*, but also later works like the Mozart–Da Ponte *Nozze di Figaro* or Rossini's *Barbiere di Siviglia*, even Strauss's *Der Rosenkavalier*. Gozzi's operatic descendants, to the contrary, would be not only the operas based directly on his plays but also such works as Mozart's *Die Zauberflöte*, the operas of Weber, even Strauss's *Die Frau ohne Schatten*.

The *commedia dell'arte* was a repertory of stereotyped comic dramas based not upon fully developed written texts but rather on *scenari*, on synopses filled out by actors improvising dialogue, along with a great deal of physical slapstick and stage business, and calling for skills such as juggling, gymnastics, and singing. The roles were "stock" characters: Harlequin, Columbine, comic servants, comic old men, braggart soldiers, and so on, some of whom wore the traditional half-mask or cat-mask, which emphasizes the degree to which they were not individuated. By a natural metonymy these traditional characters were called "masks." (Readers of high comedy in the classical European traditions will be familiar with aspects of the *commedia dell'arte* that have been absorbed into plays by Shakespeare, Jonson, and Molière.)

Gozzi, like Goldoni, substituted a written text for the old *scenario* for improvisation, but he also took over the old masks and methods and wove them into his fantastic plots. From 1761 he provided one of the few surviving *commedia* companies with a series of *fiabe*: a new type of written play mingling fairytale or fantastic elements with the old earthy fooling, with some scope still left for improvisations by talented performers. His materials involved transformations, tests, ordeals, initiations, and rituals, all elements that link folktale with myth and seem to spring from the unconscious. Gozzi's reputation declined almost to invisibility during the latter part of the nineteenth century, when realism and naturalism were the vogue, but he has been reinstated in the twentieth century as a precursor of our own preoccupations.

Turandot (1761) is based on an Oriental folktale and is recognized as Gozzi's masterpiece.[1] In the introduction to the collected editions of his *Fiabe* (1805), Gozzi described the unfavorable response to his earlier *Il corvo (The Raven)*, where he had used masks and introduced transformation scenes, writing sarcastically of his critics that

> These ungrateful people were the reason why I chose from among the Persian fairytales the comic fable of Turandot to serve as the basis for a play—assuredly containing "masks" but they play a small part—with the sole purpose of giving those actors employment, and entirely without anything magical or marvelous.
>
> I hoped that the three enigmas of the Princess of China, set in an artificial and tragic situation, might supply material for two acts of the play and that the problem of solving them might yield the subject for three more, thus creating a tragi-comic work in five acts.

Gozzi went on to point out that he chose the plot of *Turandot* in order to curtail the debate on the merit of magical transformation scenes, though he maintained that in his earlier *fiabe* he had employed that device only after adequate preparation. His preface continues:

> The fable of Turandot, the Chinese Princess, self-evidently set in motion by these impossible circumstances, and with some small use of the well-loved masks, and without the impressive magic of apparitions and transformations, was first acted by the Sacchi company at the Teatro San Samuele on 22 January 1761, and it was repeated for seven successive evenings to the applause of a full house.

Gozzi's preface encapsulates his basic approach to drama: mixing genres, using the old conventions of the *commedia dell'arte*, and refusing to be confined to the developing tradition of theatrical realism. This is the key to his popularity with Romantic writers outside Italy, such as Tieck in Germany and Musset in France. Further, it accounts for his usually being regarded in Italy as a writer of secondary importance, as the dogged opponent to the more smoothly plotted and more realistic plays of Goldoni.

Gozzi's preface also adumbrates a fundamental difficulty in the dramatic structure of his *Turandot*:

> I hoped that the three enigmas of the Princess . . . might supply material for two acts of the play, and the problem of solving them might yield a subject for three more.

It is not Turandot's enigmas, fairly handily answered by the unknown Prince on the spot, that produce the complications of the last three acts but rather the Prince's own question: what is his name and who is his father?[2] Gozzi's commitment to classical five-act structure forced him to invent a complex set of actions to keep the spectator in successive states of suspense from the Prince's solution of Turandot's enigmas until the dénouement, in marked contrast to the forward drive of the first two acts. The over-abundance of complication in Gozzi's last three acts always required simplification in later adaptations for the musical theater. Seen in the light of the genesis and final form of Puccini's *Turandot* as discussed in Chapter III, the outline of Gozzi's play that follows concretely illustrates the dramaturgic problem: the rising action in Gozzi's Acts I and II served very well for Puccini's original long Act I—eventually Act I and Act II set 2—while the falling action in Gozzi's Acts III, IV and V had to be jettisoned and replaced.

Act I of Gozzi's play opens with the Prince at the gate of Peking, which is decorated with the skulls of Turandot's failed suitors. Having escaped from his father's conquered kingdom of Astrakhan, the fugitive Prince worked for a while as a gardener for Cheicobad, king of the Caranzani, where he caught the eye of the Princess Adelma, since wrongly believed to have died.[3] He has come to Peking to join the army of the Chinese Khan, and is immediately recognized by Barach, his former tutor, now married to one Schirina, and living under the alias of Assan. Their conversation is interrupted by the sound of a dead march, and Ismaele, aged tutor to the Prince of Samarkand appears, grieving for his beheaded master, Turandot's latest victim. Cursing her beauty, the old man throws down her portrait and tramples upon it. Despite Barach's warning, the Prince picks it up, and is so entranced by the Princess's beauty that he resolves to try to win her hand. Barach redoubles his efforts to dissuade the Prince, calling upon his wife to add her arguments, and Act I ends with the Prince going off to try to win Turandot.

Act II takes place in the great hall of the Divan, the royal council chamber. The opening scene introduces Truffaldino (master of the eunuchs) and Brighella (master of the pages), two of the traditional masks. For their dialogue Gozzi supplied only a summary of what they should say, following the convention called *recitar a soggetto*, leaving it to the two comedians of the Sacchi troupe—and Gozzi's friend Antonio Sacchi (1708–1788), the *capocomico* (director of the company), was a famous Truffaldino—to improvise their own dialogue.[4] These two discuss various topics facetiously while they supervise the arrangement of the hall, scarcely three hours after the failure of the last prince.[5]

Accompanied by a march, a procession enters: guards, the eight sages who will confirm the answers of the enigmas, then Pantalone (the Emperor's secretary) and Tartaglia (the Chief Chancellor), the other two masks. Last to enter is the Emperor Altoum bemoaning the cruelty of his daughter and the deaths of so many luckless aspirants to her hand, while Pantalone complains of this world of princes who fall in love with portraits and girls who hate marriage, adding that if he were to tell his fellow Venetians about these things, they would laugh at him.[6]

The Prince is brought in under guard; his appearance stirs the Emperor's pity and he asks for the young man's name, but the Prince begs to remain incognito.[7] His demeanor and lofty sentiments persuade Altoum of his nobility, and the Emperor grants his request. Thrice the Emperor then tries to dissuade the Prince, describing his daughter as perverse, proud, cruel, vain and obstinate. Thrice the Prince says that if he cannot win Turandot he would rather die: "Morte pretendo, o Turandotte in sposa." Truffaldino and Tartaglia offer comic yet sinister reasons why the young man should withdraw, but he remains steadfast. At the Emperor's reluctant command, Truffaldino and his eunuchs go to fetch Turandot.

To a march accompanied by tambourines, Truffaldino and his minions reenter, followed by a group of female slaves; then come two veiled personal slaves, Adelma (the daughter of King Cheicobad) and Zelima (the daughter of Schirina and stepdaughter of Barach); Turandot herself, also veiled, brings up the rear. With "several facetious formalities" Truffaldino takes from Zelima a bowl containing sealed scrolls—the answers to the enigmas—and gives it to the sages. Haughtily, Turandot demands to know who longs to lose his life so miserably; her father indicates the Prince standing in awe before her. In an aside to Zelima, Turandot admits that this unknown Prince stirs her to pity, and Zelima begs her to set easy enigmas. Adelma, who has recognized the Prince as the sometime gardener of her father Cheicobad, wishes that she had known his true rank before she herself became a slave. Turandot advises the Prince to withdraw, but he holds his ground. Altoum orders the reading of the edict, whereupon Tartaglia ceremoniously proclaims that Turandot will marry only a prince who can solve her three enigmas.

Turandot now propounds her enigmas, each in a different lyric stanza—*ottava rima*, *settenario*, and *terza rima*. The Prince answers them correctly, though the last one gives him some difficulty, compounded by his distraction when Turandot approaches and drops her veil. The solutions to the enigmas in Gozzi's text are the sun, the year, and the lion of Adria (St.

Mark). Gozzi evidently intended to represent Turandot as something of a bluestocking, because she is directed to utter her first enigma "in an academic tone," and her resistance to marriage is prompted not only by a general contempt for the male sex but by intellectual pride as well.

Turandot's first reaction to being bested is to sink fainting upon her throne, but soon pride and anger reassert themselves. She proposes to come up with three new enigmas by the following dawn, enigmas that will prove unanswerable, but her father insists upon the letter of the law, declaring himself ready to adjourn at once to the temple to celebrate the marriage. Turandot declares that if she must approach the altar it will be only to kill herself upon it. Moved by her rage and suffering, the Prince offers to die if by the following dawn she can discover his name and that of his father. Reluctantly, the Emperor agrees to this new trial. The march with tambourines strikes up again, and the scene of the three enigmas, the culmination of the rising action, closes with the male characters exiting through one door and the women exiting into the seraglio through another.

Although the first two acts of the final form of Puccini's libretto do not agree with the first two acts of Gozzi's play in every detail, there is a clear and close connection between them. But even allowing for the compression of action and the suppression of peripheral characters expected when a play is turned into a libretto, the differences are striking, and most are improvements upon Gozzi. The dramatist adheres to the convention of the unity of time, and so do Puccini's librettists, but the passage of time is handled more evocatively and dramatically in the opera by appointing the hour of moonrise for the Prince of Persia's execution and by anticipating the moon's appearance with a haunting choral invocation. Having the Prince fall in love at the sight of Turandot's portrait—a stock device now perhaps most familiar from Schikaneder's *Zauberflöte* libretto—is far inferior to the Adami-Simoni solution, where the sight of Turandot herself, in a brilliant coup de théâtre, awakens the Prince's passion. And the eventual transformation of Gozzi's Venetian masks into the purely Chinese Ministers Ping, Pong, and Pang gives the libretto greater coherence.

The remainder of Gozzi's plot has little directly in common with the rest of the Adami-Simoni libretto in its final form. The problem confronting Puccini's librettists on their way to the dénouement is difficult to grasp, however, without some notion of the extraordinary thicket of complications invented by Gozzi, through which they tried at first to cut a path. In the medial stages of the libretto's evolution a number of details from the last three acts, particularly from the latter part of Act IV, found their way into the text, before eventually being discarded.

Act III of Gozzi's play begins in a room in the seraglio. The former princess Adelma laments her lot as a slave and reveals her hatred of Turandot. Hearing her mistress Turandot and her fellow-slave Zelima approaching, she conceals herself. Now Turandot exposes something of her motives. She does not hate the unknown Prince so much that she wants him to die, but men in general arouse her scorn. They are faithless, insincere, incapable of love; no sooner do they win one girl than they stop loving her, nor does shame prevent their seeking out the vilest slaves and prostitutes. This speech is the nucleus from which Turandot's inserted *aria di sortita* "In questa reggia" will develop, but it differs in two significant aspects, one mainly dramaturgic, the other mainly psychological. First, rather than being a private colloquy with a maidservant, "In questa reggia" is delivered publicly, a much more effective treatment for an *aria di sortita* coming so late in the work. Second, Turandot's motivation has been changed. The proto-feminist contempt of the Princess in the play for the social behavior and intellectual pretensions of men becomes feminism of a very different sort in the opera, where hatred for men as sexual beings is exteriorized in the Princess's desire to avenge a ravished and murdered ancestress Lo-u-ling who stands in for all oppressed womankind.

Adelma emerges from hiding and suggests that Turandot may discover the unknown names by an exercise of cunning. Hoping to gain the Prince for herself, Adelma short-circuits Zelima's suggestion that they try to trick the name out of her stepfather Barach, offending her to the point where she storms out. Now Adelma proposes her own plan to Turandot, and after the Princess leaves, Adelma declares her determination to win the Prince and escape from slavery.

In another room in the palace the Prince and Barach are talking, the former confident that his secret is safe because his death has been rumored for years, the latter fearful of treachery and sorry that the Prince gave Turandot a second chance. As Barach is assuring him that he has not revealed the Prince's name to anyone, even to his wife Schirina, three of the masks enter with guards to fetch the Prince and march him off. At this point an old man dressed in rags enters and, horrified at seeing the Prince led away by soldiers, cries out his name. Barach silences the old man, then recognizes him as his former master the deposed monarch Timur, who has come to Peking in search of his son. Joined by his wife Schirina, Barach is angry when she confirms his suspicion that she may have revealed that the Prince is their guest. Hearing Truffaldino approaching with his eunuchs, Barach begs his wife to help the old man to safety, but Truffaldino enters before they can get away. Asked the identity of the two people with him, Barach denies knowing either of them, but Truffaldino has seen Schirina in the harem and knows her to be Zelima's mother. This situation was adapted for Act III of Puccini's opera: when Liù and Timur are dragged in by the guards, Ping reports that he had seen them with the Prince (in Act I), while the Prince insists that they do not know him.

Act IV of the play begins in a columned atrium in the seraglio. The faithful Barach, his wife Schirina and old Timur are led in, in chains. Turandot tells them they may save their lives if they give her the answer to the Prince's question. Barach defies her, saying that he would rather die than utter the names. Moved by Barach's loyalty, Timur volunteers to submit to torture and, finally, to reveal to Turandot what she wants to know if she will spare Barach and Schirina. (In Adami and Simoni's libretto for Puccini, it is Liù who undergoes torture because she has revealed to Turandot that she knows the Prince's name.)

They are interrupted by Adelma, who announces that she has corrupted the Prince's guards and set in motion a plan of her own; she takes Zelima and Schirina away with her. Dispatching Barach and Timur to dungeons, Turandot, alone, reveals her divided mind. While she relishes the idea of throwing the names in the Prince's face, hoping that Adelma's scheme will find them out, she is also tormented by thoughts of the Prince. Rousing herself, she decides to shame him to retain her freedom, but then just to send him away. Turandot's ambivalence about the Prince and her idea to send him away found their way into the aria "Del primo pianto" in Act III set 2 of the Adami-Simoni libretto.

The Emperor Altoum enters and informs his daughter that he has received a letter containing the names of the Prince and his father and that she cannot possibly discover them. If she yields now, she will be spared a second public humiliation, regain the respect of her subjects, and a husband who is the worthiest man alive. Still hoping for news from Adelma, Turandot hesitates; though shaken by her father's words, she will not renounce the trial at dawn.

Meanwhile, in the room where the Prince is being detained Brighella warns him that he may be visited by temptations and the Prince, forewarned, lies down on a sofa to await events. The idea of tempting the Prince was also adapted by Adami and Simoni for Puccini's opera, though the actual temptations are quite different. Gozzi's take the form of four attempts to discover the Prince's name. Schirina appears first, disguised as a Chinese soldier. Revealing her identity, she tells the Prince that Turandot holds Barach prisoner and that Timur is at her house, lamenting the death of his wife and worried for his son. Schirina says the old man would be reassured if she could bring him a letter written and signed by his son; she produces writing materials, but the Prince does not fall into this trap. Then comes Zelima, who claims that though Turandot protests her hatred for the Prince, there are also stirrings of love in her heart, adding the asseveration formula "Let the earth open and swallow me, if I lie to you." She says that Turandot finds it impossible to appear at court and face the shame of being unable to speak the names, and again she adds "Let the abyss open and swallow me, if I lie to you." The Prince says there is still time to call off the trial: without damaging her reputation, Turandot could simply agree to marry him. Zelima replies that the Princess wants to save her self-respect by announcing that she has discovered the names, and then she will graciously descend from her throne and marry the Prince. But this time Zelima omits her formula, so the Prince bids her go to Turandot and say that though he still withholds his name and his father's, it is from excess of love, not to offend her. Zelima leaves, and the weary Prince falls asleep.

Next Truffaldino steals in, muttering that if mandrake root is placed beneath a sleeper's head he will talk in his sleep and give whatever information is desired. Truffaldino slips the root beneath the Prince's head; the Prince does not speak but stirs in his sleep. Truffaldino interprets these random movements as forming letters of the alphabet, believes he has made out a name, and goes away content.

The last to appear is Adelma herself, veiled and carrying a torch; looking at the sleeping Prince, she invokes love to aid her plan. As she removes her veil he awakes and recognizes her as the Princess Adelma, daughter of Cheicobad. She pours out her story: how her brother was beheaded for failing to answer Turandot's enigmas, how her father raised an army to avenge him and was defeated, and how all the rest of her family was exterminated. She has told him all this hoping that his blind love for the Princess will not make him scorn her for speaking the truth about Turandot's cruelty. She tells him Turandot has ordered that he be slain at dawn; he bursts out "Oh, miserable Calàf! Timur! This is the help I bring you!" Adelma urges him to escape with her: guards have been bribed, horses readied, a haven awaits them at Berlas. But thinking of Altoum's generosity, Calàf will not betray the laws of hospitality; he will not try to evade what he now supposes to be his fate. Adelma storms out, stung by his rejection, but triumphant now that she knows his name and rank. Calàf is in despair, and when Brighella arrives at dawn with his soldiers he announces his readiness to die. Brighella, surprised, marches the Prince out to the sound of "drums and other instruments."

Act V is a second enigma scene, like Act II taking place in the court council chamber. Behind a scrim a temple and altar are visible and all but Turandot and her retinue are present and in the positions they occupied earlier. The Prince enters, astonished at seeing that he has been brought not to execution (as Adelma had led him to believe) but again to the Divan. Altoum encourages him, saying that Turandot has been summoned to appear, whereupon the Princess and her suite enter in mourning, accompanied by a "lugubrious march." She declares that the Prince must be gratified by her appearance and by the sight of the altar already prepared; but she is only playing a game, for in the next breath, hoping now to shame him and drive him away, she speaks the names of Calàf and Timur and orders him to leave the court and find another bride. In a frenzy Calàf draws a dagger to kill himself at Turandot's feet; she stops him, but he refuses to consider life without her and raises his dagger again. Once again she stops him, this time saying that he must live for her sake, that he has won her. The resulting jubilation is halted by Adelma, who claims that she will die if she cannot have Calàf for herself, seizing his dagger. Calàf holds her back, takes the dagger from her, and expresses his gratitude to her, for through her discovery and betrayal of his name and his own consequent near-fatal despair, Turandot has finally been moved to recognize the depth of his love and acknowledge her own. Turandot asks her father to grant Adelma her freedom; Altoum does so, and restores her kingdom to her as well. The Emperor then gives Calàf a letter telling him that the usurper in Astrakhan has been slain and a faithful minister holds his throne for him. Turandot thanks the gods and begs their forgiveness for her obstinacy, then invites the audience's applause in a traditional *licenza*:

> Sappia questo gentil popol de' maschi,
> Ch'io gli amo tutto. Al pentimento mio
> Deh, qualche segno di perdon si faccia.

(May the mannerly world of men know that I love them all. For my repentence, pray let some sign of forgiveness [i.e. applause] be offered.)

IMITATIONS OF GOZZI'S *TURANDOT*

Out of Gozzi's complex plot, with its repeated suspensions in the last three acts, Puccini and his librettists proposed to shape a subject for the musical theater that would be attuned to the sensibilities of a post–World War I audience. Puccini's initial interest was sparked by Andrea Maffei's Italian translation of Schiller's German adaptation of the Gozzi play, before he turned to the original. More than that, Maffei's translation of Schiller had some effect on Gazzoletti's libretto for Bazzini's *Turanda*—discussed in the next part of this chapter—which played a part in the tortuous evolution of the falling action of Puccini's opera, after the Enigma scene.

From Gozzi's text to Schiller's the shift in tone is striking. Gone is the local Venetian color: the dialect of the masks, the third enigma "il leone d'Adria," and various touches of satire directed at the audience in the Teatro San Samuele. Schiller retained the masks as a purely decorative motif rather than the vivid cynics and connivers that Gozzi had made them. Gone too are their improvisatory passages and their prose: they have the same German blank verse as the others. Schiller replaced the local folk texture of Gozzi with a decorous smoothness of undeniable charm, but a charm very different from that produced by Gozzi's quirky shifts of level.

Schiller also changed the enigmas, adopting Gozzi's second (the year) as his first, and supplying two new ones, the eye and the plow.[8] Some speeches are drastically cut, and the scene of Truffaldino and the mandrake root is omitted. Schiller's most significant change, however, comes at the end of the play. He removed Turandot's concluding speech with its *licenza*, halting the dialogue after two lines of gratitude from Calàf, who has read the letter that Altoum handed him, and ending with a *tableau vivant*:

> At this moment the room opens; Timur and Barach enter, accompanied by Zelima and her mother. When Calàf sees his father, he runs to him with outstretched arms. Barach falls at Calàf's feet, while Zelima and her mother postrate themselves before Turandot, who graciously raises them. Altoum, Pantalone and Tartaglia stand, moved. The curtain falls amidst these activities.

Andrea Maffei's translation of Schiller follows him with far greater fidelity than Schiller had followed Gozzi. Few details need detain us here. Turandot's "Straniero, ascolta!" that introduces the first enigma may have come directly from Maffei's translation of Schiller; though brief, this expression is crucial, for in the original libretto that Puccini set, as discussed in Chapter III below, these were the Princess's first words. Also interesting is a footnote Maffei appended to his list of characters: "Should one wish to stage *Turandot*, it would be necessary to give other names to the four masks, who have become intolerable these days." As also noted in Chapter III, Puccini had some initial reservations about including the masks at all, and their inclusion in the guise of the three purely Chinese Ministers, *a fortiori* with changed names, may well have been suggested by Maffei's observations; at any rate, it reflects the same aesthetic premise. Maffei's verse is even less colorful than Schiller's; what in the German poet is at least graceful or eloquent becomes bombastic and pompous. To place Maffei's text beside Gozzi's is to see how dated can be a well-meaning but humorless attempt to impose a later style upon a work conceived along earlier, more lively conventions. Gozzi may not be a Shakespeare, but Maffei looks very like a Nahum Tate; in which case, Schiller is a Dryden.

TURANDOT AS OPERA
BEFORE PUCCINI

WEBER AND OTHERS NORTH OF
THE ALPS[9]

In the decades before and after 1800 virtually every spoken play in German was adorned with incidental music; Schiller's *Turandot* was no exception. Incidental music for the first production in 1802 was supplied by Franz

Seraph von Destouches; for another production in 1806 the incidental music was by Friedrich Ludwig Seidl. In 1809 the play was produced with Weber's music, in 1813 with music by Joseph von Blumenthal. In 1843 it was done with music by Vincenz Lachner, music regularly used in revivals over the next four decades, and probably once again as late as 1911.

Weber was evidently the only composer before Puccini to use a Chinese melody for *couleur locale*. In Breslau in 1804, he had composed an *Overatura* (!) *Chinesa*. Though its original form is not known, Weber revised this overture in 1809,

> adding six pieces by 12th September . . . all but one based on the single theme of the overture . . . He had originally discovered the tune in vol. 2 of Rousseau's *Dictionnaire de Musique* (1786), given as an 'air chinois'. . . . [It] was later to appeal to Hindemith when he made it the subject of the second movement of his Weber Metamorphoses.[10]

Operatic versions of *Turandot* before Puccini were all German except for the Bazzini *Turanda* discussed below. The first, by J.F.G. von Blumenthal (Munich, 1809) is known only through secondary sources and reviews; a *Turandot* by Hermann von Löwenskjold (Copenhagen, 184?) is even more tenuously documentable. Franz Danzi's *Turandot, Singspiel nach Gozzi* (Karlsruhe, 1816) was followed by Carl Gottlieb Reissiger's *Turandot, tragikomisches Oper nach Schiller* (Dresden, 1835); *Turandot, Prinzessin von Schiraz* [!] (Vienna, 1838) by J. Hoven, pseudonym of Johann Vesque von Püttlingen; and Theobald Rehbaum's *Turandot, komische Oper . . . frei nach Gozzi* (Berlin, 1888). Adolf Jensen composed a *Turandot* that was never performed; Ferruccio Busoni's *Turandot* on his own libretto (Zürich, 1917) is discussed briefly below. A curious phenomenon to which Kii-Ming Lo has called pointed attention in the conclusion to Chapter V of her *Turandot auf der Opernbühne* is the fact that in none of these operas is there the slightest touch (with one inconsequential exception) of that orientalizing *couleur locale* characteristic of so much nineteenth-century opera.

THE GAZZOLETTI-BAZZINI *TURANDA*

More significant for the student of Puccini is Bazzini's *Turanda* (Milan, 1867). The Brescian violinist and composer Antonio Bazzini (1818–1897), encouraged by Paganini, built a distinguished career as an international virtuoso in the first part of his life; from 1841 to 1845 he lived in Germany, went back to Brescia, then resided in Paris from 1852 to 1863. Again in 1864 Bazzini returned to Brescia, and devoted himself to composition thereafter, resuming an old acquaintance with the Brescian poet Antonio Gazzoletti, who completed the libretto for *Turanda* shortly before his death in

1866. In 1873 Bazzini was called to the Milan Conservatory as professor of composition, becoming director of the Conservatory in 1882; among his pupils there were Alfredo Catalani, Pietro Mascagni, and Giacomo Puccini. In *Italia umbertina*—the "Victorian" era of the new Kingdom of Italy—Bazzini's symphonic poems and chamber music were highly esteemed, and though he has been remembered in our day only as a composer of violin salon music, some idea of his command of a grander style may now be had from the powerful *Dies irae* he contributed to the composite Requiem for Rossini.[11]

The Gazzoletti-Bazzini *Turanda* was first given at La Scala on 13 January 1867 for a run of twelve performances. It was never revived there nor ever performed elsewhere. Giulio Ricordi's opinion of *Turanda* is preserved in a letter he wrote to Franco Faccio:

> an absolute zero: the first evening very bad; the second was modestly approved, thanks to some kind friends; the third was met with silence of the tomb. . . . The libretto is stupid and without interest, with an absolute absence of any genre whatever, no form that is either old or new.[12]

The distinguished progressive critic Filippo Filippi had a rather different view:

> considered musically, it is an outstanding work, full of strange and lovely things [*peregrine bellezze*]. It missed an enthusiastic success owing to its rather miscalculated subject, the *Turanda* of Gozzi as remade by Schiller and then made into a libretto [*melodrammaticamente ridotta*] by the genial poet Gazzoletti, with stupendous verses but little sense for the exigencies of the theater.[13]

Puccini was probably aware that Bazzini had composed this opera, his only stage work, though it is unlikely that he would have known even the three published fragments. Gazzoletti's libretto, on the other hand, was obviously consulted by Adami and Simoni, though few of the details that clearly originated there survive in the final libretto of Puccini's opera. Gazzoletti's libretto, called an "azione fantastica in quattro parti," derives chiefly from Maffei, but as Gazzoletti observed in his preface to the reader,

> it has been altered or supplemented by me, in tune with the special needs of music and with today's tastes . . . I have taken a path unfamiliar at least among us, which if followed by talents more fortunate than mine can perhaps lead to results that will satisfy at one and the same time the strict logic of Art and the thirst for novelty by which the musical theater of our time is assailed.

The setting is changed to "Modain on the Tigris, capital of Persia, before the year A.D. 650, or at the time of the last Sassanid kings." The Arabian Nights atmosphere given by references to the seraglio and the Divan has been eliminated. The *maschere* are omitted, their routine dramaturgic functions taken over by the *comprimario* Gandarte, the head of Turanda's guard. The female contingent is cut back to two: Turanda, the daughter of the King of Persia; and Adelma, now merely companion and confidante to Turanda. Calàf becomes Nadir, an Indian Prince, and Barach becomes Ormut, now one of the Supreme Magi of the kingdom, though, as in Gozzi's play, he had once been tutor to the unknown Prince. Altoum is now called Cosroe, King of Persia; Timur has been dropped altogether.[14]

Like other librettos based on Gozzi's plot, Gazzoletti's is most faithful to the first two acts of its source, and the answers to the enigmas are as they are in Maffei (after Schiller): the year, the eye, the plow. Act III, to the contrary, is one of Gazzoletti's new inventions. The first part takes place in Ormut's *laboratorio*, where Turanda comes in order to learn by magic the secret of the Prince's name; spirits (*incubi*) of the upper and nether worlds refuse to divulge it, however, because Ormut is determined to preserve the Prince's secret. The second part of Act III takes place in a banquet hall, where Prince Nadir and the Emperor Cosroe are being entertained by Adelma singing the legend of "the nightingale and the rose" to the accompaniment of a phalanx of harpists. Unobserved, Adelma slips a sleeping potion into Nadir's goblet; the Prince, left alone, sings an aria before he slumbers. Turanda and Adelma steal in to observe him; Adelma confesses she is attracted to the sleeper, nor is Turanda herself unimpressed. Nadir begins to talk in his sleep, confessing his consuming love for Turanda, and in his dream, he sighs "O fortunato, fortunato Nadir!" Repeating his name in triumph, Turanda and Adelma leave.[15] Ingredients from this Act III of *Turanda*, specifically the two episodes of the *incubi* and the banquet, formed some part of an "Act II" for *Turandot* that Adami and Simoni proposed to Puccini in August 1921 (see Chapter III, pp. 73–75). The intrusion of these episodes from Gazzoletti helped create the major crisis for Puccini and his collaborators that led to the fundamental rearrangement of their libretto that evolved into the form in which we know it today.

Gazzoletti's Act IV was also newly invented. It opens in "hanging gardens," with a female chorus entertaining Turanda and Adelma with a song. The brief episode closes with a recitative and aria for Turanda (aside), in which she confesses that Nadir has aroused feelings of compassion. This episode may stand behind a proposed scene for Turandot, Liù, and the slaves that once formed the second part of the three-scene "Act II" suggested by Puccini in September 1921 but soon abandoned (see Chapter III, pp. 74–75).

The setting shifts to the temple of Oromane, where Turanda and Nadir arrive with their attendants. Like Norma in her final scene, Turanda bids her father and the priests retire so that she can interrogate Nadir in private. She tells him that she knows his name, but since she wishes him no harm, she orders him away. He urges her to yield; but she remains unpersuaded until Nadir draws his dagger and tries to stab himself. Calling for help, Turanda stops him and confesses that she loves him. When the others rush in, Turanda asks her father to bless her union with Nadir.

It is possible that the duet for Turanda and Nadir in the final scene may have suggested some of the substance of the several versions of the second and final confrontation of Turandot and the Prince in the Adami-Simoni libretto. There are no verbal echoes of Gazzoletti, though, for he used the artificially poetic librettistic style, still current in the 1860s, that the Milanese *scapigliati* were seeking to replace in such librettos as those Arrigo Boito and Emilio Praga wrote for Faccio's two operas, *Amleto* and *I profughi fiamminghi*.

BUSONI'S *TURANDOT*

In 1904 Feruccio Busoni (1866–1924) made his first sketches for what he originally conceived as a *Turandot* Suite. He completed orchestrating it in May 1905, and it was performed in Bologna on 29 April 1906 as *Suite per orchestra, Opus 41*. The work had eight sections derived from the musical cues of Gozzi's *Turandot*, but it was not originally intended as incidental music for performance with the existing German version of the play by Schiller; by 1911 Busoni had added two more sections to this suite, and in this expanded form it had its first performance in Boston. Dent has suggested that Busoni may have come to think his *Turandot* suite could be used as incidental music for a new German translation of Gozzi's text, however;[16] and in 1911 Karl Vollmöller (1878–1948), perhaps at Busoni's suggestion, did adapt the play for a production directed by Max Reinhardt at the Deutsches Theater, Berlin, 27 October 1911. An interesting allusion to this production survives in Puccini's letter of 18 March 1920 to Simoni, in which he responded favorably to his first reading of Maffei's translation of Schiller:

> Yesterday I talked to a foreign lady who told me about a production of this work in Germany with a mise-en-scène by Max Reinhardt, executed in a very curious and novel way . . . in Reinhardt's production Turandot was a tiny woman, surrounded by tall men, specifically cho-

sen for their height; huge chairs, huge furnishings, and this viper of a woman with the strange heart of an hysteric. [*CP*, ltr 766, p. 490; see References, A:4]

In 1913 Busoni wrote to his wife: "What do you think about *Turandot* . . . as an opera, in Italian of course, to the words of Gozzi?"[17] When the opportunity to compose an opera on this subject arose three years later, however, Busoni wrote his own libretto, in German though preserving the spirit of Gozzi's text; Busoni believed that Schiller had distorted it. The vigor of Gozzi's play, and its fantastic atmosphere and treatment of the *maschere*, appealed to Busoni's original and radical bent, and when he finally composed the opera he responded to the hints for exotic ceremonial music in its stage directions. Busoni spent the years of World War I in Zürich, and when the opera house there accepted his one-act *Arlecchino* and asked for a companion work to fill out the evening, he decided the time for his *Turandot* had come, thereby juxtaposing two works treating *commedia dell'arte* characters in a contemporary style.[18] For the three out of Gozzi's four *maschere* that Busoni kept he retained the original names of Truffaldino, Pantalone and Tartaglia.[19]

Busoni's simplification of Gozzi's plot is masterly. Each of his two acts is in turn divided into two relatively short scenes. The score has nineteen numbers altogether, some of which contain brief passages of spoken dialogue.

Act I set 1 is a compression of Gozzi's first act. The chief alteration is the substitution of a new character, the black Königinmutter von Samarkand, who serves the function that Ismaele performed in Gozzi's plot: grieving for a prince who has failed, throwing away the miniature portrait of Turandot which the Prince picks up and to which he straightaway loses his heart.

Act I set 2 is the throne room. In an aria Truffaldino directs the arrangements for the coming test. The Emperor Altoum, in Busoni's opera a bass and a major character, enters to a solemn processional and sings an aria complaining of Turandot's intransigence. The Prince appears, and in a quartet with Altoum, Pantalone, and Tartaglia, he reiterates his intention to die if he cannot win Turandot.[20] This is followed by Turandot's processional entry, in which Busoni retained Adelma, but omitted Zelima. Adelma recognizes the Prince and also knows his name, and this seemingly slight change allowed Busoni to evade most of the complications that prolong the latter part of Gozzi's play. Busoni changed the enigmas yet again; now the answers are human understanding, custom, and art. As in Gozzi, the act ends with the Prince propounding the questions of his name and parentage, but if Turandot succeeds in answering him, he offers to release her and depart, not to die.

Act II set 1 is preceded by an off-stage mezzo and female chorus intoning a tune that one recognizes with amazement as *Greensleeves*. The curtain rises on Turandot's quarters. After a choral dance, the Princess sings an aria in which she examines her mixed feelings for the Prince. Truffaldino appears and his second aria recounts how he slipped the mandrake root under the sleeping Prince's head. Altoum enters next and tells his daughter of the letter he had received and urges her to yield, adding "he is too good for you." After Altoum's departure, Adelma tells her mistress she knows the name, and in exchange for her freedom she will reveal it. Turandot agrees, and Adelma whispers it in her ear.

Act II set 2 is connected to the preceding one by an orchestral intermezzo. The curtain rises on the throne room, and a funeral march is heard as Turandot and her maidens enter. In the brief dialogue separating this episode from the finale she announces Calàf's name. There is general consternation, and Prince Calàf bids the court farewell, but Turandot stops his departure, declaring that he has awakened her heart. The final ensemble takes the form of a pseudo-enigma, "Was ist das alle Menschen bindet?" and the answer, "Die Liebe!" (What binds all men together? Love!). Perhaps this ending suggested Turandot's final line in the Adami-Simoni libretto: "Il suo nome è Amor!"

We have seen how easily Busoni avoided Gozzi's tortuous path to the dénouement, the path that would give Puccini, Adami and Simoni such headaches. Busoni also retained the intimate atmosphere of Gozzi's play—originally written to be acted in the small theater of San Samuele in Venice—while Puccini and his collaborators came out with a massive spectacle in the vein of late-nineteenth-century opera. Instead of the fairytale atmosphere of romance or fantasy they imposed an epic scale upon the protagonists. Even if Puccini and his librettists were aware of Busoni's success in ridding himself of most of Gozzi's complications (and the chances are they were), they were determined to seek a solution of their own.[21]

CHAPTER III

THE GENESIS

RISING ACTION

THE BEGINNING

Not since *Manon Lescaut* had a Puccini opera a birth as tortuous as *Turandot*, nor such prolonged and circuitous questions about its basic structure. To follow the trail from Puccini's first favorable response to the subject, in his letter to Simoni of 18 March 1920, to his death on 29 November 1924 with the crucial final scene still in drafts and sketches, to make sense of all the tangents and backtrackings, requires close appraisal of the evidence. Letters between Puccini and his librettists survive which shed light on the evolution of text and music. Yet they sometimes give only a passing reference to meetings between composer and librettists at which important decisions must have been made, though other letters and accounts sometimes help fill in the blanks.

The story is only comprehensible if we bear in mind that both the librettists, Giuseppe Adami (1879–1946) and Renato Simoni (1875–1952), were pursuing their own careers during the time when *Turandot* was coming into being. Both men were born in Verona, in the Veneto region. Of the two, Adami had the greater experience of working with Puccini: he had already supplied Puccini with the librettos for *Il tabarro* and *La rondine*, and their collaboration had begun back in 1914 with the stillborn *Due zoccoletti* (a subject eventually used by Mascagni for his *Lodoletta*). Adami was primarily a playwright. His first play, *I fioi di Goldoni* (1905), was written in the Venetian dialect, and during the *Turandot* years (1920–24) he produced seven full-length plays as well as a number of one-act plays (at least one of which contained *commedia dell'arte* characters), not to mention five other librettos. In the interstices of all this work, he would on occasion write for and direct films. So Puccini and his *Turandot* were not always uppermost in Giuseppe Adami's thoughts.

Renato Simoni had come to Milan in 1899 to pursue a career in journalism, but he was a dramatist and librettist as well. His second play was *Carlo Gozzi* (1903), and in fact it was Simoni who first mentioned Gozzi's *Turandot* to Puccini. In 1906 Simoni succeeded Giuseppe Giacosa as director of the influential review *La lettura*, a position he held until 1924, and from 1914 until his death he was drama critic of the Milanese paper *Il corriere della sera*. Simoni's best-known libretto was for Giordano's *Madame Sans-Gêne* (1915), but he did not follow that phase of his career as assiduously as did Adami, who had important ties with the publishing house of Ricordi.[1]

Around the beginning of February 1919, after the European première of *Il trittico* at Rome, Puccini went back to his home at Torre del Lago and found himself restlessly and nervously confronting the need for a subject for his next opera. As usual with him, the road started off with what turned out to be a detour. On a visit to London in the summer of 1919, Puccini saw a dramatization of *Oliver Twist*; as in the case of the Belasco plays that eventuated in *Madama Butterfly* and *La fanciulla del West*, Puccini's lack of English did not interfere with his perception of dramatic situations that might be, to use a cogent Verdian term, *musicabile*, and he saw the possibilities for musical theater in *Oliver Twist*. Back in Italy in August, while Adami was with him working on revisions for Act III of *La rondine*, Puccini asked for a scenario for the *Oliver Twist* subject, first called *Mollie*, later *Fanny*. Adami felt that a collaborator would be a good idea and proposed his fellow *veronese* Simoni. The two writers prepared part of a scenario for *Fanny*, but shortly after the beginning of 1920 Puccini decided that he had been mistaken about its possibilities.

The meeting between Puccini, Adami, and Simoni that resulted in the choice of *Turandot* for his next opera took place in Milan in mid-March 1920. Puccini had come from Torre del Lago to have lunch with Adami and Simoni, making a detour on his way to Rome, where he was to oversee the 1920 reprise of *Il trittico* at the Teatro Costanzi. While they were eating, Simoni happened to mention Carlo Gozzi and his tragi-comic Chinese fable *Turandot*. It was nearly time for Puccini to leave for the station, and Simoni offered to get the text from his apartment and bring it to the train so Puccini could read it on his way to Rome. By the time Simoni came hurrying to the platform, Puccini was already in his compartment, and the book was handed through the window. It was not Gozzi's original text, however, but Maffei's translation of Schiller that Puccini read on the train.

He sent his reactions to Simoni in the letter from Rome of 18 March 1920 already quoted in Chapter II (see pp. 56–57 above):

> I have read *Turandot* . . . this work [has been] given in Germany with mise-en-scène by Max Reinhardt . . . for my part I would advise that we seize upon this subject. To simplify it by reducing the number of acts and to strive to make it slim and workable, and above all to intensify the amorous passion of Turandot, that for so long has smouldered beneath the ashes of her great pride . . . I think that *Turandot* is the most normal and human theater-piece among all of Gozzi's other plays.

> To sum up, a *Turandot*, by way of the modern mind, yours, Adami's, and mine. [*CP*, ltr 766, p. 490]

Puccini's imagination was fired by the idea of the icy princess transformed into a passionate woman. For him this would remain, as he would often put it, the *clou* of the subject, however difficult it might prove to effect this transformation. From the start Puccini could also see that much of the plot in the last three acts of the play would be unusable in a libretto, and this too remained a problem.

When Puccini wrote of "a *Turandot* by way of the modern mind," he was clearly thinking of presenting the heroine in terms of the repression and release of sexual conflict, made explicit rather than being buried beneath the generalities and euphemisms of Gozzi, Schiller, and Maffei. By the early twentieth century the vocabulary of librettos had become less stereotyped and more specific than in earlier periods: three examples familiar to Puccini were Hugo von Hofmannsthal's text for Richard Strauss's *Elektra* (which he had heard in Italian at La Scala, 6 April 1909), Sem Benelli's verse play *L'amore dei tre re* set by Italo Montemezzi (La Scala, 1913), and Tito Ricordi's reduction of Gabriele D'Annunzio's verse play *Francesca da Rimini* for Riccardo Zandonai (La Scala, 1916).

Puccini's next letter to mention *Turandot*, an undated one to Adami, reports that he is returning the book Simoni had given him. Since Puccini thereafter usually referred to Gozzi's play as their source, he must have soon found a copy of it. He described again the process needed to arrive at a serviceable libretto: "Choose a style for it, make it interesting, pad it, stuff it full, and squeeze it down again." He went on to tell Adami about his own preparations:

> some scenic material is coming from Germany . . . I shall get some old Chinese music too, and descriptions and drawings of different instruments which we shall have on stage (not in the orchestra). [*EGP*, ltr 176]

This letter illustrates Puccini's vivid sense of milieu; for him atmosphere was a synthesis of the aural and visual, and he felt he needed to find authentic melodies, as he had for *Madama Butterfly* twenty years earlier.

Soon Puccini's attention was engaged by the problem of how to incorporate Gozzi's masks into the text.

> Do not make too much use of the traditional characters of the Venetian drama—these are to be the clowns and philosophers that now and then inject a jest or an opinion . . . but they must not be of a type demanding too much attention. [*EGP*, ltr 177]

61

His librettists answered him at once that it might be wise to suppress them entirely. Puccini's reply shows his uncertainty.

> It is also possible that by keeping the masks *with discretion* we might have an Italian touch, which, amid so much Chinese mannerism . . . would introduce a more familiar note of our [Italian] life, and above all sincere. The keen observation of *Pantaleone and Company* would bring us back to the realities of our lives. To sum up, do a little as Shakespeare does in *The Tempest* . . .
>
> Yet these masks might spoil [the opera]. If you were to find something to enrich them, make them less bizarre, with the Chinese element? [*EGP*, ltr 178]

At this still notional phase of the libretto's development, we see Puccini grasping the double function of the masks as both participants and commentators, yet supposing they might function on a "real" level opposed to the fantasy of the rest. The final treatment of the masks is one of the most admirable and original features of the finished libretto. Their origin in the *commedia dell'arte* has vanished without a trace and they are now wholly Chinese, dramatically occupying a middle ground between the heroic plane of Turandot and the unknown Prince on the one hand and the completely exotic background of Altoum's court and Peking on the other.

THE SCENARIO

The arrival of a scenario for Act I of *Turandot* at Torre del Lago by the middle of May 1920 brought a note of enthusiasm to the correspondence, though the uncertainty has not disappeared.

> *Turandot!* Act I—very good! I like the scenic plan too. The three masks are promising. I worry a little about the effectiveness of the close, but I could be wrong. [*EGP*, ltr 180]

We know from the corresponding first version of the libretto that the scenario for this Act I will have had two scenes: the first an abridgement of Gozzi's Act I, but with some new material as well; the second, the Enigma scene. Puccini's worries about "the effectiveness of the close" refer to the conclusion of that second scene; the larger question of how many acts there ought to be in the end, and what else they should contain, also remained unsettled for the next two years.

Although intrigued by the possibilities of *Turandot*, Puccini had not yet irrevocably committed himself to it. On 5 July 1920 he wrote to the soprano Gilda Dalla Rizza: "Yesterday I left [Giovacchino] Forzano, who has been working on the second act of *Sly*.² And the decision rests on this act, whether to do it or throw it into the wastebasket" (*CP*, ltr 768, p. 491).

Forzano was a proven quantity, since he had provided the librettos for *Suor Angelica* and *Gianni Schicchi*. In the first days after the Roman *prima* of *Il trittico*, Puccini had asked Forzano to come up with a possible subject. It seems clear that for a while Puccini hoped to spur on Adami and Simoni by hints of another iron in the fire. Evidence of Puccini's tactic surfaces in a letter he wrote to Carlo Paladini in January 1921, in which he says that although he has definitely discarded the idea of composing *Sly*, he does not want to announce his decision.[3]

By mid-July 1920 Puccini had received a scenario for a second and third act of *Turandot*, accompanied by a revision of the May 1920 scenario of Act I. This now completed scenario gave Puccini a first full-length draft of the action, and only now did the magnitude and complexity of the problem emerge. Puccini's earlier librettos taken from plays had involved fairly straightforward adapatation: condensing and simplifying the action, and finding an operatic pacing for it. The problem posed by *Turandot* was much greater. The situation at first glance seems similar to that presented by the one-act Long-Belasco play *Madame Butterfly*, that of inventing a substantial amount of material. But to convert *Madame Butterfly* into a full-length libretto, only preliminary action had to be invented, for the play itself provided the catastrophe. With *Turandot* Puccini and his librettists were faced with the inverse problem, a much harder task: they had a source that gave them the exposition and the rising action through to the Princess's three enigmas and the Prince's counter-proposal, in short, Gozzi's first two acts. Now they wanted to invent a new falling action and a new preparation for the dénouement; Turandot's eventual capitulation was the only part of the rest of Gozzi's plot they would retain. The whole story of their tribulations in arriving at a definitive form of the libretto will be clearer if this aspect of their problem is kept in mind. A further complication resulted from the initial compression of material adapted from Gozzi's Acts I and II, plus the new material, into a single long Act I for the libretto; but more than a year would pass before the disadvantage was grasped.

On 18 July 1920 Puccini sent Adami his first reactions. His tone is appreciably less enthusiastic than it had been in May, and he had already glimpsed the essence of his final problem.

> Your packet received. At first glance it seems good to me, except for criticisms that I might make in both the second and third acts. In the third I had imagined a different dénouement. I had thought her yielding would be more gripping, and I would have wanted her to erupt in expressions of love before the people . . . excessively, violently, shamelessly, like a bomb exploding.
>
> We should meet. Will Renato come to Bagni di Lucca? Will you? [*EGP*, ltr 181]

One of the few surviving accounts of a meeting between Puccini and his librettists—it took place at Bagni di Lucca, early in August 1920—is found in Adami's *Il romanzo della vita di Giacomo Puccini* (Milan, 1942):

> We brought the first draft of the plot with us to read to him at Bagni di Lucca, where he met us with a surprise.[4] The reading took place in the villa of Baron Fassini, who for many years had been associated with our embassy in China and who had furnished his house with every sort of *chinoiserie*. Hardly had the manuscript been deposited on a little lacquered table when . . . the silence was broken by the clear sound of a music box playing the ancient Imperial Hymn. . . . In his hands the notes of that Hymn became the massive chorus at the end of Act II. [*RVGP*, p. 229]

In addition to the "Imperial hymn" the Fassini music box also provided Puccini with "Mo-li-hua" and the tune for the first entrance of the three Ministers.[5]

Puccini came away from Bagni di Lucca expecting to be able to start composing in the very near future, yet it was nearly the end of September before he heard anything from Adami. In his reply, Puccini described his efforts to evoke some signs of life from his librettists, and went on to say,

> this will tell you how impatiently I am waiting for Acts I, II, and III of *Turandot*. I have filled several sheets of music paper with bits and pieces of ideas, of harmonies, of continuations. [*EGP*, ltr 182]

Those "bits and pieces" would probably have been in the same form as the sketches for the latter part of the duet and final scene of Act III that Puccini left at his death, filling time until his real work could begin with the receipt of a satisfactory text. The waiting had taken a toll on his impressionable spirits, as his letter to Adami of 10 November 1920 testifies:

> I keep thinking *Turandot* will never be finished. I cannot work like this. When the fever diminishes, it ends by disappearing, and without fever there is no creation; because emotional art is a kind of illness, an exceptional state of mind, over-excitation of every fiber and every atom. . . . It is not a matter of just finishing it. One must give lasting life to a thing that must live before it can be born. . . . Will I have the strength to follow you? Who knows? Shall I be tired, mistrustful, weighed down by age and spiritual suffering, by my continual discontent? Who knows? You should work as if you were working for a young man of thirty, and I will do my best, and if I do not succeed, it will be my fault! [*EGP*, ltr 184]

This revealing letter shows Puccini's understanding of his gift and its limitations. His art was not one of inventing and solving cerebral puzzles

but rather of aroused involvement stimulated by concrete dramatic situations and verses. He had staged that little occasion at Bagni di Lucca to fire
Adami and Simoni with something of his own excitement over the exotic
potential he saw in *Turandot*. It was hard for him to feel the creative heat
ebbing a little more each day while he waited to begin serious work.

THE LONG ACT I

At last, shortly before Christmas 1920, Adami brought a completely versified Act I to Puccini's hunting retreat in the Maremma, the Torre della
Tagliata, but it was not entirely what Puccini had been led to expect, for
on 22 December 1920 he wrote to Simoni:

> On the whole, I liked it, but to tell the truth I must confess this act
> absolutely needs shortening in many places, and above all it is neces-
> sary to think of a closing curtain that will be more effective. In the
> scenario I found more promptness of action and more luminosity of
> diction. . . . Given the scenario, I expected the proportions of the
> scenes to be more concise and, may I say, less literary, although the
> verses are clever and well-turned. [*CP*, ltr 783, p. 499]

He was a little more discouraged than he admitted in this letter to Simoni,
as we learn from a letter he wrote three days later to his friend Riccardo
Schnabl (1872–1955):

> *Turandot*, Act I: as an overall plan, good, but too many words, too
> much literature, they must reduce it by half; if not, there's no saving
> it. But when will I have all three acts balanced and ready to work on?
> I believe *never*. Keep this monosyllable [*mai*] to yourself. It's my own
> notion, but I think well-founded. And so? As usual, I am without a
> libretto! I am already old, it's better that I should give up and leave
> my place to the [Gian Francesco] Malipieros, to the [Francesco Bal-
> lilla] Pratellas, to all those others who "do not want" to have ideas.
> [*CP*, ltr 784, pp. 499–500]

Before Adami left Puccini's hunting retreat, the composer promised to
come to Milan—despite his distaste for that city in the troubled post-war
years—for a round of conferences with his librettists to see if they could
arrive at a satisfactory revision of Act I. Puccini was in Milan by mid-Jan-
uary and on 24 January 1921 was able to report to Schnabl that

> *Turandot* is taking on fantastically beautiful proportions and values—
> Adami and Simoni have done and are doing very well—it will be a
> beautiful libretto, and above all, most original, full of colors, surprises,
> and emotion. [*CP*, ltr 788, p. 502]

Puccini remained in Milan much of the time until early March 1921. This period marks the first major turning point in the project, for if their work had not gone well, Puccini might have abandoned *Turandot*. The results exceeded his expectations, however, and now, fired with enthusiasm, he settled down to compose. At last he had something to work on: a satisfactory versified libretto for the two-scene Act I whose scenario had already been worked out by mid-May 1920, ten months earlier. In a letter to Schnabl on 3 March he repeated his January evaluation of the libretto—"*Turandot* takes on magnificent proportions as a libretto"—and on 4 April 1921 he sent Schnabl a copy of the two-scene Act I that Ricordi had printed out for him, inscribed

> to my friend Riccardo Rossi Schnabl, this first proof of the *Turandot* libretto, but under oath not to show it, read it, or tell about it, to anyone. Affectionately. 4.IIII.21[6]

There are two long scenes in the versified libretto for the original long Act I. The major pieces from the eventual Acts I and II in the final libretto that were conceived later—the grand *concertato* before the striking of the gong, the Ministers' *fuori-scena*, Turandot's *aria di sortita*—are of course absent. But though the original long Act I otherwise corresponds with the present Act I and Act II set 2 in many particulars, there are significant differences, and both the correspondences and the differences are important not just for a genetic account of the opera but also for its generic analysis.

Below is a summary of the long Act I libretto of 1920–21, coordinated with the rubrics for numbers and movements given in the outline of the final version in Chapter I and the Appendix.

I.A is much the same, but every place in the original versification where the unknown Prince's name "Calàf" was uttered by Liù or Timur was afterwards reworked to avoid mentioning the name.

I.B is the same, except that there is no "Hymn to Confucius" at the end of I.B.3.

I.C.1 is the same, plus a longish speech for Ping just before Turandot's handmaidens appear.

I.C.2 is the same.

The rest of what became I.C.3–4 and I.D was significantly different in the original libretto. What became Act II set 2—the Minister's *fuori-scena* (now Act II set 1) was a later addition—was only a second set in Act I, growing directly out of the first set without a lowering of the curtain. The major differences between the 1921 long Act I libretto and the libretto in the form into which it evolved between 1922 and 1924 are tabulated below, the asterisk denoting interpolated numbers.

Act I (1921)	Acts I-II (1922–24)
. . .	. . .
Ghosts 1: "Non indugiare . . ."	} I.C.3
Prince: "No! no! Io solo l'amo!"	
Ministers: "L'ami? che cosa? chi?"	I.C.4.a
Ghosts 2: "Batti quel bronzo . . ."	----------
Prince: "A me il trionfo! a me l'amore!"	} I.C.4.b
The Executioner shows the severed	
head of the Prince of Persia.	
Ministers: "Stolto! Ecco l'amore!"	
Ghosts 3: " . . . dolce fratello! . . ."	----------
Prince: "Io son tutto una febbre!"	
The Prince strikes the gong.	
Ministers: "Lasciamolo passare	} (cf. I.D.4)
Quando rangola il gong	
la morte gongola."	
Timur: "O mia povera vita! . . ."	} (cf. I.D.1)
Liù: "È finita! è finita!"	
Prince: "Non piangere, Liù . . ."	I.D.3
Liù: "Per quel sorriso . . ."	(cf. I.D.2)
---- || ----	* I.D.4
	(*concertato*)
---- ↓↓ ----	* II.A
	(*fuori-scena*)
The palace is illuminated	} II.B
and the court assembles.	
The Emperor and the Prince:	II.C
"Un giuramento atroce mi costringe"	
Mandarin: "Popolo di Pekino!"	II.D.1
(Reprise of Children's chorus ? ? ?	II.D.2)
---- ----	* II.D.3
	(*aria di sortita*)
The Enigma scene: "Straniero, ascolta!"	II.E

As can be seen above, after the surviving stanza "Non indugiare" for the ghosts of Turandot's failed suitors (I.C.3), the ghosts originally had two further stanzas, making three in all. After each of the stanzas for the ghosts came responses from the Prince: to the first "No, no! Io solo l'amo!"; to the second a repetition of "O divina bellezza! o meraviglia!" followed by "A me il trionfo! a me l'amore!" In the final version these two, minus the repetition of "O divina bellezza! o meraviglia!" were combined into a single response to the single intervention of the ghosts. In the 1921 libretto, the first of the Prince's responses is followed by the ministerial philosophizing now found in I.C.4, the second by the appearance of the Executioner with the severed head of the Prince of Persia and the Ministers' "Così la luna bacerà il tuo volto."

Following the ghosts' third stanza came a third set of responses from the Prince and the Ministers, using what are now the very last lines of Act I in the present libretto, beginning with the Prince's "Io son tutta una febbre" (now buried in the last measures of the *concertato*). After the Prince's third response he was to strike his three strokes on the gong; then follows the Ministers' third response, their snickering "Quando rangola il gong la morte gongola."[7] Then came a single line each from Timur (now expanded to five lines as I.D.1) and from Liù—"È finita! è finita" with a single sob— followed by the Prince's comforting aria "Non piangere, Liù" (now I.D.3). That aria was followed by (rather than preceded by) an aria by Liù (now I.D.2), which was the last number in the original 1921 Act I set 1.

Liù's original aria text "Per quel sorriso" had a tone very different from that of the tearful Puccinian sufferer she was to become in "Signore, ascolta":

> Per quel sorriso. . . . si. . . . per quel sorriso,
> Liù non piange più! . . .
> Riprenderem lo squallido cammino
> domani all'alba. . . . quando il tuo destino,
> Calàf, sarà deciso.
> Porterem per le strade dell'esilio,
> ei l'ombra di suo figlio,
> io l'ombra di un sorriso!

> [For that smile. . . . yes. . . . for that smile,
> Liù will weep no more! . . .
> We shall resume our wretched wanderings
> tomorrow at dawn. . . . when your fate,
> Calàf, will have been sealed.
> We shall carry, on the paths of exile,
> he the ghost of his son,
> I the ghost of a smile!]

Though much of this resembles her later text, Liù's first two lines set a very different tone for the whole. Picking up the Prince's words "per quel sorriso" from his aria as her incipit and responding to his wish that she continue her support of his aged father (the Prince's text is virtually the same in both versions of the libretto), the determination expressed in the continuation "Liù non piange più" is virtually the opposite of her present "Liù non regge più"! Her originally fatalistic and resigned strength of will is confirmed in the accompanying stage direction, which reads "repressing her tears, with firm promise."

There being as yet no *concertato* or Act curtain, following Liù's brave and stoic aria came a transition "*a vista*" into what eventually became Act II set 2. The continuity between the two scenes, moreover, was closer not only in action but in setting as well. The opening set of the 1921 libretto is not outside the walls but rather within, and "the grand white marble staircase" of the present Act II set 2 was already in view and "links the courtyard to the palace." The new set came into view merely through a change in lighting: "the interior of the palace, in the meantime, is awakening and becoming illuminated." The procession and its music are described in the stage directions more or less as in the final libretto.[8] Eventually, as in the transition from set 1 to set 2 of the present Act II, "at the the top of the staircase, seated on an . . . ivory throne, the Emperor Altoum appears" for his dialogue with the Prince (now II.C); both that dialogue and the reprise of the first part of the Mandarin's proclamation that follows (II.D.1) remained the same in the final text.

The partial musical reprise of the Children's chorus singing "Mo-li-hua" (II.D.2) is in neither the original nor the final libretto; it was supplied by Puccini, using fragments of the text from the Children's previous appearance. One assumes that Puccini used such a reprise in his initial composition of the long Act I later in the summer of 1921 in order to bring Turandot forward to open the Enigma scene with "Straniero, ascolta!"—these were then her first words in the opera—but there is no way to know.

From Turandot's "Straniero, ascolta!" to the end, the text of the original long Act I set 2 was the same as that of the concluding part of the present Act II (II.E–F).

Though Puccini and his librettists must have had something of both the person and the name of Liù in mind already in 1920, it is only in this first versified libretto, and in correspondence after March 1921, that she is mentioned by name. The one surviving earlier reference is generic. Shortly after the meetings at Bagni di Lucca the previous August Puccini had written to ask Simoni: "Have you thought hard about the new interruption of the *piccola donna?*" (*CP*, ltr 774, p. 495). That Puccini referred to this character this way suggests that at this point (28 August 1920) she existed more as a dramatic function than as a realized character. Since Liù participates in the action only at the beginning and end of the present Act I and in the concluding number of the present Act III set 1,[9] one cannot be sure whether this "new interruption" had to do with one of what became these moments or with some since-discarded intervention. What is clear, however, is that Puccini's question about her refers to something that had already come up at Bagni di Lucca in August 1920.

By the middle of March 1921 Puccini obviously believed that the momentum of the project could be sustained and that before long he would have a complete text of the rest as well, since there seems to have been talk of a satisfactory second act, of which there is no direct documentary survival: on 26 March he wrote to Simoni, urging him "on to the third act, which will be worthy of the preceding ones . . . I shall be very glad to hear the lament of Liù and the triumphant finale" (*CP*, ltr 793, p. 504).[10] So far not a word about Liù's death; that complication still lay ahead.

One other piece of evidence gives some idea of how Liù's role was taking shape that spring, as Puccini progressed through the composition of the original long Act I with increasing confidence. On 20 May 1921 he wrote to Gilda Dalla Rizza, who was appearing in the successful first run of Mascagni's *Il piccolo Marat*, to attract her attention by describing a role he intended for her.[11]

> I'm working with faithful zeal at *Turandot*. I think that little Liù will be a role for you; don't imagine that it is of secondary importance, far from it. Turandot might be adapted to la Gilda, but for now she is still in the wings.[12] Liù is becoming, it seems to me, delicious. In short, whether Liù or Turandot, I am thinking of my dear Gildina. [*CP*, ltr 796, p. 505][13]

Puccini and Richard Strauss were perhaps the last who were able to compose their operas with the unquestioning assumption that they would be performed in leading theaters by outstanding singers whose careers were based in the mainstream of the repertory, and, like composers of the first half of the nineteenth century who wrote roles with particular singers in mind, Puccini thought of voice types as represented by individuals he admired. If Dalla Rizza, as she sang in her mid-twenties, was his vocal prototype for Liù, it was the Maria Jeritza of 1922, whose Tosca in Vienna impressed him both by her acting and her tireless, easy upper register, who was to become his prototype for Turandot.

Puccini's contributions to the figure of Liù illustrate the decisive role he played in determining the direction the libretto would take, and though he may not always have exercised his authority helpfully, his central role has been affirmed by Adami.

> Repeatedly, the maestro's suggestions shed new light for us. And often, one touch, one indication, one intention, one doubt sufficed to open up new aspects, to give the plot unforeseen and original twists,

and to enrich it with a new spiritual significance. . . . In this way, abandoning Gozzi and Schiller, the masks transformed into ministers, and grafting onto the plot a particularly Puccinian character in the poetic Liù, a moved and moving antagonist, gradually a *Turandot* of our own, full of the humanity that Puccini desired, was born. [*RVGP*, pp. 228–29]

On 30 April Puccini reported to Adami that "*Turandot* is making good progress; I feel that I am on the right road. I am at the masks, and in a little while at the enigmas! I think I have made great strides. What about [Acts] II? and III? My God, don't wear me out with waiting" (*EGP*, ltr 187). By "at the masks" Puccini must have meant their first entrance, in Act I (now I.C.1), since the *fuori-scena* for the Ministers, the present Act II set 1, had not yet been conceived; and of course the Enigma scene (now II.E) was still part of the original long Act I.

The music for the Ministers' entrance, whose tune came from Baron Fassini's music box, seems to have been prepared a little ahead of time, since three weeks later, on 22 May 1921, he wrote to Simoni: "I have just finished the frightening chorus of the Executioners [now I.A.4]; I am starting on the Moon and the funeral march [now I.B.1–3]" (*CP*, ltr 797, p. 506).

And then on 7 June 1921:

I am at the phantoms [the ghosts of Turandot's executed suitors, now I.C.3]. I have nothing else to report, but I have done, "Non pianger [sic], Liù" and "Per quel sorriso."[14] [*CP*, ltr 799, pp. 506–7]

Then finally to Adami, on 20 June:

I am at the *enigmas* and can't get started.

In a joint letter to both librettists the same day he wrote:

The [original long] first act is almost ready; the last part is maddening, or at any rate, vexing me. For the third [act] I urge on you lyricism and emotion. Choruses, color, emperor, executioner, etc, are fine and beautiful things, but when the soul speaks through a single mouth the expression comes forth more directly and communicatively. [*CP*, ltr 802, p. 508]

And the following day, to Simoni:

The first two enigmas are too wordy; I would like them more concise. So that I won't have to go back to them, see if you can send me this change right away. It is urgent. [*CP*, ltr 804, p. 509]

On 17 July he asked Simoni for some additional words to accompany the entrance of the Imperial Court. To indicate the desired meter and effect Puccini inserted five lines of his own devising (in the final form of the libretto three other lines in the same meter were used instead). At the end of the letter he returned to his demands for the rest of the text.

> Clogged and stranded, I have had a relapse in my work; now I am taking it up again. And you, at what point are you? Are you working or not? Very soon I shall need the second act. Think about and work on the third. [*CP*, ltr 808, pp. 510–11]

In early August 1921 Puccini's English friend Sybil Seligman and her son visited Viareggio for three weeks, and while they were there the composer played the first act of *Turandot* for them, as it then stood (*PAF*, p. 330; see References, A:4). On 10 August Adami reported to Carlo Clausetti of Casa Ricordi that he had visited Puccini at Torre del Lago.

> I heard and re-heard the first act, and I carried away an enormous impression of it. Only Puccini could have done something so vast, original, suggestive. Richness in color, breadth of humanity, highly characteristic exoticism, are there in profusion. And clear melodies relieve the impetuosity of the drama, like deep, pure breaths. [CP, ltr 812, p. 513]

Thus, the music for most of what is the present Act I (except the final *concertato*) and for Act II set 2 (except Turandot's *aria di sortita*) was composed in a protracted and intensive bout beginning in late March 1921, picking up steam in May, and winding down about the end of July 1921, a period of a little more than four months. But Puccini had not orchestrated any of it as yet; that was a separate task taken up later. And there must have been some changes in Liù's aria as well, if not a completely new setting, and other changes too, after the decision to reverse the order of the two arias and make the Prince's aria the lead-off for a *concertato*.

FALLING ACTION

ACT II–SEPTEMBER 1921

Adami's visit in August 1921 had motives other than to hear Puccini play as much of the score as then existed. After describing what he had heard to Clausetti in glowing terms, he went on to make what turned out to be a rash prediction. "The second act which I had brought with me and read to him, pleased very much; so much so that he set to work on it promptly, and by autumn this too will be completed" (*CP*, ltr 812, p. 513). Adami also brought a draft of a contract between Ricordi and Puccini for *Turandot*, but a year would elapse before final agreement was reached.

Some idea of the "second act" that Adami had just delivered can be gathered from two letters Puccini wrote to Simoni from Munich not long after he had received it. On 16 August 1921: "Second act very good, especially after the banquet.[15] It seems to me the first sections are not entirely right" (*CP*, ltr 814, p. 514). Five days later, he wrote to Simoni again. Mentioning that he had seen fine mises-en-scène in Munich, he wrote that they would have to improve the designs for their second act in view of the machinery implied in the libretto.[16] And then come these details:

> The spirits [*incubi*] must cross above, like Chinese shades, and perhaps I can finish the act with the rustic dance [*trescone*]. My criticism of the first episodes does not amount to much. Doesn't it seem to you that the little dances should be different, one from the other? Both of them double? I think so. The duet is magnificent. [*CP*, ltr 815, p. 514]

But the more Puccini read the text of this "second act" the less he liked it. When he returned to Torre del Lago from Munich and tried to get down to serious composition, an activity that always sharpened his critical sense, he started wrestling with the problem facing him. After more than two weeks of mounting frustration he fairly exploded to Simoni on 13 September 1921.

> I am sad and mistrustful! I keep thinking about *Turandot*! . . . That second act! I find no way out, perhaps I am torturing myself because I have one fixed idea: *Turandot* should be in two acts. What do you say? Doesn't it seem to you too much, to dilute [the action] after the enigmas in order to arrive at the final scene? Telescope events, eliminate others, to reach a conclusion where love explodes . . . I don't know how to advise you about the right structure, but I feel that two more acts are too many. *Turandot* in two large acts! And why not? It is all a question of finding the idea for the finale. Why not do as in *Parsifal* with the change of scene in the third act, to find onself in a Chinese Hall of the Grail? Filled with flowers, roses, everything breathing love? Think about it, think about it, think about it, tell Adami about it. You two will surely find a way, and do it well. [*CP*, ltr 816, pp. 514–15]

The following day, 14 September, Puccini wrote a letter to Adami that begins: "I have sent Renato a plan for the second act" (*EGP*, ltr 193). This was part of his campaign to persuade his librettists to condense *Turandot* into "two large acts," the second becoming an amalgam: the "Act II" plot that Adami had just brought to Torre del Lago the month before, but now with some events telescoped and others eliminated; plus the concluding sections of the "Act III" arrived at by Puccini and his librettists at Bagni di Lucca the year before.

The "plan for the second act" that Puccini told Adami he had already sent to Simoni survives, and is printed in *Carteggi pucciniani* (p. 496) with a conjectural date "[*dicembre* 1920]" that is obviously incorrect. The correct date should be 13 or 14 September 1921, because the balance of the letter in which Puccini told Adami he had sent Simoni a plan for "Act II" (*EGP*, ltr 193 quoted above) gives a plan identical in most details with the one in the *Carteggi*, with many verbal echoes.[17] Since this outline of "the second act" has to do with what eventually became Act III, and bears no resemblance to the present Act II, for convenience it will be referred to as Act II–September 1921.

Act II–September 1921 as Puccini submitted it to his two librettists is worth examining, not only because of the light it sheds on the evolution of the libretto, mingling episodes familiar from the present Act III with materials later discarded, but also because it gives a clear sense of Puccini's continual striving after an alternative to Gozzi's unwieldy winding down of the action before the final confrontation of Prince and Princess. Puccini's plan follows below, collated from the versions sent to Simoni and to Adami: those details which occur only in the letter to Adami are placed in brackets; those parts which survive in the present Act III are placed in italics.

Here is a sort of guide to the second act. //

2d act: very much in outline form—be rapid and stop only when lyric expansiveness demands //

entrance of Turandot, nervous [after the enigmas. A short scene ending with the threat "Let no one sleep in Peking."[18] After that do away with the banquet and have a scene in which *the masks dominate the action.*]

Nessun dorma in Pekino // *romanza for the tenor* //

Temptations: [*riches*], drink, *women*, no banquet. Invitation [*they beg and beseech Calàf*] *to say his name to save their lives.* Calàf: No, I lose Turandot. Invitation [Strong proposal] to flee. "No [I lose Turandot]"—*then a little conspiracy aside and threat of death* [*with daggers*]— no spirits—[Conference of dignitaries, rapid conspiracy and attack.] *Turandot arrives*; [they flee]—duet shorter—*torture shorter.* The three declare broken hearts[19]—I have lost her; my heart, why are you beating? [Exit Turandot, with burning face and throbbing heart.]—Liù says she wants to remain, to try [to speak of] compassion to Turandot—Darkness.

[change of scene][20]—a room with draperies [yellow and rose], female slaves and Liù—[a long cloak]—Turandot stung by jealousy—not a long scene—Darkness.

Final Scene: [imposing in white and rose] large, white palace—Pegonie[21]—*all ready in position including the Emperor—Rising sun*, Calàf: farewell to the world, to love, to life—his name? I don't know it, terse. Big love phrase *with modern kiss and all, surprised, begin to express their own feelings* [*tutti presi si mettono a lingua in bocca!*]

It is clear from the instructions to get rid of the "banquet" and "spirits" that the first scene of Puccini's "plan" is a condensation of the Act II Adami had brought to Torre del Lago in August. It is plausible that the second set of his plan, and certainly the final set, formed part of what heretofore had been referred to as "Act III." One notable feature is the idea of using Liù to hasten Turandot's emotional capitulation, though the extreme of suicide is not yet in question.

Puccini's plan seems not to have satisfied any of the collaborators for very long, not even the composer himself. It is a highly significant document, nonetheless, and not only because it includes episodes that survived into the present Act III. It also marks a second turning point in their notion of what sort of an opera *Turandot* was to be, although all the consequences of this volte-face would take three years to fall finally into place. Up to this point *Turandot* had been conceived in the more traditional Puccinian fashion, consisting largely of a sequence of genre episodes; from now on it would assume an ever greater resemblance to the large-scale spectacle and design of the school of internationalized Grand Opera of the previous century. The answer was not going to be Puccini's "two large acts," however, but rather three acts containing more spacious musical structures. Up to September 1921 four such structures had yet to be conceived: the three that were to fill out the two acts resulting from the eventually divided long Act I (the *concertato*, the Ministers' *fuori-scena*, and Turandot's *aria di sortita*); and eventually Liù's death and cortège, with Timur's farewell, as a fourth. A spacious final duet for Turandot and the Prince, moreover, was also still in the future. Though some sort of final confrontation was the indispensable dénouement of Gozzi's original drama and had of course been planned for the opera from the outset, Puccini's letter of 8 November 1921 quoted below, calling for a duet (including by then the kiss) that would be "grand, bold, unforeseen, and not leave off at the beginning and be cut off by offstage cries" was the first move toward a second really large-scale number for the protagonists after the Enigma scene. (One notes that the "duet" Puccini had mentioned in his plan for the first set of Act II–September 1921 was to be made "shorter," not longer.)

Discarding the plans for the falling action as they seemed to have been settled at Bagni di Lucca in August 1920 precipitated a major crisis. This is first confirmed in a letter to Puccini's boyhood friend Alfredo Vandini, dated 16 September 1921 (just two days after Puccini sent out his "plan"), from which we learn that Puccini had just been to Rome "for two days . . . [involved] in serious work with Simoni" (*CP*, ltr 817, p. 515). On 30 October 1921 the composer urged both Adami and Simoni to come to Torre del Lago for a week to discuss that "*bene-male-detto*" second act; if they don't come, he foresees "shipwreck" (*CP*, ltr 818, p. 515).

One predictable manifestation of this crisis was Puccini's feverish groping for ideas to resolve it. A letter he wrote to Adami is dated only "Monday," but since it was sent from Bologna (where Puccini went to supervise *Il trittico* at its local première) and since he writes of the dénouement as still located in Act II, this letter may be safely assigned to the latter half of October 1921. Besides exposing Puccini's anxiety, it gives the first hint of some more details that survive in the present Act III.

> *Turandot* gives me no peace. I think of it continually, and I think we are perhaps on the wrong track in Act II [i.e., Act II–September 1921]. I think the central nub [*nocciolo*] is the duet. And the duet as it is doesn't seem to me what is wanted.[22] In the duet I think we can work up a high pitch of emotion. And to do that I think Calàf must *kiss* Turandot and reveal his great love to the icy princess. After he has kissed her, with a kiss that lasts several long seconds, he must say: "Now nothing matters to me, I will even die," and he tells his name on her lips. Here you could have a pendant to the grisly opening of the act "Let no one sleep in Peking." The masks and perhaps the officials and slaves, hidden, have heard the name and shout it out. The shout is repeated and passed on, so that Turandot is compromised.
>
> And in the third act, when everything is ready, with the executioner, etc. as in Act I, she says (to everyone's astonishment), I do not know his name.[23] [*EGP*, ltr 196]

And in his next letter to Adami, on 8 November 1921:

> I am in black despair about *Turandot* . . . I have said, and I repeat, that the second [act] as it stands is a major error. After a first act [the original long Act I] that is so beautiful, so rich and sumptuous, particularly well balanced and persuasive, it needs a second act that is the quintessence of effectiveness, and the individual events must be clear and convincing. For me, the duet has to be the *clou*—but it should have in it something grand, bold, unforeseen, and not leave off at the beginning and be cut off by offstage cries of people arriving. [*EGP*, ltr 197, 273–74]

FALLING ACTION

THE LONG ACT I DIVIDED

In November and December 1921, Puccini divided his time between Torre del Lago (where preparations were afoot to move into his new villa at Viareggio before the end of the year), the Maremma, and Rome, the latter because he served upon a committee of judges for a government-sponsored Concorso Nazionale for new operas. At some point during this period must have occurred the vitally important meeting between Puccini and one or both of his librettists in which the two sets of the original long Act I were divided to make two acts—thereby incidentally reverting to Gozzi's original act division. This change would entail revising the ending of the former first set to convert it into an effective closing for the new shorter Act I. These decisions had been reached by 21 December 1921, as Puccini's letter of that date to Adami reveals.

> I feel how much you are in agreement—in fact, how much we three, etc. etc. And now to work!
>
> I need the trio for the first [act] Finale [now I.D.4]. And with regard to the new Act I, if you find you can expand it in some way, do so freely. That will make it less rapid.
>
> And for the [new] second act, first scene, consider the daughter of heaven, high up beside the Emperor's throne, begging and praying that she should not be thrown into the stranger's arms [now II.E.4]. [*EGP*, ltr 200]

What Puccini was referring to here as the trio for the first act Finale ultimately became the *concertato*—the trio of the Prince, Liù, and Timur, accompanied by the three Ministers and finally the offstage chorus—led off by the Prince's "Non piangere, Liù," now placed after Liù's aria. (The invention of the intermezzo of the Ministers, the present Act II set 1, did not take place until the following March of 1922.) Since at this point Puccini was thinking of the Enigma scene, followed by Turandot's plea to her father "Figlio del cielo" and its aftermath (now II.E), as the "first" scene of Act II, then "Nessun dorma," the temptations, and the duet—that is, material from the first of the three sets from Act II–September 1921—must still have been intended for the balance of that act.

In another letter to Adami, written the day after Christmas 1921, Puccini described his notion of how to end the Finale to the new Act I:

> Yesterday, after so much time, I played the first act of *Turandot* again, in the new house, and [Ernesto] Consolo, who was there, said things that comforted me. If only we had succeeded in finding [the moment for] the fall of the curtain after the masks have finished their pleading and almost exhausted their insisting! The two—the father and the

77

slave girl—should finish, with the addition of the three masks, and [then] to end after Calàf's hymn, a phrase of the type of the *Faust* trio [that is a threefold sequence at successively higher pitch levels], with the striking of the great gong. I know I am preaching to the converted. [*EGP*, ltr 201]

The last sentence quoted suggests that the idea of dividing the original long Act I might have originated with the librettists. Puccini was of course still waiting for new text—"the trio for the Finale" mentioned in his previous letter—but he had at least settled on (or decided to retain) the musical design for the Prince's threefold invocation of "Turandot!" before striking the gong, and he had also decided that the invocation and the gong should come after and not before Liù's aria (and *a fortiori* after the Prince's aria). He went on: "I am in a fever to get down to work, but I don't have this material before me, and I torment myself" (*EGP*, ltr 201). Five months had passed since Puccini had been able to move ahead with the composition of *Turandot*.

In January of 1922 Puccini spent some time in Milan supervising the rehearsals for the local première of *Il trittico* at La Scala on the 29th. This was a period when his relations with Simoni were at a low ebb, as may be seen in a letter of 31 January 1922 (*CP*, ltr 827, p. 522). But whatever had caused the coolness at the end of January proved transitory, because by 7 March 1922 Puccini had received from Simoni the text of the intermezzo for Ping, Pang and Pong that opens the present Act II. Puccini even sounded optimistic about Act III, once more on the drawing board. And from this point in the Spring of 1922 *Turandot* assumed the act and set divisions that we know in the final form of the work.

I will begin at once on the *fuori-scena* [the intermezzo]. That done, and I hope I will be done quickly, I will very soon need material for Act III. Send it to me episode by episode, now that the framework and pattern are set. [*CP*, ltr 929, pp. 522–23]

By 28 March 1922 Puccini could report to Simoni that he had started work upon the new scene and that he was satisfied with the way it was planned (*CP*, ltr 830, p. 523). He had also begun to orchestrate Act I: his fair-copy pencil autograph in the Ricordi archives bears the notation "21 marzo 1922 / ore 11 pm" on its first page. But two weeks later he was back in the depths. On 10 April 1922 he confessed to Sybil Seligman that he was going through an "ugly period" and his nerves had been bothering him. At the end of the letter he explains why. "I still haven't got the complete libretto . . . those lazy fellows keep me waiting" (*PAF*, p. 341). On 1 May 1922 he wrote to Simoni again, fairly bristling with frustration and fear that it would all come to nothing.

Tell me the truth: you no longer have any trust in me! Why haven't you sent me the promised third act? Have you done it? Perhaps not, and here I am torturing myself because it seems to me that I have lost your trust; perhaps you think I work in vain. Perhaps that may be true, too. [*CP*, ltr 831]

He went on to discuss the possibility that his work was in vain because it seemed to him that his contemporaries had renounced melody, or if they wrote one it would be deliberately vulgar. And coming from the composer who turns out to have written the last Italian opera to have entered the standard repertory, a sentence a bit later on has the ring of prophecy: "It is the belief that symphonic music should dominate [*sinfonismo debba reg-nare*], and instead I believe that is the end of opera in the theater." He summed up his diatribe about the direction music was taking as "All Celtic sicknesses, real transalpine pox."

During the spring of 1922 Puccini was bothered by periods of poor health, and progress on *Turandot* remained fitful. Some time in June 1922 he finally received a text for Act III, though he wanted modifications. On the 25th he wrote to the directors of Ricordi, Carlo Clausetti and Renzo Valcarenghi, that Adami had consigned "to my complete satisfaction" the finished libretto of *Turandot*. (*CP*, ltr 833, p. 525). But since this letter deals with renewing the contract for his earlier operas and also contained clauses covering *Turandot*, Puccini's phrase should be interpreted to mean no more than that he could foresee a time when the libretto would satisfy him completely. That the text was still being tinkered with is shown by a letter Adami wrote to Valcarenghi from Viareggio on 1 August 1922.

I am preparing the passage of *Turandot* for the second act [i.e., the text of 'In questa reggia'] and the close of the third. Now he is profoundly convinced of everything, and he told me yesterday that he expected to make something extraordinary of the third act. [*CP*, ltr 835, p. 526]

To prepare himself for the coming bout of work and to have a change of scene, Puccini, accompanied by his wife and son and some old friends, set off on 20 August 1922 in two limousines to motor up through Austria and the Rhine Valley as far as The Hague, returning through the Schwarzwald and Switzerland. The trip, which lasted about three weeks, seems not to have produced the desired effect, for on 8 October 1922 Puccini informed his friend Schnabl,

Turandot is sleeping. It lacks a big aria in the second [act]. I need to graft it in and . . . find it [*bisogna innestarla e . . . trovarla*, that is, the music for it]. Then I have all the third to do. Only the first is orches-trated, but it lacks the Finale [now I.D.4], which for six months has been on the music rack, sketched. There is nothing else to report. Now I would like another libretto, and perhaps Adami and Simoni will give me [a scenario] at the end of November. [*CP*, ltr 842, p. 530]

Three things emerge from this letter. First, Puccini had not yet composed the music for Turandot's "In questa reggia." Second, he was not completely satisfied with text for Act III because he could not get immediately caught up in it, as he had been able to do with the original long Act I back in March 1921. And third, he was looking for a new libretto, perhaps as an escape hatch if the problems with *Turandot* proved insurmountable.[24]

THE DEATH OF LIÙ

One of the most important letters in the correspondence concerning the gestation of *Turandot* is one Puccini wrote to Adami on 3 November 1922. Here for the first time we find the suggestion that Liù should die.

Turandot is there with the first act complete, without seeing light because the rest of it is dark, perhaps in dense, permanent shadow! I have been thinking that I will have to put this work to one side. For the balance of the opera, we are on the wrong track. The second and third acts as they have been conceived I find a great mistake, and for that reason I have come back to the idea of two acts. Finish up everything in a [single] second act. Its foundation must be the *duet*, and it must cling to the fantastic to the limit—even exaggeratedly. In the *grand duet* as it develops, the iciness of Turandot melts; the set might be an enclosed place that changes little by little to take on the appearance of a large area of flowers, of embroidery-like marbles, and of fantastic apparitions—where the crowd, the Emperor, the Court and all the pomp of ceremony stand ready to receive Turandot's cry of love.

I believe that Liù will have to be sacrificed to some sorrow, but I think this cannot be developed—unless she is made to die in the torture episode. And why not? Her death can have a powerful influence in bringing about the thawing of the princess.

I am sailing on seas of uncertainties. This subject has caused me great distress of spirit. I would like it if both you and Renato could come here! We could talk and perhaps we might save everything. If it goes ahead as it is: *requiescat Turandot*! Give me some word. If you care for me and if your concern that I should work with you continues, then do not leave me in the lurch like this! [*EGP*, ltr 206]

It may seem extraordinary that such a moving and typically Puccinian moment as the death of Liù should not have become part of the overall plan for *Turandot* until after more than two years work had gone into the opera. Yet to put this suggestion in the perspective of November 1922, we must understand that Liù had not been in the forefront of Puccini's concern as he wrestled with the crucial scene of Turandot's capitulation. And the tone in which Puccini suggests that perhaps it would help if Liù were sacrificed sounds very much as though the thought had occurred to him only as he was writing, as a possible way to make Turandot's change of heart believable: it would be a means to an end, not an end in itself. And he seems at least fleetingly to have realized—"this cannot be developed"— that to make Liù a focus of attention might seriously deflect attention from the central figure and upset the balance of the overall design—which of course is exactly what happened.

This letter of 3 November 1922 also suggests that the idea that Liù might die may have been put forth in the first instance as part of a final effort to reanimate the crucial dénouement of a project that seemed to have lost its bearings. To illustrate the doldrums that beset *Turandot* in those days one representative, if minor, point will suffice. In Puccini's last letter to Adami before the one under discussion, he was asking for a few more words for the ensemble at the end of Act I (*EGP*, ltr 205, p. 280).[25] Some time before the middle of November 1922, the composer explained to Valcarenghi that he could not send the first act to be set up in proof because, although otherwise complete, it still lacked the lines from Adami for the chorus in I.D.4 (*CP*, ltr 848, p. 533).[26] The annoyance caused by this sort of trivial but frequent frustration helps explain the nimbus of discouragement that had come to shroud *Turandot*.

By December 1922 the air of discouragement was very gloomy indeed. On the 11th Puccini addressed Adami:

> I have no good news of *Turandot*. I am beginning to be concerned about my laziness. Could I be fed up with China after having finished the first act and almost all the second? The fact is I don't succeed in making anything good take root. Also I am old! . . . I am unable to write the *preambulo* to Act II [the *fuori-scena* for the three Ministers]— no matter how many tries I've made—and China doesn't seem to suit me. [*EGP*, ltr 208]

Back in March 1922 Puccini had been able to tell Simoni that one section of the intermezzo—"*la chitarrata*" he called it—was going well (*CP*, ltr 829, p. 523), so evidently he had reached a certain point in the *fuori-scena* and then simply lost the thread.

That December Puccini heard a performance of Pizzetti's *Debora e Jaele* at La Scala, new that season of 1922/23, and he told Schnabl that although it contained some very interesting things and he wanted to hear it again, the opera would not survive because of "the abolition of melody . . . a great mistake" (*CP*, ltr 851, pp. 534–35). He had come to Milan for the first of seventeen performances of La Scala's thirtieth-anniversary production of *Manon Lescaut*, and he returned on 1 February 1923 to attend the performance that marked the actual anniversary, which was followed by a banquet in his honor. During this period, *Turandot* lay dormant, perhaps because Simoni had been ill, perhaps because Puccini found it impossible to compose in Milan.

Puccini returned to the Lombard capital early in March 1923, at which time he received some parts of the revised libretto to Act III. Although he had reported to Ricordi at the time of the contract negotiations back in June 1922 that the libretto was finished, such was far from the case as is revealed by Puccini's letter of 6 March 1923 to Adami.

> No! No! No! *Turandot*, no! I have part of the third [act]. It won't work. Perhaps, or even with no perhaps, it is I who don't work any more. But the third act also won't work like this . . .
>
> Who knows, but if you put this together with the previous third act, maybe it could somehow be made to work. If it could? and if I will be up to it? [*EGP*, ltr 209]

On 14 April 1923 Adami received a later progress report from Puccini, giving a fairly detailed account of his recent activity.

> My work? Slow, but good. The [music for the] aria of Turandot ["In questa reggia"] is almost finished, but what an effort! It wants some modifications in the text, however. It seems to me that up there, at the top of the grand staircase, this aria might not make a bad effect. Also the trio of the masks is in good state. This piece, too, is very difficult, and it is of the greatest importance, being a *morceau* outside of the action [*senza scena*] and thus an almost academic piece. In short, amid the usual discouragements and the customary brief small joys of work, *Turandot* advances with tiny steps, but she does move forward. [*EGP*, ltr 213]

Three days later he wrote to Adami again, this time to remind him to "think about the final duet that is still needed" (*EGP*, ltr 214). He kept urging Adami and Simoni to come to see him so that they could adjust the libretto once and for all before he had to leave for a two-week stay in Vienna in May 1923. From there he informed Sybil Seligman on 2 May,

> At last I've had the third act of *Turandot*. Adami came to Viareggio and in a week we finished it very well. Now the libretto is complete and very beautiful too; it's up to me to write the music! But I shall

have to work a lot to finish this blessed opera. However, now that I have a fine third act, I have more courage and desire to work. [*PAF*, p. 347]

In spite of these sanguine expectations, Act III was not yet in its present form, and the text for the final duet would remain a problem until it was in fact too late for Puccini to complete the music for it.

Instead of the spate of letters that mark some of the earlier phases of composition, from the summer of 1923 only a few survive, and perhaps only a few were written. In one letter dated 28 June Puccini offered Adami some details of his efforts.

It is true that I am working, but you must not think it is with the proverbial fever. Yet the third [act] is begun well with the off-stage voices, and the famous *romanza* ["Nessun dorma"] is finally in place. But I have tampered with the verses a little.

Near the close of this letter he described a scene that conveys his subdued mood:

We are here, Elvira and I, the two *ancêtres*, like two ancient family portraits, frowning now and again at the cobwebs that tickle us. We sleep, we eat, we read the *Corriere*, and with a few notes in the evening the old maestro gets by from month to month [*sbarca il lunario*]. [*EGP*, ltr 217]

By mid-November 1923 Puccini had composed Act III set 1 as far as the torture scene. On 12 November 1923, he asked Adami to supply some lines:

I am producing nothing, or only a little more than nothing. Poor *Turandot*, how neglected you are! Now that I am starting to write a few notes, I lack the verses for Liù at her death. The music is there complete, minus only the words to be set to what is already done.[27] It is only a bare sketch; to develop well the sad scene needs words. They are *settenari* [7-syllable lines], easy to insert into the existing context. Do you want me to sketch them in rough form? Well then, I'll do it. [*EGP*, ltr 219]

And he proceeded to write out the words for the opening of Liù's suicide and cortège, "Tu che di gel sei cinta" (III.D.4), just as they appear in the printed libretto.[28]

THE END

The crucial problem of the conclusion of the opera still remained unresolved, however, and as Puccini composed ahead toward it, its importance loomed ever more crucially. He had come to regard as unsatisfactory the version of the duet for the Prince and the Princess that he had received from Adami before his departure for Vienna the previous May. Some glimpse of the difficulty emerges from a letter he wrote to Schnabl on 22 December 1923.

> I am working, orchestrating and composing. I am lacking, however, the grand duet for the third [act] Finale that I have had revised for the fourth time. I am waiting for it, but the poets neglect me. [*CP*, ltr 876, p. 545]

On the same day he took the matter up with Simoni:

> You have forgotten me. Remember I desperately need the duet, which is the *clou* of the opera.
>
> I have started to orchestrate to gain time,[29] but I cannot have a tranquil spirit as long as this duet is unfinished. Do me the favor of setting yourself to this final task. Be good to me as you have always been; now draw on your great experience and dedicate it to this poor old maestro who feels the urgent need to finish this "*magna*" opera. [*CP*, ltr 877, p. 545]

Puccini kept waiting for the verses for this duet. They had still not arrived by 11 January 1924, when he wrote to inform Clausetti that he was returning the (manuscript fair) copy of Act I.

> I am still waiting for the lines from Simoni! It is really a serious matter; do you want to try to telephone him? I have written him, telegraphed him. He replied: "I want to make a beautiful thing of it, and forgive me, but in two or three days you will have it all." And nothing comes. [*CP*, ltr 881, p. 547]

He went on to report that he expected to receive a bass xylophone from Siam, and he would send it on to Milan to have it reproduced, as he had included a part for it in his score.[30]

Puccini's letters to Adami from these days evoke a clear picture of his nervous tension. On 23 January 1924 he wrote:

> if you come here at once everything could be sorted out. We have the material of the first three versions, and from these we will be able to bring forth the great duet . . . I would like to return to the idea of some off-stage voices to underscore psychological moments. [*EGP*, ltr 225]

As noted just above, on 22 December 1923 Puccini had written Schnabl that he had had the duet revised a fourth time. The first three versions would be those of the "Act II" that Puccini had received from Adami in August 1921 (when the duet still preceded the torture scene), of the "Act III" that Adami had delivered in June 1922 (at the time the contract for *Turandot* was signed), and of the "Act III" of May 1923. Off-stage voices accompany the Prince's words "Mio fiore mattutino" in the second segment of Puccini's continuity draft for the final duet, which may well date from this time.[31]

On 27 January Puccini complained to Adami that he had had

no word from anyone. Renato wired me at the first of the year: *within two days you will have it all*. And you, why are you mute? I read in the *Corriere* about your projects and your activities. I stay at my desk every day. I orchestrate, and I still have much to do. I hardly ever leave the house. [*EGP*, ltr 226]

Again to Adami, on 11 February 1924:

Try to extract the duo from Renato. [*EGP*, ltr 227]

And on 21 February, now addressing Valcarenghi:

what is there to say? This is how it is: Simoni, a procrastinator, and then . . . But the material is there, and if Adami (I beg you too to tell him) will make up his mind and come here for two or three days everything can be adjusted. Now I am very anxious about it because the second act is finished, orchestration and everything. [*CP*, ltr 884, p. 548][32]

Finally, on 25 March 1924, Puccini brought himself to write directly to Simoni. That same day he had written Clausetti at the Casa Ricordi that in a few days he would be sending his son Tonio off to Milan with all of Act II and half of Act III orchestrated. From the letter to Simoni we see that the work was finished through to the end of Liù's cortège; now only the duet and the brief final scene remained to be composed, and he wrote with rather strained diplomacy:

Carissimo Renato,
    It is a long time since I have written you, since we have written one another. I have been working desperately for four months and am almost at the end; I lack only the final duet. All the rest is orchestrated . . . I have put my whole soul into this opera; we shall see therefore if my vibrations synchronize with those of the public.
    Your duet had good things in it, but it was not sufficiently varied and rapid; Adami and I have worked on it together and it seems to me successfully, especially in its successive stages. Since I am coming to Milan, if you are able and want to, we can go over it again, if only

to give it more touches of imagery and some more "Chinese" details. But I have wanted it to be a human thing, and when the heart speaks, whether it be in China or Holland, the sense is all the same and the purpose [*finalità*] is that of all people. [*CP*, ltr 892, p. 550]

If this letter suggests that everything could be settled promptly and the duet completed, such was not the case. About the end of May 1924, Puccini received from Simoni a new version of the final duet—in prose! This latest version may stem from the time of Puccini's proposed visit to Milan for the dress rehearsal of Boito's *Nerone*. On 31 May Puccini discussed with Adami turning this text into verse, and his suggestions give some sense of the scene as it had developed to this point.

It all needs to be put into meter and should seek to preserve the rhythm that has been established, especially at *mio fiore mattutino* [now III.D.2] and the accompanying chorus, and at the finale because you know the music already exists—not yet worked out, but the *motivo* is one you are familiar with.[33] [*CP*, ltr 892, p. 552]

On 4 July 1924 Puccini was still asking Adami for the text of the duet (*EGP*, ltr 231). That summer he could work only fitfully at correcting proofs and making small adjustments. Although his health was declining and his ability to work decreasing, he still hoped that somehow this massive opera could be brought to an end. On 1 September 1924 he wrote to Adami that he had passed through a fearful crisis, partly involving his health. "The pain in my throat that has tormented me since March seemed something serious" (*EGP*, ltr 232).

This is not the first mention in Puccini's correspondence of the symptoms of the illness that led to his death in Dr. Ledoux's radiology clinic in Brussels, where he went for treatment two months later, departing from Viareggio on 4 November 1924. As early as January of that year he had spoken of taking a cure "for my throat and my winter cough." From March on, the pain seems to have been continuous. On 19 August he had reported to Schnabl: "My sore throat is a great annoyance. I've seen . . . four specialists so far . . . My illness is tonsilitis and pharyngitis that have been tormenting me for seven months" (*CP*, ltr 897, p. 555). On 9 October he wrote to Clausetti that the following day he was going into Florence "for another examination of my worrisome throat" (*CP*, ltr 900, p. 556). Shortly after this visit Tonio was informed that his father had an inoperable malignancy at the base of his epiglottis. The true nature of Puccini's illness was not explained to him until just before the end of October so that he would be prepared for the trip to Brussels and for the course of treatment at the radiology clinic, but even then the gravity of his condition was not revealed to him.

As early as February 1924 Puccini had thought about the première of the opera. He had discussed it in his letter to Valcarenghi on the 21st.

> And where will *Turandot* be given next year? Will Toscanini direct it? If not, rule out La Scala; we already hazarded a "première" in that theater. I remember the bullfight of *Butterfly!*[34] And New York? You could explore it with Gatti-Casazza, but after the Italian première, of course, and I would want to go there because I *must* absolutely be there, not being able to let the opera go on without my presence. [*CP*, ltr 884, pp. 548–49]

On 7 September 1924 Toscanini came to Viareggio to discuss *Turandot* and its possible production at La Scala in April 1925. Puccini sent a report of this visit to Adami on the same day.

> Toscanini has just left here. We are in perfect and sympathetic agreement, and finally I can breathe. And so the nightmare that has been looming since April is over.[35] The duet was discussed and it does not please him much. What to do? I don't know. Perhaps Toscanini will summon you and Simoni to Salso[maggiore]. I will come too, and we shall see if there is some way to remedy the situation. I see darkness. Until now because of this duet I have been as stubborn as an elephant. Speak about this to Renato, too. . . . The little that I played for Toscanini made a very good impression. [*EGP*, ltr 223]

A week later, on 14 September 1924, he wrote to Adami again:

> I was hoping to see you at Salso with Simoni and Toscanini, but so far I haven't received any summons . . . I have some ideas about the heart of the duet. The beginning I am not changing unless something better is suggested to me. [*EGP*, ltr 234]

Finally, on 8 October 1924 Puccini could tell Adami: "At last I have received the lines from Simoni. They are truly beautiful and they complete and justify the duet" (*EGP*, ltr 235). Yet just two days later he was begging Adami to spend just two or three hours on the duet and send him some needed verses. "But do this little bit of work in such a way that it is definitive, so that we don't have to go back to it" (*EGP*, ltr 236).

Having followed the winding trail to this point, we see plenty of support for the view that Puccini was unable to finish the last section of *Turandot* because his librettists were more than usually dilatory and occupied with their own careers. If Puccini had received the almost definitive text in April 1924 instead of in October, the month before his death, he would surely have found the energy to compose and orchestrate those last fifteen minutes of music. But to Adami and Simoni it must have seemed that Puccini had become almost impossible to satisfy; one can understand how, unaware of the true condition of his health, they were tempted to put other considerations first.

Reading these letters closely, moreover, one cannot help but feel that much of the impasse stemmed from the composer's postponing coming to grips with this crucial scene, insisting on revisions of already revised revisions, as he felt himself increasingly incapable of summoning up that sense of "over-excitation of every fiber and every atom" that he needed in order to compose.

A passage from one of Puccini's last letters to Adami, dated 22 October 1924, suggests that he may also have realized—as he seems to have done in the letter to Adami back in November 1922 first mentioning the idea that Liù might die—that part of the problem with the opera's conclusion came from the attention focused on Liù in the preceding scene of her suicide and cortège:

> Simoni's verses are good and seem to be just what are wanted and what I had dreamed of. All the rest of Liù's address to Turandot were things that did not really connect up, and you rightly said: the duet is complete like this . . . We shall see—when I get back to work after my return from Brussels. [*EGP*, ltr 237]

On 16 November, he wrote Adami,

> It must be a grand duet. The two beings, almost not of the world, come amongst humans through love, and in the end this love should pervade the whole stage in an orchestral peroration. [*EGP*, ltr 238]

And from the radiology clinic in Brussels,

> . . . and *Turandot*? . . . [*EGP*, ltr 239]

CHAPTER IV

❦

THE FOUR COLORS

THE FIRST sounds heard in *Turandot* are what we have called the "Execution" motive: a ponderous *fortissimo* orchestral unison whose descending chromatic fourths—first diminished, then augmented—cadence into f♯ minor, the principal stable tonality of the opening number (I.A). The same motive at a faster tempo and different pitch level leads into a "bicentric" chord composed of a middle-register C♯-major triad superimposed over a low-register d-minor triad; the composite in this instance arrives as the dominant harmony of f♯ minor. This much is shown in Example 1 above (Chapter I, p. 16).

The frequently heard and immediately recognizable sound quality of "bicentric" harmonies such as those in mm. 5–6 of Example 1 is associated with whatever seemed "barbaric" about Imperial Peking to the colonial-era European. Each of the three ambience-setting act beginnings is built around a repeating threefold series of such "bicentric" harmonies, made with a major triad above superimposed over a minor triad or a single note below, in the same major-seventh root relationship as the paired triads at the end of Example 1.

The opening subject is one of three that have been associated with Turandot. Andrea Della Corte, reviewing the première for the Turin paper *La Stampa*, called it "the will of Turandot."[1] Mosco Carner called it "the main 'Turandot' motif which is the motto of the opera."[2] Michele Girardi has proposed that "this theme is linked by Puccini to the image of Turandot as cruel executioner of her suitors, and like the three chords of Scarpia, it introduces the spectator into an atmosphere of tension from the outset."[3] In line with Girardi's interpretation, we call it the "Execution" motive, since its embodiments in the theater are not associated with Turandot herself so much as with the physical consequences of her "will" or "cruelty," with the impending or actual beheading of the Prince of Persia, or with the anticipated or feared beheading of the unknown Prince. The Execution motive is heard throughout Act I, usually at the ends of passages, and all but twice in one of its faster forms. It is heard at two points in Act II, but one of them is in the reprise of the first part of the Mandarin's proclamation from Act I; otherwise it is heard only in the "waiting" passage between the Princess's second enigma and the Prince's response, though it is developed there at some length; once Turandot has been vanquished by the Prince's solution of her third enigma, however, it is heard no more.

If the Execution motive is to be associated with some quality in the Princess herself—"Turandot's will" as Andrea Della Corte had suggested, or "Turandot's cruelty" as suggested by Michele Girardi[4]—it can only be as a foil to the Chinese melody we are calling "Mo-li-hua," first heard in the "Children's chorus" in Act I, in E♭ Major, doubled by offstage saxophones and accompanied by humming offstage chorus as well as the pit orchestra.[5] Mo-li-hua is next heard *fortissimo* when Turandot appears on the balcony, again in the major mode of E♭, interrupting the e♭ minor of the Prince of Persia's cortège. The pentatonic Mo-li-hua melody continues to be associated directly with Turandot, on- or off-stage, throughout the opera.

If the Execution motive is conceived as "Turandot's cruelty," Mo-li-hua might well be called "Turandot's splendor." Girardi has most aptly described the opposition:

> [The Execution motive's] connection with the cruelty of Turandot is established after the voice of the Prince of Persia has echoed that of Calàf [see mm. 14–18 of Example 32 below]. The thematic play at that moment is particularly skillful in contraposing to it another [theme], also associated with the figure of the Princess, a pentatonic melody previously sounded by a children's chorus "Là sui monti dell'est" [Mo-li-hua, see Example 4]. When Calàf cries out the name of Turandot, it is this latter theme [Mo-li-hua] that echoes him, while when the Prince of Persia cries out, it is the former [the Execution] theme.[6]

The preparation for this crucial moment is shown at the beginning of Example 32: Timur's and Liù's pleas that the Prince come away and his obsessed resistance are set to a modulating sequential crescendo intensified by progressive reduction in phrase length, beginning with a harmonic sequence in measures 1–8 whose second member (mm. 5–8) is a whole step higher than the first. The modulations continue in rising whole steps coupled with reductive rhythmic intensification: the fourth measure of the second member of the original sequence (m. 8) becomes the opening three-count member of a new sequence continuing with a second three-count member (m. 9), a two-count member (m. 10), and a final three-count member (m. 11). At the climax the Prince cries out "Turandot!" three times on a rising fourth, twice up to f' and the third time up to b♭'. Under his sustained b♭' the opening motive of Mo-li-hua begins in the high brass, *fortissimo*, in E♭ major, then collapses precipitately into a *sforzando* bicentric chord, an A-major over a b♭-minor triad; the chord abruptly softens to *pianissimo* and the Prince of Persia is heard offstage, crying out "Turandot!" just once, on a rising fourth echoing the unknown Prince's third cry, but a

EXAMPLE 32. (rh I.25 + 20): The Prince's obsession, Turandot's splendor, (Mo-li-hua) Turandot's cruelty (the Execution motive) [I.B.4]

EXAMPLE 32. *(cont.)*

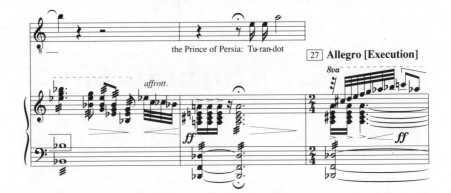

EXAMPLE 32. (*cont.*)

half step lower, rising to an a'. The Prince of Persia is brutally cut off by the bicentric chord, once again *fortissimo*, which flickers out under a descending cascade of the Execution motive in its fast form, *fortissimo* and *diminuendo*.

What is structurally significant in this moment in Act I is the juxtaposition not only of motives and tonal levels but also of musical colorations. Mo-li-hua is a melody in the anhemitonic "Chinese pentatonic," in fact a Chinese folk tune; its characteristic harmonization is a simple alternation of the tonic major triad with one or another "modal dominant" incorporating the lowered seventh scale degree of the key—I alternating with v⁷ or ♭VII—avoiding thereby the leading-tone of the key that is so essential to the establishment of a purely European tonality. The Execution motive, to the contrary, is a configuration of "irrational" melodic intervals, characterized by two non-perfect fourths (diminished followed by augmented) and harmonically associated with the characteristic color of a "bicentric" chord, dissonant with the Execution motive as well as within itself. In Example 32, then, we see a fragment of an "exotic" but simple Far Eastern song set against a "barbaric" but thoroughly European pile-up of dissonances.

The juxtaposition epitomizes a general feature of the whole work. In *Turandot* it is general colorings, rather more than motivic labels, that are associated with characters and situations; the opera is full of various kinds of that generalized *couleur locale* that Verdi scholars today sometimes call *tinta musicale* or *colorito*, following the nineteenth-century critic Abramo Basevi and Verdi himself.[7] Puccini was much more dependent than Verdi on local ambience as partial stimulus for musical ambience, from Scarpia's Roman church bells to Minnie's California cowboys. The pervasive musical "chinoiserie" in *Turandot* is *couleur locale* of an obvious sort, as the quotation from Girardi and Example 32 above suggest, but it is more than merely a Chinese equivalent of the "japonaiserie" of Butterfly's Nagasaki. In *Turandot*, far more than in any of Puccini's other operas, *tinta* is structural: it emerges from a web of interlocking resemblances and contrasts based on tempo or pacing, on instrumental and/or harmonic color, on melodic or rhythmic *topoi* and types, on the texture of accompaniment patterns, and so on. Mo-li-hua and the Execution motive represent two of the basic *tinte musicali* of *Turandot*, which for convenience of reference we may call the "Chinese" *tinta* and the "Dissonance" *tinta*. Another place where these two *tinte* occur in immediate juxtaposition is at the end of the *stretta* in the *fuori-scena* for the three Ministers (rh II.25), where the dissonant and tonally remote beginning of the Processional music rudely recalls the Ministers from their pentatonic reverie of an Imperial China to which peace and love have been restored.

The "Chinese" *tinta* and the "Dissonance" *tinta* contrast not only with one another but with two other colorations besides: an occasional "Middle Eastern" orientalism, marked by augmented seconds, drone pedal-points, and a percussively tinged orchestral accompaniment; and the normal Puccinian "Romantic-diatonic" style of *Manon Lescaut*, *La Bohème*, and *Tosca*, resting on a traditional European tonal-harmonic base colored by piquant pseudo-modal touches produced by replacing the leading-tone with the lowered seventh scale degree and by occasionally using the lowered second scale degree in the minor mode, and often featuring the so-called "*violinata*," in which strings in three or four octaves sound a strong legato melody with wind harmonies in the background.

CHINOISERIE

AUTHENTIC CHINESE SOURCES

The chinoiserie in *Turandot* is both borrowed and invented. So far as can be documented, Puccini drew from only two sources for "authentic" Chinese tunes. One was the music box belonging to the Baron Fassini that Adami reported having heard at Bagni di Lucca in August 1920, in his *Il romanzo della vita di Giacomo Puccini* published more than two decades later. The other is the booklet *Chinese Music* by J. A. van Aalst (Shanghai, 1884).

Some years ago the Fassini music box was tracked down in Rome, still in the possession of Baroness Fassini, by William Weaver and two English colleagues. In a Metropolitan Opera intermission broadcast on 28 December 1974 Weaver played tape recordings of the three items relevant for *Turandot*: Mo-li-hua; the tune the three Ministers sing at their first appearance ("Ferma! che fai?"); and the so-called "Imperial hymn."

Mo-li-hua is in D on the music box, and is exactly as it is at its first appearance in Puccini's opera in the Children's chorus (rh I.19 through to the end); like the other tunes on the music box, however, it is harmonized with ordinary and rather ill-fitting tonal successions. A slightly different version of the tune, identified with its Chinese name "Mò-lì Huā" (jasmine flower), is found in John Barrow's *Travels in China* (Philadelphia, 1805, pp. 211–12); Barrow is the primary source cited for it by Mosco Carner.[8] There is no reason to suppose, however, that Puccini saw this tune in Barrow's or in any other book, and therefore no reason to suppose that he would have known its Chinese name.[9]

The main melody of I.C.1, beginning "Ferma! che fai?" (see Example 7), is on Baron Fassini's music box in G. Again the melody is exactly as Puccini used it (rh I.28 through rh I.30 + 2); where Puccini has his 3/4 measures, however, the music-box melody simply prolongs the arrival tones at the words "fai?," "vuoi," and "questa," for an irrational duration.[10]

The "Imperial hymn" is also in G on the music box. The identification squares with the passage about the music box in Adami's *Il romanzo della vita di Giacomo Puccini*, as quoted in Chapter III. Though the piece is taken very fast on the music box, it is the note-for-note source for Puccini's "Imperial hymn" with its concluding Acclamation "Diecimila anni al nostro Imperatore" (rh II.31 + 13 through to the end).[11] Generally these two parts of the music-box tune are used as they stand, all but once together. The first appearance of the tune is prepared by a simple rising sequence of tonalities on the first phrase with motivic reduction, as shown below reckoned in numbers of quarter-note counts (rh II.30 + 9):

counts:	12	+	12	+	4	+	4	+	4	+	the full melody
keys:	E♭		E		F		A♭		C♭		E♭/A♭

This instrumental passage leads to the first full statement of the "Imperial hymn," also instrumental, and the "Acclamation" music, first instrumental then choral.

Mosco Carner's long-standing source citations for the Ministers' first music in Act I and for the "Imperial hymn" have always seemed to us implausible musically, and we are grateful for William Weaver's detective work in tracking down the Fassini music box, and for the chance to hear Puccini's sources for three of his "Chinese" tunes as Puccini himself heard them. Carner's four citations to van Aalst's *Chinese Music*, to the contrary, are correct.[12] Recently, moreover, Kii-ming Lo has found documentary confirmation in the Ricordi archives that Puccini will have used the book, and a *terminus ante quem*, in the form of a letter to Carlo Clausetti dated 21 June 1921, asking him to look out for a copy of the van Aalst book, saying that it would be useful if it were to contain musical examples.[13]

The most interesting of Puccini's four borrowings from van Aalst is from page 26 of *Chinese Music*: excerpts from van Aalst's description and his transcription of the melody follow below:

> . . . the Emperor leaves his sedan and walks to the temple at a slow, stately pace; a band of fourteen musicians and eleven ensign and umbrella bearers precedes him, while an appropriate piece of music called ⟨dào yīn⟩ (Tao-yin), the Guiding March, is played.
>
> I give here this march, which is played by two *sheng* [small mouth-blown organ], two *ti-tzu* [transverse flute], two *hsiao* [pipes], two *yün-lo* [small gong-chimes], two *tou-kuan* [woodblocks], two drums, and two pairs of castanets. [The piece then follows, in *gōng-chè* notation.] In foreign notation this may be rendered somewhat as follows:

EXAMPLE 33. The Guiding March (The little circles and dots at the side of the Chinese notes and above the Western notes indicate that the drummers and castanet players must sound their instruments.)

The first eight measures of this melody appear in the Ministers' *fuori-scena* (rh II.19 + 12) at van Aalst's pitches, with the a's in measures 4 and 8 protracted, and with f♯ instead of f; this is where the Ministers describe how they would wish to guide the unknown Prince and the Princess Turandot to the bridal chamber. Near the end of Act II, when the Emperor similarly wishes that the unknown Prince might become his son-in-law

(II.F.2), eleven and a half measures of this melody, set a semitone lower, are heard (rh II.67 + 2). Both occurrences of the Guiding March are penultimate in their respective numbers: the one leads into a light-hearted *stretta*, the other precedes a grand ceremonial conclusion. The one over which the Emperor's final words are sung was obviously the first to have been conceived and drafted, since the Emperor has the text of the passage in the libretto for the original long Act I; it will already have been set by August of 1921, along with the rest of the original long Act I (see Chapter III, pp. 71–72). In the version of the Guiding March accompanying the Emperor, moreover, Puccini followed van Aalst's melody at greater length and exactly, except for the transposition a half-step downward.[14] But more than that, Puccini followed the instructions for the rhythmic accompaniment given in van Aalst's transcription, and may have figured out enough about the instruments to try to approximate their texture and color. The melody is played offstage by muted brass plus saxophones, while the percussion rhythms in the pit—supplied by snare drum, bass xylophone, celesta, and solo cello *pizzicato*—precisely follow the "dots . . . above the Western notes" in van Aalst's example. Rather than the Emperor's version of the Guiding March being heard as a weighty reminiscence of that of the three Ministers, therefore, the Ministers' version should be taken as a lighter prefiguring of the Emperor's version to come. Both of course have to do with the hope that the marriage will take place.

On pages 27–31 of van Aalst's *Chinese Music* appears what Carner—evidently following Puccini himself, as one sees in the letter quoted just below—has called a "hymn of Confucius."[15] Puccini used only the opening four-note configuration, re-fa-sol-la, in equal note values; this is the only configuration (at various transposition levels) that is common to all six stanzas of the hymn. In the opera the phrase is sung four times by a chorus of priests at the very end of the cortège for the Prince of Persia (see Example 37-A below). The words they sing are missing in Puccini's fair-copy autograph in the Ricordi archives, and as late as 4 July 1924 Puccini had to write to Adami,

> Try to send me the definitive [text for the final duet], and the verses for the priests, at the end of the march for the Persian prince. The "Hymn of Confucius"—I have the score here and will put them in.[16]

Where the Guiding March and the Hymn to Confucius are ceremonial tunes, ceremonially used, the other two melodies Puccini took from van Aalst's book are from the chapter on "Popular Music," on pages 44–45. Like "Ferma! che fai?" from the music box, each occurs in only one movement of a single number, and like "Ferma! che fai?," these two belong to the

Ministers: the first is the lead melody for the *Tempo d'attacco* of their separate scene (II.A.1, see Example 12 in Chapter I); the other is the principal theme of the "Tempting of the Prince" (III.B.2), at rh III.10 and returning at rh III.14 after an interlude (rh III.12–13).

PUCCINIAN PENTATONICISM AND THE CHINESE *TINTA*

There are also many melodies in *Turandot* with the Chinese *tinta* that are of Puccini's own invention. There is no reason to suppose that the melody of Liù's sweetly pathetic pentatonic aria "Signore, ascolta" or the soaring pentatonic tune for the Princess's *maggiore* peroration "Mai nessun m'avrà" (see Examples 10 and 20) are anything but pure Puccini. Example 34 below furnishes a nice illustration of Puccini's natural pentatonic penchant placed in service of the Chinese *tinta*. The two nearly identical contours there aligned are musico-dramatically related only in their "Chinese" attributes and references: to the one Liù sings "Nulla sono . . . una schiava, mio Signore" (rh I.8)—she had been a native-born Chinese slave in the court of an alien dynasty—while the other is sung by the Ministers in farewell to the ancient glories of their Han race: "Addio stirpe divina" (rh II.18).

EXAMPLE 34. (rh I.8 and II.18): Puccinian pentatonic parallels (Liù and the Ministers)

The Chinese *tinta* comes most exotically to the fore in the scene of the Emperor and the Prince (II.C.1), discussed in Chapter V, and there too the *tinta* is of Puccini's own making (see Examples 17 and 18 in Chapter I).

The pervasive Chinese *tinta* is not necessarily confined to simple and obvious pentatonic tunes. On 30 March 1921 Puccini wrote to Adami

> I call your attention to Liù in the third [act]. It will be necessary to make an irregular meter [*metro inuguale*]. I have the bit of music with a Chinese flavor [*la musichetta di sapore cinese*] and it will be necessary to adapt it a little. [*EGP*, ltr 186]

The expression "irregular meter" suggests something like the eventual text of Liù's "Tanto amore segreto" (III.C.2), with its mixture of mostly un-rhymed *imparisillabo* lines of different lengths. The irregular lines of Liù's lyric apostrophe to her secret love were adapted to an instrumental melody of an exceedingly regular, even repetitious, phrase design (rh III.24 through rh III.25), in the manner called *parlante melodico* by Abramo Ba-sevi, in which the orchestra carries a continuous melodic line that the voice or voices join and leave in a more or less unpredictable fashion. That the somewhat tentative and hesitant effect produced in the first part of Liù's aria by the superposition of an irregular poetic meter over regular musical phrases was part of Puccini's conception from the outset is strongly sug-gested by the above letter of 30 March.

This aria is the first static movement in a number whose opening kinetic movement—III.C.1, the first torture of Liù—is erected over a low-E pedal sustained throughout. G-major and F-major triads alternate over the pedal-point low E while the melody of the Prince's outburst "Sconterete i suoi tormenti!" (you shall pay for her torments) is repeated over and over in the orchestra. That motive is replaced just once, by Mo-li-hua, right at the moment when the stage directions call for Turandot to regain her calm (rh III.21). The low E—and the low register altogether—vanish as the Princess asks Liù the source of her courage: "Chi pose tanta forza nel tuo cuore?" (rh III.23 + 9). "Principessa, l'amore," replies Liù, and Turandot repeats the word "Amore?" questioningly.[17]

The long pentatonic melody is composed, in Puccini's typical manner, of two short motives combined and recombined at various levels and in slightly varied shadings. In the first half of the aria only middle- and high-register instruments are used. The tonality is F major, but only in the sec-ond half does it begin to be stabilized; at this point the low register is reestablished in the orchestral texture with a pedal-point low F in the bass that finally resolves the pedal-point low E of the preceding kinetic move-ment. Even so there is no actual arrival at a tonic triad over this bass F until the last word of the aria (rh III.25), and that only as the resolution of a suspension. The extra sense of suspended time, of "stasis," so brilliantly achieved by this technical means is expressively matched in the text that was supplied for the aria, a young girl's dreamlike fantasy: Liù declares that her love, secret and unconfessed, makes even her torments seem sweet, because by refusing to reveal the Prince's name she can sacrifice her own hopeless love and give him what he most wants, Turandot's love.

The "sapore cinese" of the melody of "Tanto amore segreto" is height-ened by its overall tonal-melodic design, which—though Puccini is hardly likely to have been consciously aware of it—happens to be Chinese at a level sophisticated far beyond that of the usual superficial exoticism of colonialist Europe. The evolving melody is based on a technique of modulation—"metabole" would be a better word—that shifts from one pentatonic module into another through the conversion of an accessory tone into a principal one; the Chinese technical term is *biàn yīn*, "exchange tone." The process may be seen in the eight-measure excerpt from the aria's melody given as Example 25 in Chapter I. The "exchange tone" in measures 1–2 of the example is e, used only as upper-neighbor-tone to d (and elsewhere almost imperceptibly as lower-neighbor-tone to f), in the pentatonic module c–d–f–g–a. In measures 3–4 of the example, e is exchanged for f and becomes a principal tone, effecting a change to another pentatonic module, g–a–c–d–e. In measures 5–6 of the example pitch-class f returns, but the a is momentarily exchanged for b♭, which is used as a lower-neighbor-tone to c, thereby introducing a brief and subsidiary third pentatonic module b♭–c–d–f–[g], which then leads the melody, in measures 6–8 of the example, back into the first module.

One can hardly suppose, however, that Puccini would have been thinking of a change of pentatonic module such as the one in measures 3–4 of Example 25 as an "exchange-tone *metabole*"; it was rather part of an overall expressive scheme that involved the "Chinese" pentatonic on the one hand, and on the other an accompaniment that would suggest tonal centers and allow for harmonic progression without too strongly evoking normal European tonal-harmonic successions inappropriate to the "sapore cinese." Though the aria is in F major, the harmonies for the first phrase of the melody (as in Example 25, mm. 1–2) are clusters emphasizing notes of predominant harmonies (in F major, pitch-classes f–g–b♭–d) plus pitch-class c completing the pentatonic module; for the second phrase the emphasis is on the a-minor triad, which acts as a weakened substitute for the dominant of F major, containing as it does the leading-tone and the fifth degree (e and c) of the key of F major, while its second and dissonant fourth degrees (g and b♭) are replaced with a.

DISSONANCES AND HALF-STEPS

DIABLERIE

The "Dissonance" *tinta* represented by the Execution motive is partly an outgrowth of the nineteenth-century convention of representing mystery and/or terror with the so-called "diabolus in musica," an unprepared and unresolved augmented fourth, the "tritone," as in the Wolf's Glen scene in *Der Freischütz* or Fafner's music in Act II of *Siegfried*. The "Scarpia motive" with which Puccini's *Tosca* begins—rising triads of B♭ major, A♭ major, and

E major over the descending bass line B♭, A♭, E—is a classic instance of the "diabolus in musica" embodied in a "diavolo sulla scena"; the repeating set of three "bicentric" harmonies with which Act II of *Turandot* begins follows exactly the same tritone-outlining relational pattern: E♭ major over low E, D♭ major over low D, A major over low B♭. The concluding A major over low B♭—last heard as an A-major triad over a b♭-minor triad under the Prince of Persia's final despairing "Turandot!"—then becomes the dominant harmony preparing the modal d minor of the ensuing *tempo d'attacco*.

The most striking passage based directly on the "diabolus in musica" is the *tempo di mezzo* (III.C.3) of the last number in Act III set 1, Liù's torture and death, where the interval F♯–c' dominates the whole passage; its beginning is shown in Example 26 in Chapter I. This final return of the Executioners' chorus tune at its original tonal level reinforces a primary association with cruelty of f♯ minor, the tonality of the opening number (I.A), an association that also includes the f♯ minor that is the principal key of Turandot's *aria di sortita* "In questa reggia" (II.D.3). The climax line of the contrasting episode in the first part of that aria—"Un'uomo come te, [come te] straniero"—is also harmonized with parallel tritones (rh II.45 + 10).[18]

Tritones combined with adjoined or infixed whole steps and/or major thirds make whole-tone scales and augmented triads, the source of many of the tonally amorphous textures associated with Mussorgsky (as in the Clock Monologue in *Boris Godunov*), late Liszt, and Debussy. Augmented triads were used by Puccini in *La fanciulla del West* for color and (no doubt by then) simply for their up-to-date sound; in that work unstable augmented triads have replaced the unstable diminished sevenths of nineteenth-century *melodramma*.

Tritone and augmented triad are combined with the most prominent interval contributing to Puccini's Dissonance *tinta*, the unresolved major seventh, in the eerie music for the ghosts of Turandot's executed suitors in Act I, a particularly outré local manifestation of the Dissonance *tinta*. Its unique sonority, instrumental as well as harmonic, is a function of its unique status as the only place in the opera where the supernatural is overtly represented. In the final form of the opera its intrinsic interest is somewhat weakened by its extrinsic discontinuity, utter remoteness combined with a single isolated appearance. As noted in Chapter III, however, in the original long Act I the ghosts were to be heard not once but three times, and we know from his letter of 7 June 1921 (see Chapter III, p. 71) that Puccini had written their music. In that context, they would have been balanced against not one but three sets of responses by the Prince and the Ministers; three supernatural interruptions would have been followed by three successive returns to a more real world, musically as well as dramatically, thus integrating the stylistically remote ghosts' music through simple formal recurrence as part of a patterned cycle.

MAJOR SEVENTHS AND SEMITONES

Much of the music of Arnold Schoenberg's so-called "atonal" period is dominated texturally by whole-tone chords along with three-tone harmonic aggregates of augmented fourth plus perfect fourth adding up to a major-seventh span; the ghosts' music in *Turandot* is vaguely reminiscent of *Pierrot lunaire*, though Puccini evidently heard that particular work of Schoenberg's for the first time only in 1924. Puccini's rapprochement with modernism in *Turandot*, however, for the most part follows the "bitonality" of the Stravinsky of *The Rite of Spring* (*Vesna svyashchennaya*) in the manner of the E♭-major "dominant-seventh" chord over an F♭-major triad of the "Dance of the adolescent girls" (*Plyaski shchegolikh*) or the d♯-minor over d-minor of the introduction to Part II. In *Turandot*, as in *The Rite of Spring*, one or both of the two tones of a dissonant major seventh is expanded harmonically by a triadic harmony, producing that "bicentric" chordal sonority that accompanies the Mandarin's proclamations and the other act beginnings, that is heard under the faster and more bloodthirsty appearances of the Execution motive, and that appears sporadically elsewhere.

The Dissonance *tinta* as semitonal adjacency is manifested not only locally and coloristically, however, but in the larger shape of the opera too, for the potential "bitonality" of two triads whose roots are a semitone apart is reflected in antitheses of two keys a semitone apart that pervade the opera, above all in the juxtaposition of the major and minor tonalities of E♭ and D, as in numbers I.B (the Moonrise chorus and Prince of Persia's cortège) and II.E (the Enigma scene). E♭ major and D major are also the tonalities for most of the major musico-dramatic arrivals at Mo-li-hua: the Children's chorus and first appearance of Turandot in Act I, and the crowd's reaction to the Prince's triumph in Act II, are in E♭ major, while the reprise of the Children's chorus introducing Turandot's second appearance for "In questa reggia" is in D major.

A juxtaposition of the tonal centers e♭ and D also characterizes the concluding moments of Act I. The *concertato*, and of course the Prince's aria "Non piangere, Liù" that turns out to be its lead-off solo, are unremittingly in e♭ minor. Then at the climax of the *concertato* the unknown Prince cries out "Turandot!" three times on a rising fourth (rh I.47 + 13): first b♭–b♭–e♭' over the final tonic e♭-minor triad of the ostinato ensemble, then c♯'–c♯'–f♯' with an f♯-minor triad, finally e'-e'-a' with an A-major triad; after each cry of "Turandot!" the ensemble responds "la morte!" on the respective triad. At last the Prince breaks through to the gong; he strikes it three times, as stage brass and timpani sustain the A-major triad (most tenors will also sustain their own high a' through the striking of the gong if the director's staging allows for it). The A-major triad turns out to be the preparatory dominant for a final *fortissimo* return of Mo-li-hua, in D major (rh I.48), down a half-step in the overall tonal context of e♭ minor, an e♭ minor immediately vehemently reasserted to end the act.

This was not the original tonal plan for the end of the new Act I, however. Timur's speech in I.D.1, the transitional passage that prepares Liù's aria (rh I.41 + 3–10), now begins in e minor and slips down a half-step to e♭ minor without warning in the fifth measure. As Puccini first composed this passage, however, there was no such sideslip of tonality; in his pencil fair-copy autograph score in the Ricordi archives the passage is in e minor throughout, as shown in Example 35 below, and the whole conclusion of the act is a half-step higher than it is now. Liù's forthcoming aria is in G major, and the rest is in e minor to the end of the act, except for the final Mo-li-hua, which is in E♭ major rather than its present D major. The transposition down a semitone to the present form was made at Ricordi, under instructions from Puccini in a letter to Renzo Valcarenghi on 21 February 1924 (*CP*, ltr 884, p. 548): "I remind Maestro [Guido] Zuccoli that it is necessary to transpose the whole Act I Finale down a key, because as it is it's too high. But it's not a difficult matter, since it is taken from e to e♭."[19] That is, it was largely a matter of changing the initial signature from one sharp to six flats and changing some accidentals here and there; except for the four measures where the final Mo-li-hua had to be transposed from E♭ major down to D major, few actual positions on the staff lines and spaces would have had to be altered.

That original act-final reprise of Mo-li-hua—in E♭ major in an overall tonal context of e minor—would have been set up by a "Turandot!" from the Prince reaching high b♭'; whereas now that last Mo-li-hua—in D major in an overall context of e♭ minor—is set up by a "Turandot!" from the Prince culminating at high a'. And whatever Puccini may have meant by "as it is it's too high," the two tonal positions a half-step apart for the Act I Finale—the one Puccini originally conceived, and the one resulting from his act of transposition—lead to two radically different though equally valid musico-dramatic interpretations, interpretations that extend over the whole span of the Act I Finale and its relationship to the rest of the opera.

These two interpretations are most succinctly adumbrated in terms of the act-final reprise of Mo-li-hua—the original E♭ major in an e-minor context or the actual D major in an e♭-minor context—considering the reprise in light of the Prince's act-ending cry of "Turandot!" on a rising fourth that prepares it. That cry is to be heard in light of the two similar cries of "Turandot!" on a rising fourth heard earlier in the act, in the passage cited by Michele Girardi quoted above and shown in measures 11–16 of our Example 32. In Puccini's original untransposed form of the Act I Finale, the unknown Prince's third cry of "Turandot!" just before striking the gong culminated on b♭′ and would have been heard as a reminiscence of his previous third cry of "Turandot!" (rh I.26 + 10–12, or see Example 32, mm. 13–15); it would have seemed like defiance arising from confidence in anticipated triumph. The immediately succeeding *fortissimo* Mo-li-hua in the original key of E♭ major would then have been heard both as an echo of the brief Mo-li-hua that had followed the unknown Prince's previous cry and as a return of the *fortissimo* E♭-major Mo-li-hua heard at Turandot's first appearance (rh I.23 + 4), to be echoed most forcefully again by the *fortissimo* E♭-major Mo-li-hua following the unknown Prince's achieved triumph in Act II (rh II.62 + 7).

In the Finale in its actual form, transposed a half-step downwards, the musical relationships call forth a very different interpretation on stage. The unknown Prince's last "Turandot!" culminating as it actually does now on high a′, recalls not his own earlier cry but rather the "Turandot!" that had echoed that earlier cry, the dying cry of the Prince of Persia, which had also culminated on high a′. The Prince's act-final third cry of "Turandot!" and the D-major Mo-li-hua that it prepares will now be heard as expressing defiance not so much confident as fatalistic; this is much more in keeping with the text of the Prince's aria "Non piangere, Liù," and with his verses newly added for the *concertato*—"son io che domanda pietà . . . ho troppo sofferto . . . io seguo la mia sorte . . . " etc.—which of course do not appear in the original long Act I libretto. The still *fortissimo* but now D-major act-final Mo-li-hua in the transposed Finale echoes the *fortissimo* Mo-li-hua of Turandot's appearance only dynamically. Tonally it connects not with the E♭-major climax of the Moonrise and cortège but rather with its equally striking D-major opening, a D major that had arrived as a deceptive resolution of the final cadence of the f♯-minor Executioners' chorus closing the first number of the opera. That deceptive cadence is made with the second and last appearance of the Execution motive in the imposing and dramatic slow form whose first appearance had opened the opera, where it had cadenced authentically in f♯ minor. The two middle numbers of Act I themselves are tonally closed in the key reached at that deceptive cadence, with D major at the beginning of the Moonrise chorus (I.B.1) and d minor for the appearance of the Chief Executioner with the severed head of the Prince of Persia (I.C.4, end, and see Example 9 in Chapter I). The dissonant piccolo f♯‴ over the final d-minor triad of I.C.4 harks back to the principal key of the sunset world, the f♯ minor of the opening number (I.A); it is prefigured at the end of the ministerial warnings in I.C.2.

The D major that begins the Moonrise chorus, in short, is a D major that is still part of the lurid sunset and the cruel f♯ minor of the Executioners' world; the moon has not yet risen on Turandot's Act I E♭ major. Thus in Act I the two appearances of Mo-li-hua in E♭ major (the Children's chorus and the appearance of Turandot), as well as the e♭-minor funeral cortège for the Prince of Persia, are in contrast with the D major of sunset, not the D major of sunrise that will be adumbrated in "Nessun dorma" and fully manifested at the very end of Act III; the brief explosion of D major in the Mo-li-hua at the end of the act is still tonally tinged with the sunset color of that world. It also tonally prefigures the D-major reprise of the Children's chorus singing Mo-li-hua that prepares the introductory phrase "In questa reggia" of Turandot's f♯-minor *aria di sortita* in Act II, just as the E♭-major Children's chorus had tonally anticipated her first musical appearance, wordless but equally imperious, in Act I.

If the Act I Finale had remained untransposed, the e-minor tonal realm in which Timur begins his last plea to his son (rh I.41 + 3) would have remained in force until the end of the act. Example 35 is a piano-vocal transcription of the passage as it appears on folio 61 of Puccini's fair-copy orchestral autograph in the Ricordi archives; the asterisk marks the place where the shift a half-step downward occurs in the engraved scores (cf. I.41 + 7). This speech of Timur's is the last of only three that he has in Act I that is longer than a single phrase, and like the other two—his *arietta* "Perduta la battaglia" (rh I.7) and the passage beginning "No, no! stringiti a me!" (rh I.25 + 11)—it belongs to a general e/G/a/C "white-key" tonal realm, one that is surrounded by more remote tonal areas on its two earlier appearances. Had it continued as in Example 35, the Act I Finale, tonally speaking, would have become a continually augmenting outgrowth of Timur's pleading with his son (e minor), moving on through Liù's plea (G major) and the Prince's response to her in "Non piangere, Liù" (back to e minor), and on to the *concertato* in e minor, with an abrupt but temporary shift to E♭ major for the act-final reprise of Mo-li-hua, before the act-ending cadences in e minor. In that case, the juxtaposition of tonalities e minor and E♭ major at the end of Act I would have been embodied on stage as the struggle of the Prince's father and his allies to hold the Prince to his old ties to his father (diatonic music in e minor) and separate him from his new obsession with the Princess Turandot (*fortissimo* Mo-li-hua in E♭ major). Once transposed, however, the Finale is brought into the melancholic e♭-minor tonal area previously established in the cortège for the Prince of Persia, picked up later in the third of the three enigmas in Act II, and finally in Liù's suicide and cortège in Act III. The temporary D-major act-final reprise of Mo-li-hua is in direct juxtaposition with e♭ minor, and the end of the act thus reflects the whole of I.B (from the Moonrise chorus

EXAMPLE 35. The earlier version of I.D.1 (after Puccini's autograph, folio 61)

beginning in D major through the Prince of Persia's cortège in e♭ minor);
it also prefigues the d-minor and e♭-minor juxtaposed tonalities of the
Enigma scene, as well as the D-major Children's chorus Mo-li-hua leading
into "In questa reggia" and the triumphant E♭-major Mo-li-hua after the
Prince has solved the third enigma.[20]

If the particular semitone/major seventh relationship D/d and E♭/e♭ be
taken as a primary "bicentric" tonality for Turandot in its final form, whose
embodiments on stage—the pairings of Prince/Princess, fire/ice, sun/
moon, and silver/gold suggested in Chapter I—are the primary dramatic
and symbolic elements of the opera, then we might consider the tritone-
related pitch classes and tonalities of f♯ (minor) and C (major) as a secondary dissonant coupling whose representatives on stage are the Executioners
and the Emperor. Earlier in this chapter we noted the diabolic tritone F♯/
c′—literally of course a diminished twelfth—that pervades the *tempo di
mezzo* between Liù's "Tanto amore segreto" and her death and funeral cortège. The association of f♯ minor with the Executioners and with blood-
thirstiness, be it of the crowd (I.A) or the Princess (II.C.3), taking pleasure
in pain, has also been noted, and in Chapter V we shall be proposing that
the C major of Act II set 2 is embodied on stage as the impersonal, semi-
divine authority of the Emperor, beyond both pleasure and pain (see pp.
120–21 below).

PERSIAN PRINCE AND
CHINESE SLAVE

There are only three passages in *Turandot* grounded in the "Middle Eastern" *tinta*, and two of them, moreover, are only *couleur locale*: the musics
for the handmaidens of the Princess (I.C.2) and for the Ministers' offer of
dancing girls as a bribe to the Prince (III.B.1) merely denote slave women
of Middle Eastern or Central Asian origin, as colorfully exotic in ancient
Imperial China as in the pre-war Imperialist West. The third passage in
Middle Eastern *tinta*, to the contrary, is fundamental to the large design of
the opera, though only one movement is actually involved, the cortège for
the Prince of Persia (I.B.3).

Despite his brief and silent appearance in the cortège and his single off-
stage death cry, the Prince of Persia is pivotal in the structure of the opera
as it finally took shape. In his person he embodies the whole corpus of
Turandot's failed suitors; his bloody execution brings the cruelty of the
Princess into vivid focus. Puccini saw a powerful musical potential in the
Prince of Persia and his fate, and made the most of it—perhaps too much,
in the light of his subsequent difficulties with the dénouement of the opera.
The Middle Eastern Prince of Persia is the unsuccessful shadow of the un-
known Prince in the same way that the Chinese slave-girl Liù is the unsuc-

cessful shadow of the Princess Turandot. Liù's death and funeral cortège in Act III, with Timur's farewell, parallels the funeral cortège for the Prince of Persia in Act I. Both pieces are in the same e♭-minor tonality, and the full authentic cadences followed by a pause that conclude the two pieces are the first full stops in Act I and Act III, respectively. And both pieces are manifestations of the funeral-march *topos*—in Act I for the Prince of Persia with frequent Middle Eastern tonal coloring, in Act III for Liù and Timur with Romantic-diatonic tonal coloring—a *topos* evoked not so much by the minor modality and the slow pace as by the steady and monotonous short-short-long anapaest rhythm that dominates them both.[21] But where the funereal anapaests in the Act I cortège for the Prince of Persia have melodic direction, with frequent "Middle Eastern" augmented seconds and other not-quite-diatonic intervals (see Example 5 in Chapter I), in Liù's diatonic cortège in Act III the slow anapaest is simply three attacks at the same pitch, thus without melodic content (see Example 27 in Chapter I). The third stroke of Liù's anapaest, moreover, is prolonged not by being sustained, as in the melody for the Prince of Persia's cortège, but rather with a melodic extension of consistent contour. The openings of the two melodies are shown aligned in Example 36 below.

EXAMPLE 36. (rh I.21 and rh III.27): Funereal anapaests for the luckless suitor and the faithful servant [I.B.3 and III.C.4]

In the basic eight-measure melody for the Prince of Persia's funeral cortège the anapaest rhythm of the funeral-march *topos* is manifested in three adjacent scale degrees moving in the same direction, either up or down. In each of the four occurrences of the melody (rh I.21, rh I.21 + 11, rh I.22, and rh I.23 + 14), the most obvious of the musical emblems of a Middle Eastern *tinta*, the "exotic" augmented second interval, is gradually replaced as the melody completes its overall rise and fall. For instance, in the initial appearance of the melody (see Example 5 in Chapter I), the anapaest begins as a stepwise rise including the augmented second g♭–a–b♭, scale degrees ♭3–♯4–5, answered by a falling stepwise anapaest a–g♭–f, scale degrees ♯4–♭3–2; then a stepwise rise in measure 3, still including the augmented second interval, breaks the anapaestic rhythm for half a measure. At the top of line, in measures 5–6, the descending contour in anapaest rhythm returns, bounded by a diminished fourth (f–e–c♯), and again comes twice more bounded by perfect fourths in measures 5–6 and 6–7 (e–d♯–b and e♭–d♭–b♭) as the overall line curves back downward. In the penultimate measure of the melody the anapaest rhythm is fully broken as the line makes a final and purely diatonic descent, and when the anapaestic 4–3–2 of measure 2 finally returns in the last measure of the melody, it is as a purely diatonic a♭–g♭–f.

After the final diatonic stepwise anapaest in the respective last measures of the first and the second statements of the Prince of Persia's melody, the Middle Eastern augmented-second rising stepwise anapaest comes back, for the opening measures of the second and the third statements respectively. The corresponding last measures of the third and the fourth statements, conversely, are each extended in passages that wipe out the Middle Eastern *tinta* in the large, as the diatonic conclusion within the melody proper wipes it out in the small. After the third statement of the melody comes a development of its final a♭–g♭–f anapaest in the seven-measure passage of progessive reduction and rhythmic transformation illustrated in Example 6 in Chapter I. As may be seen there, the a♭–g♭–f line is kept to the fore and elaborated for four measures; then (at rh I.23 + 1) it is melodically reduced to g♭–f, which is in turn kept central and elaborated, culminating in the contour g♭–f–d♭–e♭ leading into Mo-li-hua for Turandot's appearance on the balcony. At the same time, the four-stroke repeated-note rhythm to which the chorus tenors and sopranos sing "Principèssa" in the three measures before rh I.23 is reduced to an iambic choral "Pietà!" at just the point where the orchestra's a♭–g♭–f is melodically reduced to g♭–f; at the end all join in the final g♭–f, g♭–f–d♭–e♭ for "La grazia, o Principèssa!" This tremendous buildup thus includes a reductive transformation of the Prince of Persia's Middle Eastern *tinta* into the Chinese pentatonic *tinta* of Mo-li-hua, *fortissimo*, for Turandot's appearance on the balcony.

After Turandot's withdrawal the Prince of Persia's melody, with its augmented seconds, is begun one last time, but now the only voice heard is that of the unknown Prince, as he sings the line in which his obsession is made explicit, "O divina bellezza! o meraviglia! o sogno!" over its opening measures. The concluding two and a half diatonic measures of the melody, and its extension to the end of the cortège, are shown in Example 37-A. This time the final ab–gb–f anapaest is extended in simple fourfold repetition, over which the Prince repeats fragments of his line, leading finally to a full authentic cadence in eb minor, the first and last in the piece. The cadential arrival is extended by the priests with "O gran Koung-Tzè," the four-measure "Hymn to Confucius" discussed earlier in this chapter; this constitutes the second replacement of an orientalizing Middle Eastern *tinta* with an "authentic" Chinese *tinta*, paralleling in muted form the transition into Mo-li-hua just discussed. The movement concludes with three solemn eb-minor triads sounding the last and slowest anapaest of the Prince of Persia's funeral cortège.

EXAMPLE 37. (rh I.24 + 4 and rh III.34 + 4): The first full stops in Acts I and III [I.B.3 and III.C.4]

As is illustrated through Example 37-B above, the manner in which Liù's funeral cortège is concluded is very closely parallel with the ending of the Prince of Persia's funeral cortège. The anapaests in the respective third measures of Example 37-A and B are prolonged by further precadential anapaests filling in between scale degrees 2 and 4 and harmonized with various sorts of pre-dominant ii chords and iv chords. In the final authentic cadences in eb minor the pitch class d-natural, the leading-tone of the key, is of course present in the respective dominant harmonies, but in Liù's cortège its appearance as leading-tone at the end of the number is one of only two such places in the piece where the true dominant harmony of the key is heard.[22] And though d-natural appears several times earlier in the Prince of Persia's cortège, it does so either in passing or as part of a D-major triad (as occurs at the downbeat of m. 4 of the melody as shown in Example 36-A or Example 5), a harmony deliberately far removed from the principal tonality; the first and only occurrence of d-natural as part of a true dominant in e♭ minor is similarly at the end of the number.[23] The instrumentation too, including the prominent use of the piccolo in an otherwise very low-lying texture, contributes to making the parallel between these two medial endings clearly audible, so that the three final chords in each case are easily heard as anapaestic medial conclusions in the funereal *topos*, expressing the same kind of finality in death for both these "shadows" of the protagonists. It has already been noted that the authentic cadence, followed by pause, that concludes each of these pieces is the first such conclusive ending in the respective act in question, which of course confirms not only the structural but also the expressive parallel.

THE PUCCINIAN NORM

In Example 38 the end of the Prince of Persia's cortège melody is aligned with the beginning of Liù's, to show how the melodic extension of Liù's anapaests strongly resembles that moment in the Prince of Persia's melody where the anapaestic rhythm is broken and the diatonic replacement of the exotic opening has been completed.

EXAMPLE 38. (rh I.21 + 4 and rh III.27): Diatonic descents [I.B.3 and III.C.4]

The diatonicism thus temporarily established for the Prince of Persia, like the diatonic melody of Liù's suicide and Timur's grief, is part of the general coloring we have referred to as "Romantic-diatonic." Each of the exotic *tinte*—the pentatonic Chinese *tinta*, the modernist Dissonance *tinta*, the orientalizing Middle Eastern *tinta*—in its own way conveys remoteness and alienation from the expectations represented in the late Romantic familiarity of Puccini's normal melodic-harmonic style. But that style is not only the background against which the more exotic colors are highlighted; it is also specifically embodied in the unknown Prince and his father, who—though they too are personages in an Oriental fairy tale—are the manifestations on stage of the Romantic-diatonic *tinta*. Only when the Prince is overwhelmed or surrounded by forces outside himself does he participate actively in an exotic *tinta*. His first reactions to the sensual impact of the Princess, for instance, are incorporated in passages of Middle Eastern languor: his "O divina bellezza! o sogno! o meraviglia!" fitted into the beginning of the fourth and final statement of the Prince of Persia's melody (rh I.21); and his bewitched echoing of the Princess's Middle Eastern handmaidens' "Si profuma di lei l'oscurità," sung to their music (rh I.35 + 12). The Prince also shares fully—respectfully—in the very strong Chinese *tinta* of his scene with the Emperor (II.C); but when he sings measures 5–8 of Mo-li-hua at the climax to the coda of the Enigma scene (rh II.65), he absorbs, rather than is absorbed into, the Chinese *tinta*, through the tonal harmonization, with full authentic cadence in C major, of the crucial phrase "Ti voglio tutta ardente d'amor." This is the Prince's dominant sentiment, and one that was hardly alien to Puccini's conception of universal humanity:

> when the heart speaks, whether it be in China or Holland, the sense is all the same and the purpose [*finalità*] is that of all people. [*CP*, ltr 892, p. 550]

In his two arias the Prince embodies most fully that conception of Romantic love as the touchstone of all mankind, expressed in two different shades of the Romantic-diatonic *tinta*: the passionate in the tonal-diatonic *motivo* of the Prince's name in "Nessun dorma" (III.A.2), couched in the amorous vein of the Cavaradossi of "Recondita armonia"; and the melancholic in the pseudo-modal "Non piangere, Liù" (I.D.3), in the despairing vein of the Cavaradossi of "E lucevan le stelle." Particularly effective is the way in which "Non piangere, Liù" is made to serve as leadoff for the interpolated *concertato*, as illustrated in Example II in Chapter I. The rising-falling half-step f'–g♭'–f' of "Chiede colui" (rh I.45 + 6–7) is first expanded intervallically in the two succeeding phrases, reaching up to a♭' and then b♭'; the rising step d♭'–e♭' that concludes the second of the two repetitions of "Che non sorride più" is then brought down in sequential replications to d♭–e♭ an octave lower; finally (at rh I.46) the two—the g♭–f of "[chiede] colui" and the d♭–e♭ of "[che non sorri]de più"—are combined to make the *ostinato* figure g♭–f–d♭–e♭ for the *concertato*. And it will be remembered that this same figure g♭–f–d♭–e♭ had earlier been generated in another way, by rhythmic-melodic reduction from the Prince of Persia's melody, in a single appearance making the transition into Mo-li-hua at rh I.23 (as discussed above and illustrated through Example 6 in Chapter I).

The Recognition music with which the unknown Prince is reunited with his aged father Timur, right after the Mandarin's opening speech (rh I.4, and see Example 2 in Chapter I), is perhaps the most typical passage for the Puccinian Romantic-diatonic *tinta* in *Turandot*. And as we have noted several times, the old man is always represented in this *tinta*. The strong presence of the Romantic-diatonic *tinta* in Liù's funeral cortège is the most telling confirmation of Timur's share in embodying the Puccinian musical norm. This magnificent composition, with its inexorably repeating slow anapaest marking the funeral-march *topos*, is the last Puccini completed. It is often thought of as though it were simply an aria for Liù with an epilogue, but it is as much or more the major piece for the principal bass. The 28 measures up to Liù's suicide comprise only the first episode in the movement. The 28 parallel measures that follow (rh III.29) begin with a cry of "Parla! il nome!" from the crowd followed by the Prince's sorrowful "Ah! tu sei morta, o mia piccola Liù," but they are otherwise Timur's.[24] The final cadence of this second 28-measure episode, climaxing to bass high e♭' at Timur's line "L'anima offesa si vendicherà" (rh III.31 + 8–10), is even more conclusive than the cadence to which Liù sings her last words "Io chiudo gl'occhi / per non vederlo più" (rh III.29), since his penultimate harmony is a true dominant, as hers is not; it is one of the most powerful and magical moments in the opera. And then, after the interpolated contrasting 10-measure choral prayer that Timur's warning provokes (rh III.32), his are the first 20 measures of the final 28-measure episode as well (rh III.33). Most significantly of all, the piece does not show the characteristic Chinese *tinta* of Liù's two solo arias; it is rather in the mournful Romantic-diatonic vein of the Prince's "Non piangere, Liù." It is akin to Timur's Act I *arietta* "Perduta la battaglia" (rh I.7), in short, rather than to Liù's *arietta* "Nulla sono" (rh I.8), let alone her "Signore ascolta" (I.D.2) or the immediately preceding set piece "Tanto amore segreto" (III.C.2).

The Romantic-diatonic *tinta*—being the Puccinian norm—is also reflected even where other *tinte* are being highlighted. In the first part, the *minore*, of Turandot's "In questa reggia," for example, though the parallel seventh chords in the accompaniment constitute a modernism of the Dissonance *tinta*, the melody itself is purely diatonic, and indeed, diatonic in the same manner as Liù's cortège. Example 39 shows the continuous instrumental melody to which Turandot's lines are fitted at the return to the principal subject in f♯ minor (rh II.46 + 3)—it is the same as the undoubled vocal melody at the beginning of the *minore*—aligned with the melody of Liù's cortège.

EXAMPLE 39. (rh II.46 + 3 and rh III.27): Romantic-diatonic melodies for the Princess and the slave-girl

The contours, both in the large and the small, are virtually the same, except for the absence of repeated-note anapaests in Turandot's melody; the same contour is of course found towards the end of the Prince of Persia's melody (compare Example 39 and Example 38). These resemblances may reflect no more than pure force of melodic habit on Puccini's part; one might also like to think of them, however, as reflecting the common humanity in Turandot's feeling for her "Principessa Lo-u-ling / Ava dolce e serena" in the text set to her f♯-minor melody at its first appearance, however barbaric the consequences of that feeling towards the men addressed when the melody returns: "O principi . . . io vendico su voi quella purezza."

CHAPTER V

THE TWO DUETS

IN eighteenth-century *opera seria* the paradigmatic scene type was the solo aria, in which lyric verse was set in a formal and continuous musical texture, with much text repetition for musical extensions. Each aria would express an affect or a reaction, on the part of a single character, to preceding action and dialogue set in recitative verse and texture. Needless to say, solo scenes and arias of various kinds continued to play a prominent role in the *melodramma* of the Great Tradition, but by the second and third decades of the nineteenth century duet scenes, and a grand medial Finale, had become as obligatory as the solo scene for the *prima donna*. Like the aria scene, the medial Finale was a development out of eighteenth-century predecessors, having already been adapted from *opera buffa* in the last years of the eighteenth century. Duets also occur in eighteenth-century opera, of course—very frequently in *opera buffa*, and even once in a while in *opera seria*—but the standard and obligatory four-movement Grand Duet of Italian Romantic *melodramma*, with its direct confrontation of two characters in conflict, singing lyric verse in *tempo giusto* in all movements, was a nineteenth-century invention and convention. The sequence of four movements is usually introduced with a recitative *scena*; the first and third lyric movements are "kinetic"—open-ended as to both stanzaic and musical design, with little or no text repetition for musical purposes—while the second and fourth lyric movements are "static," that is, cast in regular stanzas, formally rounded and closed musically, with much musical extension carried on repeated fragments of text already heard in full.[1]

In a duet confrontation on this plan, the two formal movements normally conclude in an extended passage, often as much as half the movement, in which the two characters sing simultaneously, repeating text previously sung alone; such duets we might call "ensemble duets." There are also duet scenes in nineteenth-century Romantic *melodramma* with little or no ensemble for the two principals. Many of these are ad hoc modifications of the normative four-movement ensemble duet in which the concluding ensemble portion in a formal movement, or even the whole movement, is bypassed, or aborted after having been prepared. Other duets, however, are made on a different kind of design altogether, in which a two-person confrontation entirely in dialogue—still in lyric verse (though often without change of verse meter) and continuous musical texture(s)—is presented as a complete and closed number, as though the duet consisted entirely of one or more kinetic movements; such duets we might call "dialogue duets."[2]

During the course of the nineteenth century the traditional multi-movement ensemble duet lost its pride of place, through reduction or elimination of *cabalette*, through withering away of ensemble conclusions in its slow movements, as well as through displacement in favor of the kinetic approach of the dialogue duet. By the end of the century, while ensemble singing in the old manner continued to be acceptable for larger groups from trio to choral ensemble, only traces and echoes remained of the traditional ensemble conclusion for formal movements in the Grand Duet, typically in such effects as the climactic octaves *con slancio* of the Santuzza-Turiddu, Mimì-Rodolfo, Butterfly-Pinkerton, and so many other tenor-soprano duets.

The Enigma Scene

The confrontation scene in Act III of *Turandot* that we have called "The Thawing of the Princess" (III.D) was clearly expected to be a dialogue duet of some kind—though whether Puccini would have found a way to conclude it with tenor-soprano octaves in the vein of

$$\text{a 2: Gli enigmi sono tre,} \quad \left\{ \begin{array}{c} \text{la morte è una} \\ \text{una è la vita} \end{array} \right\} \qquad \text{(rh II.48 + 3–5)}$$

is forever moot. The Enigma scene (II.E) is also a two-person confrontation in dialogue, but such a symmetrically structured challenge-and-response sequence might not at first seem so easily construed as a dialogue duet. In the Verdian canon such passages always form part of a larger structure, usually functioning as a kinetic movement preparing a more static formal movement to follow, and the balance of forces between challenger and respondent is usually uneven, with ensemble and chorus fully participating on one side or the other.[3] In the Enigma scene, to the contrary, though the Prince's responses have much less text and many fewer measures of music than the Princess's challenges, they are composed so as to be of equal weight musically, and therefore dramatically as well. As for the onlookers, they are only onlookers, despite their sympathies with the Prince as respondent; they participate in neither challenge nor response. Their function in the scene, dramatically and musically alike, is merely to confirm the concluding responses, and vocally to participate in the suspenseful delay in the second challenge-and-response sequence (there is no delay in the first sequence, while the still more suspenseful delay in the third sequence is purely gestural and instrumental). And though the challenge-and-response sequences in the Enigma scene are not a preparation for a more formal reflective movement, the extended coda that caps and continues the Prince's triumph—sung by the Princess, the Emperor, the chorus, and finally the Prince himself—is built on a different structural plan and establishes a different tonal center. The Enigma scene as a whole is a single number in two divisions, then, tensely begun in one manner and heroically concluded in another: a "dialogue duet" with ensemble coda; or an "ensemble duet" whose concluding ensemble augments while it separates the two principals.

THE SHAPE OF ACT II SET 2

The overall plan of Act II set 2 is laid out in Figure 1 according to the rubrics used in Chapter I, amplified by lower-case letters marking further points of articulation. Solid double horizontals mark the three complete breaks in continuity, where a very final and *fortissimo* tonic triad followed by *Generalpause* is succeeded by a radical change of texture and tonality (in the third case, by the act-final curtain itself). Solid arrows indicate musical continuity separated in the Figure merely for graphic convenience to the analysis. The three broken arrows, conversely, mark the presence of composed transitions (at rh II.25, rh II.40, and rh II.49). It will be noted that these transitions occur at just those junctures where a musical number was interpolated when the original long Act I was divided, as a comparison of Figure I with the summary of the 1921 libretto in Chapter III will illustrate; in Puccini's fair-copy autograph score in the Ricordi archives, moreover, there are slight but arguable traces of the grafting in of the interpolations at these points (see notes 5 and 6 below).

In the libretto of 1921, scene-changing and processional music (now II.B) had followed the end of the first set, which had comprised the Prince's striking of the gong, his aria "Non piangere, Liù," followed by Liù's aria "Per quel sorriso"; we know from Puccini's letter to Simoni of 7 June 1921 that he had already composed these arias, in that order, before the division of the original long Act I into two acts.[4] To suggest how the transition from Liù's original aria "Per quel sorriso" into the Processional music might have been drafted would be of course pure speculation—but assuming that her present "Signore, ascolta" is not a completely new piece but was rather an adaptation of "Per quel sorriso," it is worth remembering that "Signore, ascolta" was originally composed in G major, and that the offstage brass that presently breaks in so dissonantly with the first of the three Processional tunes at rh II.25 does so over the conclusion of another piece in G major, the *stretta* of the Ministers' interpolated *fuori-scena*.[5]

Figure 1. Tonal and thematic correspondences in *Turandot*, Act II set 2

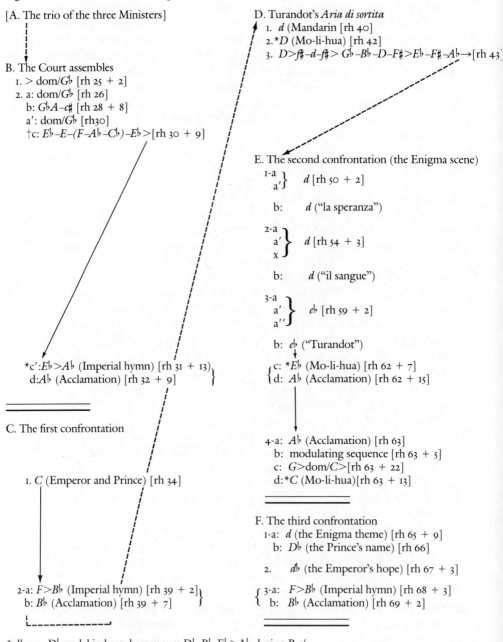

[A. The trio of the three Ministers]

B. The Court assembles
 1. > dom/G♭ [rh 25 + 2]
 2. a: dom/G♭ [rh 26]
   b: G♭A–c♯ [rh 28 + 8]
   a′: dom/G♭ [rh30]
   †c: E♭–E–(F–A♭–C♭)–E♭>[rh 30 + 9]

*c′:E♭>A♭ (Imperial hymn) [rh 31 + 13]
d:A♭ (Acclamation) [rh 32 + 9]

C. The first confrontation

 1. C (Emperor and Prince) [rh 34]

2-a: F>B♭ (Imperial hymn) [rh 39 + 2]
 b: B♭ (Acclamation) [rh 39 + 7]

D. Turandot's *Aria di sortita*
 1. d (Mandarin [rh 40]
 2.*D (Mo-li-hua) [rh 42]
 3. D>f♯–d–f♯> G♭–B♭–D–F♯>E♭–F♯–A♭→[rh 43

E. The second confrontation (the Enigma scene)
1-a
 a′} d [rh 50 + 2]

 b: d ("la speranza")

2-a
 a′} d [rh 54 + 3]
 x

 b: d ("il sangue")

3-a
 a′} e♭ [rh 59 + 2]
 a″

 b: e♭ ("Turandot")

c: *E♭ (Mo-li-hua) [rh 62 + 7]
d: A♭ (Acclamation) [rh 62 + 15]

4-a: A♭ (Acclamation) [rh 63]
 b: modulating sequence [rh 63 + 5]
 c: G>dom/C>[rh 63 + 22]
 d:*C (Mo-li-hua)[rh 63 + 13]

F. The third confrontation
1-a: d (the Enigma theme) [rh 65 + 9]
 b: D♭ (the Prince's name) [rh 66]

2. d♭ (the Emperor's hope) [rh 67 + 3]

3-a: F>B♭ (Imperial hymn) [rh 68 + 3]
 b: B♭ (Acclamation) [rh 69 + 2]

*all over D♭ pedal in bass; bass moves D♭-B♭-E♭>A♭ during B.c′

The dialogue of the Emperor and the Prince with its concluding Imperial hymn and Acclamation (now II.C) that follows the Processional music is in turn followed by a transition into the reprise of the Mandarin's proclamation (now II.D.1). The Emperor scene and the Mandarin's proclamation in the present libretto are as they were in the 1921 libretto; their musics and the transition between them would have needed no change. As has been pointed out in the summary of the original long Act I libretto in Chapter III, there is no way to know whether the present D-major reprise of the Children's chorus singing Mo-li-hua (II.D.2) that now follows the Mandarin was part of Puccini's original composition, though it seems highly likely. In any case, the Mandarin's proclamation was originally a preparation not for the D-major beginning of Turandot's "In questa reggia" but rather for her "Straniero, ascolta!" and the d-minor beginning of the Enigma scene, with or without a preparatory D-major reprise of the Children's chorus for her entrance. One can surmise how this might have worked before the interpolation of "In questa reggia" by simply omitting everything in the present score from the end of the Children's chorus (just before rh II.43) up to the d'/d''–a'/a'' blare of the stage trumpets before Turandot's "Straniero, ascolta!" (two measures before rh II.50).[6]

In any event, whatever changes in transitional passages the grafting in of Turandot's "In questa reggia" may have brought about, the essential structure of what was once set 2 of the original long Act I and is now Act II set 2 needed no change; while the *aria di sortita* may well heighten the effect of the eventual beginning of the Enigma scene, it is still an interpolation into—or better, a prolongation of—a musico-dramatic preparation already completed with the reprises of the Mandarin's proclamation and the Children's chorus. "In questa reggia" (rh II.43), beginning from the D major of the Children's chorus, is an introductory passage. The principal key of the aria proper (rh II.44) is f♯ minor, the tonality of cruelty, beginning with Turandot's rhetorical address to her ancestress (see Example 19 in Chapter I) with its accompaniment in parallel sevenths. In the contrasting period in d minor (rh II.45) she tells how her ancestress was dragged away, ravished, and killed by a man, and in the passage harmonized with tritones already noted—"un'uomo come te, [come te] straniero" (rh II.45 + 10)—she addresses the Prince directly. In the return of the f♯ minor music (rh II.46 + 3), she sings of her vicarious vengeance on the destroyer of Princess Lo-u-ling, while the pace of the accompaniment in parallel sevenths is doubled. The aria follows the tradition of the Italian Romantic *melodramma* in capping this *minore* opening with a grandly rhetorical *maggiore* conclusion. The expansive G♭-major melody sung to the words "Mai nessun m'avrà!" is the third theme sometimes called a "Turandot" motive, but in fact it only recurs once later in the opera, in Puccini's draft for the music preceding the Prince's violent kiss in the final duet.

From the outset of the planning the Enigma scene (II.E) was the constant structural apex of the opera, the high point of the rising action. This first vocal confrontation of Turandot and the Prince is prepared by the confrontation of Prince and Emperor (II.C), parallel to the Enigma scene in dramatic structure yet highly contrasted with it in tone and color, and introduced by an exotic fanfare completely divorced in its pitch content and brassy timbre from the impressive and harmonious conclusion of the Processional entrance music that opens Act II set 2. The Emperor Altoum's confrontation with the Prince is the only vocal scene in the opera for one who had been a principal character in Gozzi's play as well as Busoni's opera. Yet the Emperor is a central figure here too, literally as positioned on stage and in dramatic time, and musically as prepared. His dramatic importance resides in the fact that the enabling power that actualizes Turandot's cruelty flows from this old and semi-divine personage enthroned high above the rest, revealed only when incense clouds drift away; the power is not hers but his, even though it is constrained to her ends by an unspecified unbreakable oath.

The mythic encounter of the old Emperor and the young Prince is achieved with an overwhelming sparseness of means. The Emperor's seat is almost literally in the clouds of Heaven, the Prince stands firmly on Earth at the foot of the staircase. Neither moves during their dialogue, and the crowd and the Court are silent as well as immobile; all is still between Heaven and Earth. They are both tenors, the aged Emperor a *comprimario* tenor singing in the middle and low register, the youthful Prince a heroic tenor whose one phrase is placed in the very best part of the mid-high register. The Emperor makes three pleas that the Prince desist from his challenge, with different words and similar melodic lines; the Prince's three answers are identical textually—"Figlio del cielo! io chiedo d'affrontar la prova!"—and identical musically but for some increase in dynamic and rhythmic intensity. The orchestra is heard only between vocal phrases: the Emperor is answered with two regularly alternating exotically colored orchestral unisons, *pianissimo* on A, *fortissimo* on C; the Prince's one phrase is merely echoed, in equal note-values, with some increases in instrumental and/or rhythmic intensity each time; just before the Emperor's last words the Chinese gong is sounded once alone.

This ritual scene (II.C) prefigures the ritual Enigma scene (II.E) in its abstract dramatic design: three longer propositions from above, from the Emperor and the Princess respectively, that are somewhat varied textually and musically; three shorter answers from the Prince below, identical (or nearly so) musically, and in the Emperor scene textually identical too. Tonally and coloristically, however, the two scenes are in the strongest possible contrast: C major and "Chinese pentatonic" for Prince and the Emperor, for the mythic encounter in the Imperial Court; d minor/e♭ minor and "Romantic-diatonic" for Prince and Princess, for the intensely poetic encounter of two strong-willed individuals.

The central second confrontation of the Princess's three enigmas (II.E) is discussed in detail just below; it is followed by a more loosely structured third confrontation (II.F), comprising the Prince's single challenge, Turandot's responding silent gesture accepting the challenge, and the Emperor's concluding expression of hope, set to the "Guiding March."

The three confrontations are framed and separated by four arrivals at the choral Acclamation "Diecimila anni al nostro Imperatore." Its occurrences are symmetrically and chiasmically paired: twice *fortissimo* and final (B.d and F.3.b), and twice *pianissimo* and leading onward (C.2.b and E.3.d); twice in A♭ major (B.d and E.3.d), and twice in B♭ major (C.2.b and F.3.b). Normally the Acclamation is merely the conclusion to the Imperial hymn (B.c–d, C.2.a–b, F.3.a–b), part of the Imperial glory; one time only it is heard independently, prepared instead by Mo-li-hua (E.3.c–d), when the Emperor's daughter addresses her father directly.

A second shaping relationship for Act II set 2 is the tonal closure after and before the two abrupt medial breaks in the continuity. The central continuity between the two breaks begins and ends with C major. C major is heard for the first time in the Emperor-Prince confrontation, having been introduced abruptly and brutally by the aforementioned brass fanfare, which shatters the tonic A♭ major established in the Acclamation concluding the Processional music. The central continuity concludes with the C major of the culminating Mo-li-hua, a C major again reached from A♭ major, but now by way of a most careful modulating crescendo away from the gentle A♭ major following the triumphant E♭-major Mo-li-hua capping the Prince's resolution of the third enigma. This climactic C major is shattered in its turn by the unprepared reappearance of the d-minor Enigma motive at the beginning of the Prince's challenge (rh II.65 + 9).

The two unifying musical principles for Act II set 2 considered in isolation, then, are the variously interlinked features of the Imperial Acclamation's recurrences, and the tonal closure in the Imperial C major that frames the central numbers. What ties Act II set 2 in with the rest of the opera are the three occurrences of Mo-li-hua, marked with an asterisk in Figure 1. The Mo-li-hua of the Children's chorus reprise preparing "In questa reggia" and the Enigma scene, and the Mo-li-hua capping the third enigma, are in D and E♭ respectively, the paired keys of the enigmas themselves, as they are the paired keys of the Moonrise and the Prince of Persia, and of the Act I conclusion, as has been discussed earlier; in short, they reflect the "bi-tonal tonality" of the opera as a whole. The C-major Mo-li-hua at the grand conclusion of the Enigma scene, to be sure, is tonally connected only with the C major of the Emperor scene; but as we have noted, the Emperor, bound though he may be by his own frightful oath, is nonetheless the ultimate source of Turandot's power, of all power, and the long buildup and triumphant arrival at Mo-li-hua at the return to C major is nothing if not a musical affirmation and confirmation of power. The C-major Mo-li-hua, in effect, is a sign of both the active working of power in Turandot and of its real source in the Emperor. Here her theme appears in his key, as earlier her plea to him had begun over his theme, simply continuing the music of the preceding choral Acclamation (E.3.d > 4.a).

THE ENIGMAS

Figures 2 and 3 and Examples 40 and 41 illustrate the Enigma scene proper, number II.E, in a more closeup view. In Figure 2 the three enigmas, along with the onlookers' reactions, the Prince's solutions, and the sages' confirmations, are aligned vertically with more detail represented. The tonality of each challenge-and-response cycle is given at the far left, and the harmonic functions are indicated at the top and bottom, with $_{o}ii^7$ standing in for the whole functional class of pre-dominant harmonies, that is, those using scale degrees 1, 2, 4, and ♭6 of the key in various combinations. Arabic numerals represent the number of measures in the several phrases; above them are lower-case letters corresponding with the rubrics within E.1–2–3 on Figure 1. The lower-case letters below the measure counts correspond with the thematic content identified in Example 40, which gives the vocal parts and texts for the beginning of the second enigma (Example 40-A) and for its whole solution (Example 40-B). The basic tempo for the three cycles of enigma and solution is *Andante sostenuto*. There are two elements constant in all three cycles. The more stable element is the eight measures for the Prince's solution, grouped 2 + 2 + 4 (as in Example 40-B), plus the six-measure confirmation by the sages. Turandot's first ten measures, grouped 5 + 5 (as in Example 40-A) are also parallel in all three cycles, though the instrumentation changes considerably in the second d-minor cycle, while in the e♭-minor cycle not only are there further differences in instrumentation but also the second 5-measure phrase drops into the lower octave. What succeeds the opening ten measures of each of her enigmas, to the contrary, differs considerably from cycle to cycle.

Example 40-A shows the vocal part for the first 14 measures of the Princess's second d-minor enigma ("il sangue"). The first d-minor enigma ("la

Figure 2: The three enigmas (II.E.1-3) (rh II.50 + 4 > rh II.62 + 6)

Turandot's Enigma	onlookers' reactions	[2]Prince's solution	sages confirm	onlookers' reactions	Turandot's reaction	orchestra
$_\circ$ii⁷		$_\circ$ii⁷ – V – i	(i)			
d a 5 + 5 x x a' + 5 + 5 + 6 x y x		b 4 + 4 x x–cad.	+ 6		+ 1	+ 5
d a' 5 + 5 x x¹ a' + 6 + 4 yzz y	x +14 mm. 3/4 "Execution"	b² 4 + 4 x x–cad.	+ 6	+ 1	+ 1	+ 6
cb a 5 + 5 x x a' + 7 + 4 yz y a'' + 4 x	+ 7 y	b 4 + 4 x x–cad.	+ 6	+ n (see Figure 3)		
$_\circ$ii⁷		$_\circ$ii⁷ – V – i	(i)	(I) (see Figure 3)		

[1] See Ex. 40-A   [2] See Ex. 40-B

EXAMPLE 40-A. (rh II.54 + 3): The second enigma [II.E.2.a-a′]

EXAMPLE 40-B. (rh II.57 + 2): The second solution [II.E.2.b]

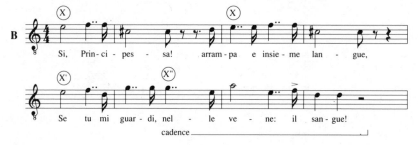

speranza") does not use the motive marked *z*, the downward-octave scale ending with upward leap above the starting point, but the unprepared suspension-resolution figure marked *y* in Example 40-A—"come un lamento" (also shown instrumentally in Example 23 in Chapter I)—is used in all three enigmas, associated with weakness or despair: "il fantasma *sparisce*," "*l'inerzia* lo tramuta in un *languore*," "*trepido*," "se per *servo* t'accetta," "ti senti [*perduto*]." This figure is heard as part of the soft passages throughout Turandot's enigmas, finally and most fearfully through seven long measures of immobile waiting in the instrumental passage after the third enigma (rh II.60 + 9).

In the Prince's eight-measure solutions the motives *y* and *z*, associated with weakness and fear in Turandot's enigmas, never appear. His responses, shown for the second cycle in Example 40-B, are melodically the same all three times: twice two measures with the head motive *x*—the Enigma theme—then four more measures in which its variant form from

Turandot's second five measures (x') is sung, then raised one degree higher (x'') to lead into a final authentic cadence in the local tonic, d minor or e♭ minor as the case may be. Turandot's music frequently reaches up to the high scale degree 4, g″ or a♭″ as it may be, of the local key, but never goes beyond it (the upbeat sixteenth-note b♭″ for "baglior" at the end of the second enigma is not linearly significant). The Prince's responses, to the contrary, always carry the rising line one degree further, from scale degree 4 up to scale degree 5, a′ or b♭′ as the case may be. Harmonically, Turandot's enigma music ends each time as it began and continued throughout, in questioning suspense, stretching out the pre-dominant harmonies in various inversions. Pre-dominant harmonization is prolonged throughout the interpolated fourteen measures of 3/4 *Allegro moderato* for the onlookers' reactions to the second enigma, developing the Execution motive at this, its final appearance, as well as being sustained during the seven measures of silent tension waiting for the Prince's response to the third enigma. When the Enigma motive returns at the beginning of the Prince's responses it is still only a continuation and reaffirmation of the pre-dominant harmonies of the music for the enigmas; but in measures 6–7 of his solutions the pre-dominant moves on to the dominant triad of the key in question, for the first time in each cycle, and in measures 7–8 occurs the V–i cadence, the only full cadence in the cycle. Each time his answer to the question posed in the enigma arrives with the tonic triad of the key: "la sperànza" (d minor), "il sàngue" (d minor), "Turandòt" (e♭ minor).

Setting the Prince's solutions to the same theme as that for the Princess's enigmas has struck some observers as weak. In fact, that is precisely what lends strength to the scene: the Prince's response continues the irresolute and dissonant pre-dominant harmony of the enigma music and then goes on to take it to a climax on the dominant harmony and resolve it on the tonic. Each challenge-and-response cycle thus constitutes a single prolonged cadential succession—pre-dominant, dominant, tonic—with both the climax and the resolution coming entirely within the Prince's response (the sages' confirmation is merely a prolongation of the tonic harmony already reached). And more than that, the 2 + 2 + 4 phrase structure of the Prince's answers is decisively symmetrical, as well as formally closed, while the 5 + 5 + n phrase structure of the Princess's questions is both asymmetrical and open-ended. Puccini has coordinated the change from question to answer in this central ritual confrontation not with obvious ad hoc thematic or coloristic change but rather with the central musical principles underlying tonal harmony and meter, as befits the central moment in the dramatic action. General musical movement from instability to stability—from suspension to resolution, from dissonance to consonance, from irregularity to regularity—is embodied on stage in each move from the challenge of Turandot's enigma to the response of the Prince's solution.

The transposition scheme of the Enigma scene has also seemed lopsided to some. The instrumentation is increasingly elaborate through all three challenge-and-response cycles; but instead of following the traditional sure-fire technique for heightening tension in a "ritual scene"—raising the pitch level of each successive member of the musical sequence—Puccini kept the first two cycles at the same pitch level, raising it only for the third cycle. But by eschewing the more obvious local intensification in moving into the second cycle—risking thereby an excess of tonal stasis in an already rather static harmonic plan—Puccini in the end not only increased the local effect of the rise in pitch when it finally does come in the third cycle; much more significantly, he established the semitonally adjacent tonalities of d and e♭ as the central "bitonal tonality" of the opera right at the opera's central point.

THE CLIMAX

In Chapter I we noted that "of the three themes with which the Princess Turandot herself has been connected, the only one used as an index to her person is also the one most used in a purely formal way." Sometimes Mo-li-hua is little more than an index calling attention to an entrance (rh III.16 + 6) or an action (rh III.21) of the Princess. But usually even the indices have a long-range formal significance as well. The contrast in tonal center between the D-major reprise of the Children's chorus in Act II, for instance, and the E♭ major of its first appearance in Act I, mark it as one pole in the D–E♭ bipolar tonality already adumbrated in Act I.

Figure 3 is a tonal and phrase-structure summary of the coda to the Enigma scene, picking up from what is in fact the first occurrence of Mo-li-hua with the Princess already on stage and involved in the action. The plot pretext for Mo-li-hua here is referential, in that the Princess's name has just been heard from three different sources: from the Prince, at the cadence of his solution to the third enigma; from the eight sages in confirmation of his solution; and from the crowd, jubilantly echoing the sages. The repetition of the Princess's name by the crowd that just precedes Mo-li-hua, however, is in neither the 1921 nor the final libretto; it is a repetition introduced by Puccini to reinforce the referential justification for bringing Mo-li-hua back. Considered purely as a thematic label, Mo-li-hua needs justification, for the text provided in the libretto for the choral jubilation at this point is not at all focused on Turandot but rather on the victorious Prince and the Emperor.

Figure 3: Enigma scene concluded (II.E.4) (rh II.62 > rh II.65 + 8)

sages confirm	onlookers' reactions	Turandot's reactions		crescendo, reduction	Prince's reaction	onlookers' reactions
			sequence modulating to G			
eb	Eb	Ab			C	
+ 6	+ [4 + 4]	+ [4 + 4]	+ 4 + [4 + 4 + 4 + (2 + 3)]	+ [21]	+ [4 + (4	+ 4]
– – – –	Mo-li-hua – – –	Acclamation – – – Recognition – – –		(see Ex. 41) – – –	Mo-li-hua – – –	– – – //

Gloria! gloria, o vincitore!
Ti sorride la vita! Ti sorride l'amore!
Diecimila anni al nostro Imperatore!

The Acclamation text at the third line has its usual music, but Puccini used the two lines addresssed to the Prince to carry Mo-li-hua, brought in here neither with relevance to the text nor to announce the Princess, but for grander and more long-range reasons. This *fortissimo* recurrence in E♭ major not only climaxes the Prince's success with a grandiloquent outburst but also strongly echoes the similar presentation of Mo-li-hua that had accompanied Turandot's entrance in Act I, dynamically and timbrally as well as tonally. It raises to the conscious surface the other of the two poles in the bipolar E♭–D tonality of the whole opera, linking the moment of the unknown Prince's triumph over Turandot at the climax of the challenge-and-response sequence with the moment of Turandot's triumph over the Prince of Persia at the climax of the Act I cortège. In short, Mo-li-hua does not index Turandot; "Turandot!" indexes Mo-li-hua.

Following the Mo-li-hua at II.E.3.c comes the unique appearance of the Acclamation music without the Imperial hymn, sung *piano* in a richly contrapuntal harmonization, followed by a repetition of its first four measures *pianissimo* for the beginning of the Princess's plea to her father the Emperor (rh II.63). Her plea continues in a sixteen-measure symmetrical modulating sequence tinged with augmented chords whose *motivo* seems to be a transformation of the first measure of the Recognition music from Act I. A five-measure continuation leads on to a 21-measure passage in which Turandot turns from fearfully begging her father to abjure his sacred oath to pridefully repulsing the Prince who has just honorably defeated her ("Non guardarmi così!" at rh II.63 + 22); after nine measures the Emperor and crowd begin to join in with reproofs, building majestically toward the climactic recurrence of Mo-li-hua in C major. But where the Princess's plea to her father was built on a modulating sequence in regular phrases of 2 + 2 measures, her repulse of the Prince is made over a rhythmically sophisticated phrase-structure cycle whose only tonal movement is from G major as tonic to G^7/G^9 as dominant of C major. The passage is shown in melody-and-bass outline in Example 41.

There are two motives: one of three measures paced in half notes and quarter notes; and one of two measures paced in quarter notes and eighth notes, whose second measure is stretched to two measures the second time. The intensification of the buildup toward Mo-li-hua is made not only with increasing dynamics and instrumental density but also rhythmically; the pattern (as shown below the staves in Example 41) is as follows.

$$\{[3 + 3] + [2 + (1 + 2)]\} + \{[3] + [2 + 2 + (1) + (1) + (1)]\}$$

The slower-paced three-measure motive is gradually eliminated. There-upon the remaining two-measure motive is intensified with a developmen-tal "liquidation of the motive": after returning twice in altered form it is further reduced to single measures, three of them, that lead up to the tre-mendous return of Mo-li-hua.[7]

Turandot's part in the C-major Mo-li-hua is marked chiefly by two high c'''s, the second doubled by chorus sopranos. In devising the coda to the Enigma scene so that Mo-li-hua will arrive in C major after what amounts to 21 measures of dominant preparation, Puccini set up those high c'''s to powerful advantage. But once again, Puccini used Mo-li-hua for musical reasons that overrode the text provided by Adami and Simoni. Their text for the concluding exchange between Turandot and the Prince follows; the *virgolette* around the bulk of Turandot's speech mark the portions Puccini did not use in his musical setting.

Turandot: Mi vuoi "cupa d'odio?"
    "Vuoi ch'io sia il tuo tormento?"
    "Mi vuoi come una preda?"
    "Vuoi ch'io sia trascinata"
    Nelle tue braccia a forza,
    Riluttante e fremente?

Principe: No, Principessa altera!
    Ti voglio tutta ardente
    D'amore! . . .

Here Turandot is speaking directly and personally to the man, not to the Prince, and not in enigmas but with four anaphoric questions marked by "vuoi." Yet in his musical setting, Puccini went out of his way to avoid making his musical crescendo with the mounting anaphoras of the Prin-cess's speech. To do so he had to repeat earlier text in the usual way; but by doing that, he reduced Turandot's six lines to two, thus matching the dimensions of her single remaining question to those of the Prince's single answer. He eschewed the poetic crescendo provided by Simoni and Adami in favor of a purely musical crescendo, a crescendo designed, moreover, to arrive at a balanced pair of short texts that could be set to a balanced pair of short musical phrases: to arrive, in short, at Mo-li-hua.

To use the chorus rather than a solo voice or pair of voices to build up such a crescendo is not without reason; but to bring in the solo voice with her single question at the dynamic climax, above the chorus, completing the orchestral *tutti* with the heavy brass, is to ensure that while the *prima donna*'s high c'''s may be heard, the Princess's words will not. But though Mo-li-hua was the musical goal of the passage, its four-measure opening—for once—is not the goal of the musico-dramatic design; the second four-

EXAMPLE 41. (rh II.63 + 22): Reductive dominant preparation for Mo-li-hua in C Major [II.E.4.c–d]

EXAMPLE 41. (*cont.*)

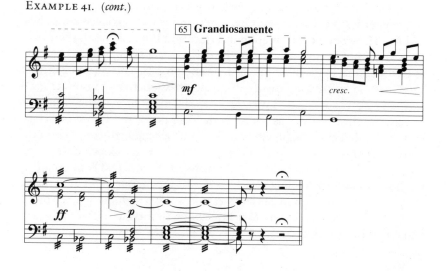

measure phrase, setting the Prince's answer to Turandot's question, is the highlighted moment. An unexpectedly lowered dynamic level, with lightened instrumentation and the dropping out of the chorus, ensure both that the Prince's solo line, placed in the brilliant register of the tenor voice, will stand forth, and that his words will be heard. The Prince's music here is more than just a consequent to an antecedent musical phrase: as we have pointed out already, his words—"Ti voglio tutta ardente d'amor!"—express Puccini's notion of the central theme of the drama and of what is common to all humanity "whether it be in China or Holland," and the harmonization of the second phrase of Mo-li-hua here is unadulterated tonal-diatonic. An enormous crescendo has reached its climax in the opening phrase of Turandot's Chinese pentatonic melody, whose responding phrase is then harmonized with the Prince's purely tonal authentic cadence.[8]

THE FINAL PROBLEM

It will have been clear from the correspondence quoted in the closing pages of Chapter III that the second *scène à faire* for Turandot and the unknown Prince was an ever-growing frustration to Puccini. The material he and his librettists had adapted earliest and most directly from Gozzi's first two acts—the Enigma scene, and in altered and improved form, the general ideas for the exposition leading up to it—had presented familiar problems of adaptation. But having decided to replace all the complexities in Gozzi's last three acts that came before the actual dénouement, they had to find some other way of dealing with the inhuman Princess's conversion to humanity. The second confrontation of Prince and Princess was the "nub"—the *nocciolo*—of the matter newly to be devised, as Puccini realized as early as October 1921, in the letter in which he also proposed his own universally valid method for thawing the icy Princess: a passionate kiss, in short, sex.[9]

Their task was not made any easier by the intensification of the Princess's cruelty they had themselves added in the cortège for the Prince of Persia and the grisly details of his decapitation, further highlighted by contrast with the sympathetic and pathetic ingenue they had developed during the creation of Liù. We can only suppose that—as Wagner said regarding the illogicalities in the rounding off of the *Ring*—the music would have made it all clear, even though in Puccini's case it was his own music—for most of Act I, for Turandot's *aria di sortita*, above all for Liù in Act III—that had raised the greatest obstacles.

THE DRAFTS

From the beginning of the duet through the ensuing colloquy up to the Prince's last words before the kiss (now "il bacio tuo mi dà l'eternità" at rh III.38 + 8–9), Puccini left music written as though in piano-vocal or short score, that is, with voice line(s) and two to four staves of accompaniment with occasional notes on instrumentation. Up to that point this musical material, though messy as ever and with many cross-outs and scribble-overs, is continuous, and therefore would more aptly be called a "draft" or "continuity draft," rather than being referred to simply as "sketches." The continuity is completely interrupted at the kiss itself, but resumes afterwards, from the Prince's words "mio fiore mattutino" (now at rh III.39) up through the Princess's words "la mia gloria è finita" (now at rh III.40 + 13–14). For all of the music for which Puccini's drafts are more or less continuous, Alfano's second setting—the one available in current Ricordi scores—may be taken as a reasonable representation of Puccini's last known intentions: in short, from what is now rh III.35 to rh III.38 + 9, and from rh III.39 to rh III.40 + 14. For instrumental music to accompany the kiss, however, there is no unambiguous draft or sketch, and after the music for "la mia gloria è finita" the few scattered continuities are at most four to eight measures in length. All this sort of material really is fragmentary and may quite properly be designated "sketches"; at any rate, some distinction should be made between the two kinds of material.

The details of how Puccini's materials for the final duet are related to the two versions of the completed duet that were composed by Franco Alfano have been ably sorted out in a study by Jürgen Maehder published in 1984 (in Italian translation in 1985); an English abridgement of that essay that includes all the reproductions, as well as Maehder's valuable tabulations showing where Alfano used Puccini's materials, is available in the English National Opera Guide to *Turandot*.[10] To sum it up briefly, Alfano had followed Puccini's continuity drafts relatively closely up to the preparation for the kiss music, and after the kiss so long as they last, but he evidently regarded the fragmentary sketches as non-definitive, and felt free to set the rest of the text with or without having recourse to them. Alfano's first version of the ending—Alfano I—jibed so poorly with Toscanini's recollection of what he had heard of Puccini's own musical ideas in September 1924 that he persuaded the Ricordi firm to require Alfano to do it over. In light of Maehder's work, and in expectation of an eventual facsimile edition of the drafts and sketches, we confine ourselves to four significant moments: the beginning ("Principessa di morte!"); the kiss, its preparation, and its aftermath; the beginning of Turandot's aria "Del primo pianto"; and the Prince's revelation of his name ("Il mio mistero? non ne ho più").

Puccini drafted the opening of the final duet on a page many times reproduced.[11] This first leaf, recto and verso, contains the music to which the Prince's first eight-line stanza is sung, from "Principessa di morte!" through "Guarda, guarda o crudele / Quel purissimo sangue / Che fu sparso per te!" This is a last remnant of the idea that Liù, alive or dead, might have been made to have some part in the eventual thawing of the Princess, and indeed, the raucous *motivo* with which Puccini firmly intended to begin the duet—"unless something better is proposed to me"[12]— is a grisly transformation of the mournful funeral-march subject of Liù's suicide and cortège, as may be seen from Example 42.

EXAMPLE 42. The beginning of the end

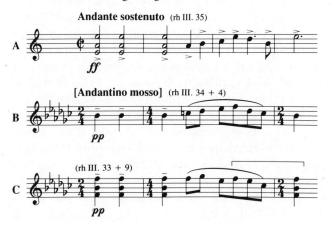

The rhythm and contours from Liù's funeral cortège are preserved but the tempo is changed and the dynamics and voicing are nastily distorted. The three-stroke repeated-chord anapaest is there, a little faster and a lot louder as though in rude parody of the immediately preceding soft chordal anapaest that ends the funeral cortège (see Example 37-B), and in hollow fourths and fifths, like the open fourth-and-fifth orchestral voicings of all four of the b♭-minor interstices after Liù's death, between rh III.29 + 8–9 and rh III.33 + 9–10. Following the vulgar opening anapaest comes an equally vulgar transformation of the stepwise melodic expansions that had followed Liù's anapaests. The tonality of the Prince's description of the cruel Princess is just as abrupt and savage a departure: a minor, a tritone away from the preceding e♭ minor.

The continuity draft continues more or less uninterrupted up to the kiss, as we have noted, and then breaks off altogether, only to resume with "mio fiore mattutino," the Prince's response to Turandot's first reaction to his forcible embrace. The interruption at the kiss itself is a heartrending sign of the artistic cul-de-sac in which Puccini found himself, where he had to resolve a dramatic impossibility of his own making by purely musical means. What instrumental music Puccini would have made for this all-important moment, as well as for the Princess's initial verbal responses, we shall never hear with any such fair approximation as was possible for Alfano to make for the music before it and for a short while after it. The closest we can come is to see how Puccini might have begun the kiss music, by extrapolating from the passage in Act II on which the draft pages containing the preparation for the kiss are modeled; and from one of his sketches we can see his last thoughts on how to conclude the kiss music and move on into "mio fiore mattutino."

In Puccini's continuity draft the preparation for the kiss music is directly modeled on the *maggiore* conclusion of "In questa reggia," from rh II.47 + 9 through rh II.48 + 6.[13] The model is outlined across the top of Figure 4, aligned vertically with outlines of the corresponding material on folios 10 and 11 in the continuity drafts for the final duet. The model passage in Act II begins from the third and final sequential statement in D major of the "Mai nessun m'avrà" melody, including those words. In the duet draft the first three measures of the same four-measure passage, again returning to the words "Mai nessun m'avrà" but now a whole step lower in C major, appear at the top of what is now numbered folio 10ᵛ, after an incomplete beginning crossed out; the fourth measure is at the top of 11ʳ (folio 11ʳ is reproduced as Example 5 in Maehder's essays as cited in note 10. The rest of 11ʳ continues with a two-measure declamatory warning by the Princess over an E-major triad, followed by the Prince singing "É nella bocca tua l'eternità" to the *motivo* of "Gli enigmi sono tre, una è la vita" in

FIGURE 4. The preparation for the kiss (III.D.1, end)

rh II.47 + 9	Mai nessun m'avrà . . .	Straniero, non tentar la fortuna		Gli enigmi sono tre, la morte/vita è una (three times)		Mai nessun m'avrà . . . (choral)
	D ▸———	$F\sharp$ ———————————		▸$E\flat$, $F\sharp$, $A\flat$	$=$	$A\flat$
	4	+ 2		+ 2 + 2 + 2		+ 4
draft 10ᵛ/11ʳ	Mai nessun m'avrà . . .	Non mi toccar, straniero		E nella bocca tua l'eternità		Mai nessun m'avrà . . . (instrumental)
	C ▸———	E ———————————		▸$C\sharp$ $(= C\sharp)$	$=$	$D\flat$
	4	+ 2		+ 2 $(= 2)$		+ 2 . .
draft 10ᵛ/11ʳ plus 11ᵛ, and see rh III.38	Mai nessun m'avrà . . .	Non mi toccar, straniero	E un sacrilegio	No, il bacio tuo mi dà l'eternità		*Mai nessun m'avrà . . . (instrumental)
	C ▸———	E ———————	∦ $A\flat$ ———	▸F	$=$	*F . .
	4	+ 2	+ 2	+ 2		*2 . .

C♯ major, and at the bottom of the page come the first two measures of the "Mai nessun m'avrà" melody in D♭ major, instrumentally. As Maehder has pointed out, these two measures will have been intended by Puccini as the beginning of the kiss music, the Prince suiting his action to his words.

As one sees, the first two phases of the derived music on 10ᵛ and 11ʳ follow the model exactly, except that the succession of keys is a whole step lower: D > F♯ > E♭ becomes C > E > C♯, ending with music that corresponds with the first setting of "Gli enigmi sono tre, le morte è una." At this point in the model from Act II the *motivo* for "Gli enigmi sono tre" comes twice more: the E♭-major position is followed by repetitions in F♯ major and A♭ major, with the soprano and tenor peaking at high c″/c‴ in the last. In the draft derived for the final duet, to the contrary, the *motivo* for "Gli enigmi sono tre" was needed only once, for the Prince's words "É nella bocca tua l'eternità" (an empurpled sentiment that would not bear repeating and in fact was shortly reworded). Having reached this *motivo* in the derived draft as he had reached it in its first statement in the model, but needing to use it only once, Puccini then left it as he had left the third statement in the model, joining on the "Mai nessun m'avrà" melody continuing on in the same key: C♯ major = D♭ major. In other words, the C♯-major music in the draft corresponds with the E♭-major first member of the sequence in the model as it arrives, but in departing it corresponds with the A♭-major third member.

Having drafted this much, Puccini then realized, as Maehder has pointed out, that he had provided no music for the Princess's words "É un sacrilegio." He thereupon crossed out on II^r the C♯-major music for "É nella bocca tua l'eternità" and the two D♭-major measures of the "Mai nessun m'avrà" instrumental melody and rectified the omission on the overleaf (II^v). He continued to use his Act II model, however: first he gave "è un sacrilegio" exactly the same setting as "non mi toccar, straniero," over a simple triadic prolongation now transposed a major third higher to A♭ major. He then continued with the Prince's impassioned declaration just as he had done in the now crossed-out passage at the bottom of II^r, setting it to the key a minor third below the immediately preceding triadic prolongation, but of course rather than shifting from E major down to C♯ major as he had on II^r, on II^v he was shifting from A♭ major down to F major. He also changed the Prince's words to "No, il bacio tuo mi dà l'eternità," ending with multiple-octave Fs. At that point, on II^v, the continuity draft breaks off.

Despite the initial pitch level a whole tone lower, and despite tonal connections obscured by abridgement of the model on the one hand and rectification of an omission on the other, it is clear that Puccini's revised draft of the preparation for the kiss is still completely dependent on the concluding *maggiore* measures of "In questa reggia." Thus it is quite possible that at the stage of his work represented by the draft completed on II^v, as outlined across the bottom line of Figure 4, Puccini meant to lead the preparation for the kiss on into the instrumental music for the kiss itself as he had done on II^r, continuing the Prince's impassioned declaration (sung to the music of "Gli enigmi sono tre, una è la vita" in F major) into an instrumental rendition of the "Mai nessun m'avrà" melody in the same key; that is, just as C♯ major = D♭ major on II^r, on II^v F major = *F major.[14]

No doubt the preparation for and return to the "Mai nessun m'avrà" melody was to be heard as coordinated with an initial resistance by the Princess to the importunate physical demands of the Prince. It is also possible, however, that Puccini changed his mind about simply continuing on into the "Mai nessun m'avrà" melody for the instrumental kiss music; we have already noted that the continuity drafts cease after the Prince's "Il bacio tuo mi dà l'eternità" to resume only at his "mio fiore mattutino" (now rh III.39). Puccini's music making the connection into the continuity on the farther side of the kiss appears on staves 4–10 of folio 14^r, of which we offer a tentative diplomatic transcription in Example 43 (with the kind consent of Casa Ricordi). Perhaps by that time Puccini may have been thinking of this as a draft for the whole of the kiss music, on second thought deciding rather to abort the expected reprise of the "Mai nessun m'avrà" melody: the draft starts with an octave f'/f'' in the melody, which could connect with the bare octave Fs with which the Prince's last words on II^v conclude. The f'/f'' octave is filled in with a D♭-major triad, over E♭

in the bass, to be sure, but that could perfectly well be a deceptive resolution to the Prince's cadence in F major concluding the draft preparation for the kiss. If this had been a revision of the earlier plan based on the "Mai nessun m'avrà" melody, then the passage drafted on folio 14[r], an unexpected new departure musically, would suggest that the Princess's resistance broke almost immediately—an unexpected new departure for her too, but fully in keeping with Puccini's expressed belief in the universal power of physical love.

EXAMPLE 43. The kiss? (after Puccini's sketches for the final duet, folio 14[r], staves 4–10)

Our hypothesis as to the order of events represented on folio 14[r] is described with the help of the measure numbers added within square brackets. The passage will have begun with the two-measure idea on staves 6 and 7 moving on to a downbeat over the barline (mm. 1–2–5A). Then the original idea was to have been repeated (mm. 1–2–3–4) and taken over the barline to the bass octave A/AA at the very end of staff 10 on the sketch leaf. At that point Puccini wrote "mettere mio fiore" in the right margin and noted its opening harmony at the end of staff 8, and extended the printed staff lines by hand, to make room for showing that the chord accompanying "mio fiore" was to be repeated in quarter-note values (mm. 1–2–3–4–7A). Then he decided to return to the original downbeat harmony (mm. 1–2–3–4–5A) and inserted a two-measure prolongation of it on staves 4 and 5, all to precede "mio fiore" as noted at the end of staff 4. The final continuity, then, would have comprised measures 1–2–3–4–5B–6–7B.

THE SKETCHES

The continuity recommencing at the Prince's "mio fiore mattutino" may be seen on folio 5^r (Maehder, Example 2); its concluding measures at the Princess's "la mia gloria è finita," sung to Mo-li-hua in B major, may be seen on 7^r (Maehder, Example 3). From this point on, as we have noted, there are no continuities of more than a few measures in the surviving materials. Among these fragments, however, are the beginnings of music for two important dramatic moments. The first four measures of the melody and accompaniment for Turandot's aria "Del primo pianto" (III.D.3) appear on sketch folio 13^r, in f♯ minor, the cruel key of the opening number of the opera (beginning with the Execution motive and ending with the Executioners' chorus), as it is of the *minore* of Turandot's other aria "In questa reggia." But though Alfano kept Puccini's four-measure beginning, he transposed it to e♭ minor, starting the aria in the polar tonality so often used by Puccini in the more tense or gloomy pieces (the cortège for the Prince of Persia, the aria of the unknown Prince with its *concertato* concluding Act I, the third enigma, Liù's suicide and cortège).

Alfano's first composition of "Del primo pianto" ran to 105 measures; they were cut down to 64 measures for the second composition by hacking out a half-dozen chunks of from 3 to 13 measures each. It was butcher-work on what is a crucial piece dramatically, for only here is there any real remnant in the opera of Gozzi's original plausible preparation for Turandot's otherwise implausible conversion: she was affected as she had never been before by her first sight of the Prince, and his heroic bearing thereafter, though she had been trying fiercely to resist her incipient softening. "Del primo pianto" needs all the time and emphasis it can get, and if the opera is to be done with Alfano's completion at all, for this piece the longer version should be used (apart from the fact that it is an instance of the art of Franco Alfano that is well worth hearing on its own merits).[15]

Immediately following "Del primo pianto" is the Prince's speech offering the Princess not only his name but his life (III.D.4), beginning "Il mio mistero? non ne ho più" and ending "Io son Calàf, figlio di Timur." A draft of the music for the whole passage appears on sketch folio 16[r], but Alfano made no use of it in his first composition of the final duet, once again providing an original and much more up-to-date treatment of his own. The realization based on Puccini's draft that was evidently required of him by Toscanini and the Ricordi directors for the shortened second composition may be seen at rh III.46 (see Example 31 in Chapter I).

For Turandot's immediate reaction to hearing the Prince's name there is a most interesting sketch on folio 17 (Maehder, Example 7), with the beginning of her text "So il tuo nome! Arbitra son [del tuo destino, etc.]" at the top. There are eight untexted measures, the first four with a lush and wide-ranging diatonic melody in b♭ minor/D♭ major with richly moving inner parts, followed in the second four measures by a Straussian shift to E major and back to D♭ major. Alfano did not use this material in his first composition, nor in his second, where all that is now left of the Princess's originally rather complex reaction is the twice-sung expression "So il tuo nome!" Of the text to the Prince's rejoinder to that reaction a version may be seen even now in the current printed libretto: "Che m'importa la vita! / É pur bella la morte!" As Maehder has rightly observed (ENO Guide, p. 44), the idea expressed here must account for the words Puccini wrote at the bottom of the sketch: "Poi Tristano." Alfano made a very interesting setting of some similar text for the Prince in his first composition of the duet—though there is nothing in it either of Puccini's draft or of Wagner's *Tristan*—all of which was cut for the current version.

Other scraps of music in the sketch leaves are even more fragmentary: a bit of the fanfare for the "cambiamento scena" back to the Emperor's court after the duet; the theme of the Prince's name, which we know Puccini had meant for the final scene from the letter of 31 May 1924 quoted in Chapter III (see p. 86); and other jottings.[16]

THE END

From 25 April 1926 until this writing there has been, and will no doubt continue to be, speculation as to how—and more recently, whether—Puccini might have handled the thawing of the Princess and completed the work that, even uncompleted, is his masterpiece, and a fitting Finale to the Great Tradition of the Italian *melodramma*. Puccini died at 66. Had Verdi died at the same age, we would have had *Aida* and the *Requiem*; we would not have had the revised *Simon Boccanegra* nor the final *Don Carlo* revision, and we would not have had *Otello* and *Falstaff*. *Turandot* is not *Aida*, Puccini was not Verdi, and above, all, 1924 was not 1879. But like Verdi in his later years, Puccini kept in touch with what went on around him as well as complaining about it. Suppose he had not only completed *Turandot* but also redone *Manon Lescaut* yet again and (let us say) *La fanciulla del West* as well, and produced two new operas in his old age. Where would our sense of the Great Tradition stand now? or would all have gone on just as (perhaps inevitably) it has? Time will never tell.

CHAPTER VI

※

TURANDOT STAGED

The *Prima assoluta*

Puccini's letters to his librettists reveal how often he imagined action in terms of quite detailed stage pictures. It is not surprising, therefore, to find him taking the initiative in consulting with scene designers and costumers. He was already concerned about the stage picture in early June 1921, while he was composing music for the two sets of the original long Act I. On 7 June 1921 the composer reported to Simoni (*CP*, ltr 759, p. 506) that he had received sketches from Pietro Stroppa (1878–1935), a notable scenic artist, and also floor plans (*piante*) for the two sets of the long Act I.[1]

Stroppa was the first of a number of potential collaborators to be consulted by Puccini, though as it turned out he was not involved in the final designs for the *prima* of *Turandot*. Three months later, on 3 September 1921, Puccini told his friend Schnabl that he had had a visit at Torre del Lago that day from Umberto Brunelleschi (1879–1949), a Tuscan painter. They had discussed possibilities for sets and costumes, and Puccini had found his ideas "original and good" (*LRS*, ltr 87, p. 151; see References, A 4). Apparently either in this year or the next, a formal agreement was reached between Casa Ricordi and Brunelleschi, engaging him to provide designs for *Turandot*. But Puccini had also been thinking of "Caramba"— the pseudonym of Luigi Sapelli (1865–1936)—whose *atelier* in Turin was the principal supplier of costumes for La Scala in the 1920s. Caramba was a formidable designer, famous for his ability to create costumes directly on the material, without recourse to intermediate sketches, and by October 1924 Puccini was confiding to Adami that

> I am very sorry now not to have the collaboration of Caramba, but you know better than anyone how we are placed vis-à-vis Brunelleschi.
>
> I hope that Clausetti will make an effort to cancel the agreement, particularly as it is not impossible that Brunelleschi might back out, being terrified by the shortness of time and the two hundred or more costume-sketches [*figurini*] that must be drawn. [*EGP*, ltr 235, p. 209]

It is not clear to what extent Brunelleschi contributed costume designs for the *prima* of *Turandot*, or whether he withdrew from the project completely. Some reference books, such as the *Enciclopedia dello spettacolo*, credit

141

him with supplying some designs for *Turandot*, but his name does not appear on the La Scala program for the première, where the costumes and properties are credited to Caramba.

Puccini's active concern with scenery and costumes for *Turandot* falls mainly into two periods: the summer of 1921, when the work first seemed to be making steady progress, and again after February 1924, when much of the score was orchestrated, only the final duet remained to be written, and Puccini could again start thinking seriously about the visual aspects of a first performance. In that month it seemed possible that the première could be scheduled for late 1924, though after Puccini's contretemps with Toscanini over *Nerone* and their subsequent rapprochement only in September 1924, the date was postponed to April 1925.

On 14 February 1924 Puccini wrote to Carlo Clausetti at Ricordi about the stage designs.

> I am thinking about the scenery. I had already talked a long time ago in Paris and here with Brunelleschi about the costume sketches.[2] He welcomed the idea with great enthusiasm; the matter, however, was premature and remained in limbo. Now I have seen [Galileo] Chini, who did the set for *Schicchi*, and who lived in Siam and China for four years.[3] He would be happy to sketch the scenery for me. Before telling him yes, I am waiting for you and Renzo [Valcarenghi] to tell me what you will pay him. I maintain that with Chini and Brunelleschi we might have a mise-en-scène that would be artistic, and above all unusual and original. To go looking abroad (Vienna, Berlin) is inappropriate, and, to tell the truth, I am in favor of entrusting this important task to our native artists. [*CP*, ltr 882, p. 548]

Galileo Chini, a fellow Tuscan like Brunelleschi, did design the scenery for the première of *Turandot*. Chini's experience as a scenographer had been primarily for the spoken stage; he had worked particularly closely with the dramatist Sem Benelli. Chini's first set designs for La Scala appeared on the occasion of the *prima assoluta* of Giordano's *La cena delle beffe* (20 December 1924), an opera setting one of Benelli's plays. Chini worked comparatively infrequently at La Scala, however; Antonio Rovescalli and Edoardo Marchioro were then the house set designers.

The first performance of *Turandot* finally took place on 26 April 1926, at La Scala. The delay of a year from the April 1925 date proposed by Toscanini in the fall of 1924 was needed to allow Franco Alfano time to complete the missing portion of the score.[4] Alfano had been recommended by Toscanini for the task of working up the final scene from the thirty-six pages of continuity drafts and fragmentary sketches left by Puccini at his death, and had finally been commissioned to do so by Casa Ricordi on 25 August

1925. He completed the first version of his music (Alfano I) well before the middle of January 1926, since there are letters from that month confirming that the second version (Alfano II), as required of him by Toscanini and Casa Ricordi, had been completed.[5] Some aspects of these two versions have been discussed in the text and notes of Chapter V, and the question of whether and where Alfano's original ending may have been performed before its resuscitation in the 1980s is discussed below.

Arturo Toscanini conducted at the première; subsequent performances at La Scala in that first season were conducted by Ettore Panizza, with the following inaugural cast:[6]

> The Princess Turandot – Rosa Raisa
> The Emperor Altoum – Francesco Dominici
> Timur, deposed Tartar king – Carlo Walter
> The unknown Prince (Calàf), his son – Miguel Fleta
> Liù, a young slave – Maria Zamboni
> Ping, Lord Chancellor – Giacomo Rimini
> Pang, Majordomo – Emilio Venturini
> Pong, Chief Steward – Giuseppe Nessi
> A Mandarin – Aristide Baracchi
> The Prince of Persia – N. N.
> The Executioner – N. N.

This cast included none of the singers Puccini had in mind when he composed the opera. As noted in Chapter III, he had suggested to Gilda Della Rizza that she would be an ideal Liù, and he had thought of Maria Jeritza as *Turandot*; as early as April 1922 he had written to Gatti-Casazza that he could imagine no other singer for the title role.[7] And as also noted in Chapter III, for the role of the Prince Puccini had made approaches both to Beniamino Gigli and Giacomo Lauri-Volpi, but both tenors, like Jeritza, were then under contract to the Metropolitan in New York. This was a period of active estrangement between Gatti-Casazza and Toscanini, and Gatti-Casazza had made it clear that participation in this première to be conducted by Toscanini by artists under contract to the Metropolitan would mean the immediate termination of their profitable engagements in New York.

THE PRODUCTION BOOK

The régisseur for the first performance was Giovacchino Forzano, the superintendant of staging at La Scala from 1922 to 1930. Forzano had first directed at La Scala on the occasion of the local première of *Il trittico*, a choice in the historic vein of nineteenth-century librettist-director, since

Forzano was the librettist for *Suor Angelica* and *Gianni Schicchi*. Forzano's production book (*disposizione scenica*) for *Turandot* survives, albeit not in the published booklet form in which Ricordi had at one time published such documents.[8] It consists of detailed typewritten directions interleaved in a copy of the first edition of Ricordi's piano-vocal score of *Turandot*. These instructions are keyed to the music by numbers placed in the appropriate measure. The directions are by Forzano, who consulted with Adami; they frequently provide a considerable amplification of the staging indicated in the printed score.[9] This document was a working copy actually used during rehearsals, as the various corrections and modifications upon it in both pen and pencil testify. It contains occasional diagrams to indicate the position of characters on stage, for instance at the beginning of Act I where the crowd is addressed by the Mandarin, accompanied (according to the production book) by a servant holding a parasol over his head.

Some sense of the progress of the rehearsals and the adjustments made as they proceeded appears early on in Act I, at the episode of the sharpening of Pu-Tin-Pao's huge scimitar (I.A.4). Forzano had originally wanted a symmetrical center-stage distribution of the twelve servants of the Executioner and their implements. The outsized whetstone was to have been in the middle; kneeling on either side of it were to have been two men to turn the wheel, and four more seated behind it to supervise the work. To the left of the wheel there was to have been a servant squatting with a cauldron of water and another servant on foot to pass the wet rags; on the right there was to have been a similar pair with the cauldron of grease. Standing in front of the wheel, facing up-stage, were to have been two men holding the sword, one by the hilt, the other by the blade. The stage space required by the servants and their equipment meant that part of the chorus would have had to move to the wings to sing the "Ungi, arrota" passage (I.A.4) from offstage.

At some point this arrangement was changed to move the action of sharpening the blade to another playing area, on top of the bastions. The overall symmetry was retained, but the shallower space available meant that now ten of the servants stood in a row behind and on either side of the whetstone, while the two who held the scimitar were to face the others as before. Although this change involved some loss of detail by moving this action farther away from the audience and to a more constricted space, it must have become obvious at some early phase of the staging rehearsals that cluttering the central area with a large grindstone and two imposing cauldrons that then had to be carried off created distracting activity just before the Moonrise chorus. Further, situating the Executioner's servants upon the bastions meant that the general chorus could be onstage for "Ungi, arrota," thereby increasing its impact.

From this example we see that Forzano's first impulse was to emphasize picturesque detail, making modifications later if some idea proved awkward or impractical. For instance, he found ways to take advantage of relocating the whetstone on the bastion. He sought to heighten the interaction between the servants of the Executioner above and the crowd below.

> Let me say once and for all that during this episode the movements both of the Executioner's servants and of the crowd, should be violent, full of ferocious anticipation, often vulgar, interspersed with bursts of laughter, grimaces and exaggerated gestures.

Near the end of this passage the Executioner's servants are directed to sit on the ramparts, some of them eating, others sticking out their tongues and sneering at the crowd below.

The shift of mood between the animated business of sharpening the sword and the hushed expectancy of the apostrophe to the moon finds a visual counterpart in Forzano's instructions for the second (and last) appearance of the Execution motive in the *fortissimo* and slow form with which it had opened the opera.

> At these five measures the crowd, as though worn out by the savage frenzy which until now had dominated them, sinks to the ground. It should be visible from the motions of their arms that they relax. Indolent, Asiatic poses.

And a little later:

> Note the expressions on the faces during the evocations; at every epithet—"faccia pallida," "o testa mozza," "o squallida,"—all must bend their bodies forward, undulating, raising their faces (but keeping their arms still).

The same preoccupation with striking detail recurs throughout the funeral cortège of the Prince of Persia, accompanied by Pu-Tin-Pao, the white-robed priests, and the others. The grisly fairytale atmosphere is heightened by such action as this:

> Immediately following Turandot's imperious gesture [the death-sentence], Pu-Tin-Pao approaches the Prince of Persia and kisses his hands. Then he goes to the two sword-bearers and takes the scimitar, which he brandishes before placing it on his shoulder. The procession starts up once more and disappears into the Executioner's house, at stage left.

When the three Ministers first appear they come down the flight of five steps below the gong, middle right. Forzano characterizes them like this:

Ping, Pong, and Pang, without being three true Venetian masks, must however call to mind at the most appropriate moments the characters of Pantalone, Brighella, and Arlecchino, with their traditional poses and gestures (but never exaggerating their comicalness).

The tension of the climactic part of Act I is stretched between the gong on the right—access to Turandot—and the Executioner's house on the left—the risk of decapitation. Forzano has designed, one could almost say choreographed, the movements of the Ministers as they distract the Prince from the gong or impede his path to it.[10] The significance of Pu-Tin-Pao's house is emphasized when the Executioner himself appears with the severed head of the Prince of Persia and impales it upon a stake. That Forzano did not see the Ministers merely as bizarre, artificial figures becomes clear from an instruction in the final ensemble of Act I:

> The desperate words of the unknown Prince produce an ever deeper impression on the three masks. They would like to save him at all costs.

It is only after they realize the futility of their efforts that they give way to cynical laughter. When the Prince finally succeeds in reaching the gong, the basic polarity of the staging is reinforced by causing the Ministers to move toward the Executioner's house, and "if they are in time before the curtain closes, they can knock" on Pu-Tin-Pao's door.

One of the last letters Puccini wrote to Adami, dated 8 October 1924, offers his suggestion for staging the *fuori-scena* of the Ministers that opens Act II. Not long before, he had received from Galileo Chini a sketch for the embroidered curtain (the tent), in front of which this scene takes place.

> I beg you to look at the libretto again, along with Renato [Simoni] and change the stage directions, and please try to make up your minds about the mise-en-scène for the trio in front of the curtain. For the staging keep in mind the pictorial ideas of Chini, following the lines of his work where you can . . . you could introduce an openwork marble balustrade with a gap in the center, like this: [here Puccini inserted a linear sketch]. And this could be retained in the following scene with the staircase. The masks play their parts on this balustrade, sitting or lounging on it, or astride it, as the case may be. I am not explaining clearly what I mean, but I know that in Strauss's *Ariadne* at Vienna, they did something of the sort with the Italian masks, only there the masks climbed up a little stairway from the orchestra pit. That would scarcely be tolerated at La Scala. [*EGP*, ltr 235, pp 298–99]

Instead of adopting Puccini's balustrade, however, Forzano's *disposizione* patterns the three Ministers' movements around three portable stools that doubled as lanterns, could be sat upon, stood on, moved about, and at the end of the scene carried offstage by the three singers.

The second set of Act II begins with the massive assemblage of the whole Imperial Court. The stage is dominated by a grand staircase in the center, divided from top to bottom into three sections of six, eight, and four steps respectively, separated by landings. On either side of the steps are, at the top, a passageway to permit entrances from either side, and, below that, four risers that fill up with supernumeraries representing guards, mandarins male and female, the eight sages, and standard bearers. Again, Forzano's taste for strict symmetry is apparent. Among his detailed directions, one notation almost allows us to hear him addressing the more than a hundred participants rehearsing this scene.

> I emphasize that all the various movements until the end of the procession are to be executed walking *slowly* and that, once the assigned position has been assumed, the members of the procession are to remain until the end of the act with their arms folded across the chest (in the Chinese manner).

The chorus was divided into two groups: downstage left (tenors and sopranos) and right (mezzo-sopranos, baritones and basses). The spectacle of this crowded stage with its sense of *horror vacui* suggests two sources: the mass scenes of Parisian Grand Opera that influenced the Italian *melodramma* from *Tell* and *Poliuto* to *Aida* and *La gioconda*, but also the crowd scenes of silent film epics with their myriads of extras; of this latter medium Forzano was an acknowledged master.

With most of the stage crowded by choral groups and supernumeraries, the interaction between Turandot and the Prince takes place on the landings and foot of the open staircase. Their movements against the largely static human and decorative background are designed to emphasize the rising emotional arc of the scene. During the propounding of the enigmas Turandot descends stage by stage to the Prince, bent on intimidating him by her formidable proximity. In Forzano's directions for this scene there is little if any preparation for Turandot's eventual capitulation, to warrant her confession in the aria "Del primo pianto" (III.D.3) that "quando sei giunto, / con angoscia ho sentito / il brivido fatale / di questo male / supremo!" (when you came I felt, in anguish, the fateful trembling of this supreme evil). At the conclusion of "In questa reggia"—that is after the unison phrase for the soprano and tenor with the high Cs—"They remain unmoving, one in front of the other, looking at one another, the Prince filled with his enthusiasm and faith, Turandot always in her paroxysm of rage and cruelty." At the beginning of the enigmas she is confident of her victory, and as the Prince solves the first and then the second enigma, her disappointment and anger show clearly, but the only indications that she might be experiencing some inner conflict are in a series of inconclusive directions that follow immediately after the Prince's successful solution of her third enigma. First, "Turandot does not dissemble her desperation, just as the chorus does not disguise its immense joy"; then as the sages confirm the correct answer, "Turandot, bewildered, climbs the stairs to the lower landing; she is convulsively agitated." Yet soon the serene demeanor of the Prince "further exasperates" her, as she seeks to persuade her father not to enforce his edict, and after her plea to her father, when she addresses the Prince directly, she is once more at the bottom of the staircase, turning to face him "with absolute rebelliousness" and "in her words is now the urgency of extreme resolution." It seems that her desperation and bewilderment were a result only of shock and anger, even though later on Turandot is instructed to "detach her glance from the Prince, discomfited," and as he asks her to discover his name, "Turandot fixes him with an enigmatic look." Throughout this scene Forzano's directions clearly project the struggle between two powerful wills, and though Turandot's emotional stances are certainly more complex than the Prince's, there is no real hint that desire might have been mingled with her fear in the way she eventually recalls it in "Del primo pianto":

> C'era negl'occhi tuoi / la luce degl'eroi, / la suprema certezza, / e per quella t'ho odiato / e per quella t'ho amato / tormentata e divisa / tra due terrori uguali: / vincerti od esser vinta.

> [There was in your eyes the light of heroes, the supreme confidence, and for that I hated you, and for that I loved you, tormented and divided between two equal terrors: to conquer, or be conquered.]

The set for Act III set 1, like that of the Ministers' *fuori-scena*, was planned as a relatively shallow one, positioned in front of the massive court set used both in the preceding scene (Act II set 2) and in the short concluding episode (Act III set 2). One of Forzano's rubrics makes it clear that a little more depth of playing area was achieved by detaching the lowest section of the grand staircase (from Act II set 2) and using it here to form the steps leading up to Turandot's pavilion on the right. Balancing this structure on stage left was a shrine, containing the figure of an idol, with another set of steps leading up to it. At the back of the playing area was a painted flat depicting distant mountains, and, directly in front it, a raised walkway (formed from the risers in the court scene) allowing access from both wings; in front of this walkway and on either side of the three steps leading down from it were placed flowering shrubs.

In Forzano's directions for Act II set 2, there are few indications of changes made during rehearsal, probably because the restricted space available for movement and the formalized nature of much of the action allowed little leeway for alteration. For Act III set 1, however, a number of adjustments were made, almost always involving the chorus and supernumeraries, and resulting from the problem of manipulating them within a restricted space. The gradual coming together of the populace, drawn by concern for their lives, underwent modification so as to leave sufficient room for the Ministers to tempt the Prince with women and riches, and at the same time let the chorus be on stage in sufficient numbers to make an impact when they begin to sing.

Another point in Act III set 1 that underwent modification came just before the entrance of Turandot. Eight guards enter to form a barrier to contain the crowd upstage; at first they were directed to face the chorus, but a penciled "no" seems to reverse their position; then another addition causes them to be armed "with halberds." Still another addendum at this point, apparently to justify somewhat brightening the stage lighting, brings on six lantern bearers, two of whom are instructed to stand at the foot of the steps leading to Turandot's pavilion.

Something of the acting style envisioned by Forzano comes across in his detailed directions for Liù from her entrance in this scene until her death. Once again we are reminded not only of the overblown gestures of late nineteenth-century acting traditions but also of Forzano's experience as a director of silent films, in which those traditions survived. His instructions, keyed to the various relevant spots in the score, we recast in narrative form:

> Her fear of not withstanding torture and of revealing the secret in a moment of weakness drives her to frenzy. First she backs away from the sight of the Executioner; then she circles the stage, convulsively. Now she turns toward the public to say "Più non resisto!" She goes to the right in search of an opening through the crowd, but she is repulsed by the people and by the brutal guards [*sgherri*]. Then she runs desperately to the left, but there too she is repulsed. On the words [of the chorus], "Parla! Parla!" one of the guards seizes her. She struggles with him; then, as if he had brutally pushed her, she staggers away and after several steps falls full-length on her side. All through this episode she is as though gripped by some mad fear until she falls . . . She raises only her face. She is exhausted physically, but the phrase ["Sì, Principessa, ascoltami"] is uttered vigorously and solemnly, because by now Liù has determined to kill herself . . . During these measures for the orchestra [the introduction to "Tu che di gel sei cinta"] she slowly raises herself a little, falls back, raises herself again so that her body is supported by her left arm . . . She looks at

Turandot and addresses her in the prophetic tone of one who knows she must die.

At the climax of her part of the movement, Liù extends her right arm and points her index finger at Turandot. Then, after her final phrase,

> she rises, determined on death. She wheels around and unexpectedly seizes a dagger from one of the guards (whose identity and position have been determined beforehand). She stabs herself. Staggering, she moves to fall to the left of the Prince's feet.

According to Forzano's directions, Liù's corpse is to be carried away by four women, while the rest of the chorus processes after them to the raised passageway and exits into the right wings, where some of the chorus have already been stationed to sing "Liù, bontà!" from offstage. This whole episode seems designed to keep Liù the focus of attention and to generate the maximum amount of sympathy for her, by keeping the rest of the figures relatively stationary while her movements are both agitated and striking. Forzano's approach stressses Liù's pathetic courage to such an extent that it imperils the dramatic effectiveness of the following episode.

The stage directions for the final duet do nothing to diminish the suddenness of the Prince's transition from initial invective ("Principessa di morte!") to ardent wooing. The turning point of the scene is described in these terms:

> The Prince draws [Turandot] violently down from the pavilion, while she struggles to free herself from his frantic grasp . . . He seizes her in his arms and kisses her frenziedly. A long kiss. Slowly, she draws away from the embrace, as though she has awakened from a dream.

Forzano presents a Turandot who does not yet understand what has happened to her.

> During the words of the Prince ["O! Mio fiore mattutino"] Turandot seems like a vanquished creature that does not know how to offer further resistance. She listens to his words almost automatically, more preoccupied with her own defeat than aware of the victor's tenderness.

Her weeping is motivated in this fashion:

> She looks around and notices that it is dawn. Suddenly she thinks that this has occurred without her being able to discover the Prince's name. She is, therefore, bound to him forever! And then she weeps.

From this point on the emergence of Turandot as a responsive, aroused woman is depicted clearly and consistently.

Forzano's directions allow us to see how the rapid scene-change to the courtyard Finale was accomplished.

> During the blackout, while the backdrop is being raised, the two gar-
> den-pieces . . . will be taken away quickly and also the lanterns placed
> at either side of the steps to the pavilion. These steps will figure again
> as the lowest section of the grand staircase. The walkway at the back
> of Act III set 1 will become the bottom riser, where the *Mandarinesse*
> and the standard-bearers will take up the same positions they occupied
> in Act II set 2. Thus when the lights come up and reveal the scene,
> there will be exactly the same view of the complete court as in Act II.[11]

A penciled addition at this point directs that if any variations have to be introduced because of the exigencies of the setting, these should not be such as to produce on the audience any impression of difference from the earlier setting.

Since the final chorus was a few measures longer in Alfano's first ending, Forzano originally supplied more movement to fill the time. After hearing Turandot proclaim his name as "Amor!" Calàf impetuously climbs the steps that separate him from Turandot.

> They embrace and kiss. But suddenly Calàf detaches himself and
> climbs the remaining steps to bow to the Emperor, whereupon he
> returns to Turandot, throwing himself into her arms, while she in turn
> abandons herself in his. They remain like this to the end.

In the shorter second version of Alfano's ending there is time for only one uninterrupted embrace, and the obeisance to the Emperor is omitted.

Forzano's *disposizione scenica* impresses by his resourcefulness in revealing motivation and character, in heightening conflict through movement.[12] The tumultuous episodes of Act I memorably catch the blood-thirsty mood of Peking in the days of the Princess Turandot. Following the entrance of the Ministers, who try to prevent the Prince from reaching the gong, the dynamic of the conflict gains tension through the logic of the shifting positions of the four characters. Particularly successful is the projection of successions of mood for Ping, Pang and Pong during their *fuori-scena*—ironical and cynical (II.A.1), nostalgic (II.A.2), wistful (II.A.3.a), optimistic (II.A.4), and only at last, dejected (at the beginning of II.B)—and their ingeniously patterned movements keep this rather formal scene from becoming too static.

Today Forzano's staging of the Enigma scene might strike us as overproduced, particularly if the spectacle of what seemed like acres of human background proved monotonous once the original impression had passed.[13] Forzano's shift in Act III set 1, from fantasy for the Ministers' temptations to a veristic style for the agonized intensity of Liù's final moments, juxtaposes two approaches that coexist uneasily at best. The potentially lasting psychic energy generated by the heroic contest of wills that emerges so vividly from Forzano's manipulation of Turandot and the Prince during the second set of Act II is dissipated by the distraction of Liù's suicide, and the episode of the final duet does not begin to generate a comparable energy until the moment of the Prince's kiss. Forzano's directions leave no clue that Liù's sacrifice produced any profound impression in helping to bring about Turandot's capitulation, but of course that motive is only barely hinted at in the final text of the libretto. Puccini's original reason for suggesting the death of Liù—that her sacrifice might somehow "have a powerful influence in bringing about the thawing of the Princess" (*EGP*, ltr 206, p. 282)—has disappeared virtually without trace.

The first performance of *Turandot* on 25 April 1926 ended with Liù's cortège. Eugenio Gara, who was present, gives a firsthand report of Toscanini turning round to face the audience and saying "in a voice hoarser than usual: *Qui finisce l'opera, perchè a questo punto il Maestro è morto*" (The opera is ending here because at this point the Maestro died; *CP*, 563). The appropriateness of Toscanini's gesture was generally appreciated because the evening was dedicated to Puccini, seventeen months after his death. Toscanini's words have been variously reported, but were frequently interpreted to suggest that Puccini had died shortly after composing the episode of Liù's death, which allowed the sentimental to regard the passage as Puccini's own requiem. The facts are quite otherwise, as we know: Puccini had finished orchestrating the passage in late February 1924, nine months before he died, and in it he probably utilized material—the "musichetta di sapore chinesa"—that dated from 1921, the first year of intense work upon the score.

Nor should it be overlooked that Toscanini's remarks could have served him as a diplomatic excuse for not conducting Alfano's ending to *Turandot*. Though Alfano's completion of Puccini's score was not performed on the evening of the *prima assoluta*, it had been played and sung at the *prova generale*, the dress rehearsal two days earlier, to which the critics, many of them from abroad, had been admitted. It was no secret that Toscanini's dissatisfaction with Alfano's first attempt was because the conductor did not regard it as conforming sufficiently closely to his memory of Puccini's playing and discussion of the final duet in September 1924, and that a revision had been ordered. Alfano had come ruefully to realize that he had accepted a thankless task, and he suffered growing resentment at the cavalier treatment accorded him by Toscanini and Casa Ricordi. In fact, Alfano had not even been given a chance to see Puccini's orchestration of the score (through Liù's cortège) until he had nearly finished his first ending around the turn of the year 1925/26, at which time he asked the publishers to allow him to examine it so that he could score the closing pages of the final scene, where the theme of the Prince's name from "Nessun dorma"—"Ma il mio mistero è chiuso in me"—returns. Alfano's *amour propre* was so hurt that it took three telegrams to persuade him to attend the final rehearsal.[14] His ending was played at the second and subsequent performances of *Turandot* at La Scala, but Toscanini was not on the podium, his place being taken by Ettore Panizza. We can only infer that Toscanini's sense of musical integrity was offended by the hybrid nature of Act III of the score, and to the best of our knowledge Toscanini never conducted *Turandot* again.

Puccini's relationship with the Milanese musical establishment had been guarded at best since the cruel reception accorded the first version of *Madama Butterfly* at its first performance, at La Scala on 17 February 1904. Not only did he refuse to allow that opera to have a second performance at that theater during his lifetime; until the last year or so of his life he would not contemplate giving the *prima assoluta* of any of his subsequent operas there. Thus the Metropolitan was the theater selected for the premières of *La fanciulla del West* and *Il trittico*, and Monte Carlo for the introduction of *La rondine*. It was not until after the thirtieth anniversary production of *Manon Lescaut* at La Scala (with Toscanini conducting) during the 1922/23 season that there was anything like a rapprochement between Puccini and the artistic administration of that opera house.[15] Puccini regarded Toscanini as the best conductor in Italy, one whose participation lent enormous prestige to any artistic event, though in January 1922 he had become angry with Toscanini, who had steadfastly refused to conduct *Il trittico* when the triple bill had its first Milanese performance (Ettore Panizza conducted), even though Puccini had tried to influence him to change his mind. But Puccini determined upon La Scala as the arena for introducing *Turandot* because he wanted that opera to demonstrate once and for all his premier position among his Italian contemporaries and to dispel the inimical atmosphere that clouded his relationship with what in terms of prestige was acknowledged to be the foremost opera house in Italy.

THE PRESS

Nor was Puccini very happy with the Milanese press. Ricordi had its own house organ, *La gazzetta musicale di Milano*, which regularly touted the achievements of composers—Puccini among them—under contract to the publisher, but the partisan stance of this journal seems to have produced a compensatory strictness and reticence on the part of other Milanese critics.

Puccini felt that *Il corriere della sera*, the leading newspaper of Milan, was never fair to him, and writing to Simoni, its drama critic, shortly after the Bolognese première of *Il trittico*, Puccini complained that "in the *Corriere* I read an insipid telegram that did not adequately reflect last night's success. Along with Forzano I telegraphed you [how it actually went]. But I am never favored in the pages of the *Corriere* and never will be" (*CP*, ltr 918, p. 515).

Critics who attended only the *prima assoluta* of *Turandot* had to judge the work on the basis of an incomplete performance, which omitted a crucial ingredient of the plot: the coming together of the protagonists. By being ended with the death of Liù the overall effect was distorted, in that a plot designed to end happily was made to conclude tragically with an event that is in no way central to the main line of the action. The atmosphere of the performance was further distorted by the emotional impact of Toscanini's terse, and for many present, misleading announcement. Generally, the first-night critics seem to have been impressed by Puccini's advances in orchestration, by his powerful evocation of atmosphere, by the effective deployment of the chorus, but to varying degrees less persuaded by the drama.

Andrea Della Corte, who must have been present at the *prova generale*, was one of the few who recognized the centrality of the title role. In the Turinese paper *La stampa*, he wrote that

> an opera constructed along these lines was truly new for Puccini . . . [He] does not take plot as a fable, that is, he did not conceive it in terms of artificial fancy or transparent paradox; instead he gave it realistic substance, treating it as a human action shot through with bizarre effects . . . For the first time Puccini has succeeded in presenting a cruel, violent situation, without artifice but with true art, in the scene of the enigmas. Well defined in the libretto beyond the other characters, Turandot is effectively prepared before beginning her singular battle of wits with the unknown Prince. The brief theme of "*la volontà di Turandot*," with its harsh intervals and strange modulations, that stridently begins the opera, and whose dark echo seems to go on resonating in tragic chords, leaves no doubt about the dramatic essence that the composer recognized as fundamental to Turandot herself.[16] Her silent appearance before the crowd (in Act I), her gesture refusing clemency and underlined by somber orchestral sonorities, predisposes our attention to center upon the protagonist.

Della Corte found Turandot's *aria di sortita*

> of little interest. But when the tortuous Enigma theme bursts forth in the orchestra, and hatred lashes out in the vocal line of the Princess,

and there is in the orchestra a thrilling commentary on the dramatic moment, we are at the best page in the opera, and an important point in the art of Puccini. The three enigmas are amplified by the power of music, and raised to symbolic significance.

But for Della Corte the dramatic focus is eventually lost "in stupefying *féerie*" and marred at the end by the composer's unanticipated death and the consequent impossibility of working out the dramatic implications; there is not enough of it to provide "that consistency vainly expected from the preceding parts of the work." Della Corte concluded:

> Thus, the "new woman" was only dimly perceived by the composer who gave us Mimì and Manon. And it is to these gentle creatures that Puccini's name remains entrusted.[17]

Gaetano Cesari, in his review for *Il corriere della sera* appearing the day after the première, saw less deeply into either the merits or the defects of the work; he took it primarily as a contest between Turandot and Liù.

> On the lyric side, Turandot and Liù engage in a decisive battle, won at last by the one who surpasses in the area of sentiment: Liù. Lyrically she occupies the foreground of the opera. Turandot, to the contrary, does not always succeed in being convincing as the source of the dramatic energy of the opera. Her enigmas belong to the world of fable and of symbols, which, though capable of suggesting poetic elements, present material difficult to suggest in terms of musico-dramatic sensibility. The music does not succeed in communicating fully the Sphinx that exists in Turandot, that is, in translating the dark and static states of her spirit into sensation, let alone into emotion. No wonder, therefore, that Liù, overcome by Turandot in the drama, succeeds in supplanting her in the soul of the listener.

Cesari's review reveals with particular force how much the incomplete hearing of the score that first night must have misled most of the audience.

Another critic who took Liù unequivocally for the outstanding personage in the work was Michele Lessona, writing in *La gazzetta del popolo* of the last of Puccini's completed numbers.

> It is fine and comforting that this page, the last of the last opera by the Maestro, belongs to him so intimately and with such direct, sincere and spontaneous expression of his character . . . [and] this page shows that Puccini's creative energy was not enfeebled. He remained until the end an acute investigator of the feminine soul; he was until his death the compassionate poet of simple human passions. This conviction we owe not only to this page, but to every note in Liù's part.

While the rest of the opera might lead us to believe in a weakening of Puccini's inspiration, yet still we cannot believe this, having in the score proof to the contrary; and so we are forced to seek some explanation of this apparent contrast, and the explanation is possibly this: that Liù is the only truly human figure in the opera.

Adriano Lualdi used his review of *Turandot* in *Il secolo* as an opportunity to contrast the new work with Puccini's earlier operas, pointing out that

in no other of the recent operas of Puccini more than in this posthumous *Turandot* is the inspiration and the drive toward the new so moving and constantly evident . . . The composer who had won worldwide fame and fortune with his *verismo* abandons his old platform and approaches in his sixties the theater of the imagination. At an age when others think of retirement, the sensitive painter of intimate scenes and little effects has confronted grandiose scenes and intoxicated himself with vast horizons. The genial minstrel of beautiful solo arias tests himself with choral music and asks for a libretto in which the chorus takes a part that is, if not predominant, at least very large. The harmonist of simple tastes adds herbs sometimes rather pungent to his always flavorful harmonies; the refined orchestrator is not content with what he has already done, and finds new combinations and creates new colors.

But Giulio Cesare Paribeni, in *Ambrosiano*, saw continuing progress rather than a new direction in *Turandot*.

[In] fact *Turandot* sums up the composer's entire musical life, in the sense that it reviews all the evolving pages of the career of one who, while remaining faithful to himself, did not disdain to observe how much the restless modern age was continuing to find in the feelings and forms of art.

THE TRAVELS OF *TURANDOT*

The dissemination of *Turandot* throughout the principal centers of Europe and the rest of the operatic world was uncommonly rapid, but scarcely surprising in the light of the continuing popularity of *La Bohème*, *Tosca*, and *Madama Butterfly* and of the particular interest aroused by a composer's final score. By the end of 1926, in the eight months subsequent to its introduction at La Scala, it had traveled far.

The Roman première of *Turandot* took place at the Teatro Costanzi four days after the La Scala première, with the leading roles sung by Bianca Scacciati and Francesco Merli; the opera continued its initial round of Italian theaters, reaching Venice's Teatro La Fenice on 9 September 1926. *Turandot* came to South America in the summer of 1926 as part of the repertory of the Italian company that the impresario Walter Mocchi used to take there every year. He introduced the score to Buenos Aires on 25 June, with Claudia Muzio as Turandot, Giacomo Lauri-Volpi as the Prince, Rosetta Pampanini as Liù, and Gino Marinuzzi on the podium; some two weeks later the same forces performed it in Rio de Janeiro.

Often erroneously cited as having taken place on 4 July 1926, the first German-language performance, using a translation by Alfred Brüggemann, occurred at Dresden on 6 September of that year.[18] On 14 October it was introduced at the Vienna Staatsoper, the roles of Turandot and the Prince in the hands of Lotte Lehmann and Leo Slezak, but they were followed by the alternate principals, Maria Nemeth and Jan Kiepura, who performed those assignments more frequently. On 6 November *Turandot* reached Berlin. Ten days later—16 November 1926—the Metropolitan in New York gave the work its North American première, with Jeritza and Lauri-Volpi, Tullio Serafin conducting. On 17 December a French-language version, the work of Paul Spaak, was introduced at the Théâtre de la Monnaie, Brussels, the city where Puccini had died two years earlier.

The year 1927 saw first performances in a number of other Italian opera houses. *Turandot* was staged at the Teatro San Carlo in Naples, 15 January 1927, beginning a run of eighteen performances. The title role was shared by Bianca Scacciati and Iva Pacetti, while Antonio Bagnariol sang the role of the Prince. On 12 February *Turandot* was given at Parma, on 17 March at Turin, and it was introduced at Bologna in October of that year.

Behind the progress of this opening round of performances stood the efficient organization of Casa Ricordi. The translations of Brüggemann and Spaak were those that appeared in printed scores and had been commissioned in advance by Puccini's publishers. Toscanini's late rejection of Alfano's first conclusion caused problems for the publisher because piano-vocal scores containing Alfano I, including a de luxe edition of 120 numbered copies, had already been prepared and were ready for distribution at least by March 1926.[19]

The circulation of piano-vocal scores containing Alfano I raises the question whether the original ending was performed during any of these earliest stagings of *Turandot*. The last part of the opera involves only the roles of Turandot and the Prince (with Emperor and chorus at the very end), and unfortunately neither the pairings of Raisa and Fleta at La Scala nor Jeritza and Lauri-Volpi at the Metropolitan have left any evidence of their various ways with *Turandot*, although all four were active in recording studios. There are, however, two early recordings in Brüggemann's German translation of Turandot's aria "Del primo pianto" that employ Alfano I, sung by the first Dresden Turandot, Anne Roselle, and by her Viennese counterpart, Lotte Lehmann. It seems highly unlikely that these sopranos would record this aria in the version of Alfano I if that were not the version they were singing in the opera houses.[20] More than that, another kind of evidence can be adduced, thanks to the fairly detailed description of the various editions of *Turandot* in Cecil Hopkinson's bibliography of Puccini scores.[21] Hopkinson's discussion of the German-Italian scores, with the plate number 120150, shows that they were circulated in May 1926, for an exemplar of this German edition with that plate number in the Library of Congress was received on 26 May.[22] Since Alfano II is over 100 measures shorter than Alfano I, piano-vocal scores with the earlier, longer ending run to 398 pages, those with Alfano II have 384 pages. Hopkinson's bibliographical description specifies that the Library of Congress copy of the German edition (plate no. 120150) contains 398 pages, a sure sign it contains Alfano I.[23] At some later time, probably June 1930, Ricordi issued a German score containing Alfano II but retaining the original plate number of 120150.[24] These details suggest that German-language theaters almost certainly performed the opera with Alfano I at least through the spring of 1930. Given the potential problem of persuading leading sopranos and tenors to relearn a part in a modified version, the practice may have continued even longer.

The earliest piano-vocal scores to contain Alfano II (and these contained only the Italian text) appeared during the summer of 1926. Assuming that Casa Ricordi would want to dispatch a copy to Washington immediately, to protect its copyright (particularly in light of the announced Metropolitan première set for November), the reception date of 9 August 1926 for the Library of Congress copy of the score with Alfano II suggests that the scores of this edition (plate number 119772) will have come off the presses not before June or July 1926. If this is so, then there is a possibility that the South American performances of that year by Mocchi's company, which sailed from Italy in May, may also have used Alfano I. But since scores containing Alfano II were available in time for both the Metropolitan première (16 November 1926) and the first Covent Garden performance (7 June 1927), it seems certain that the revised ending was used from the start in both those theaters. French-Italian piano-vocal scores 384 pages in length were available at the time of the French-language première in Brussels in December, so it is certain that those performances and later ones at the Paris Opéra used Alfano II. Needless to say, however, questions about the early survival in performance of Alfano I cannot be answered from the evidence of piano-vocal score and their dates with anything like the assurance given by the German-language recordings; only the performing materials employed for the premières of *Turandot* in these theaters, if such material survives, could be conclusive.

As *Turandot* spread throughout the opera world a rather surprising inconsistency of acceptance is demonstrable. Nowhere did it prosper so well as in Vienna, where singers well-adapted to its demands helped it to achieve a vogue. By the summer of 1965 it had reached there the respectable total of 240 performances, two and a half times as many as it received at La Scala in the same period, and nearly eight times as many as the Metropolitan had given of it in those forty years. On the other hand, *Turandot* proved least hardy in French-language performances. At the Monnaie where the chief roles were introduced by Jeanne Bonavia and the tenor Verteneuil, the opera's career came to a close after the twenty-seventh performance; yet this was nearly twice the total it attained at the Paris Opéra, where after its local première on 29 March 1928, with Maryse Beaujon as Turandot and Georges Thill as the Prince, it survived for only fourteen evenings, the last of these on 14 January 1929.

After a somewhat shaky start, *Turandot* made a more secure niche for itself at Covent Garden than it did during its four-season first run at the Metropolitan. London initially heard the opera sung by Bianca Scacciati (Turandot), Lotte Schoene (Liù), Francesco Merli (the Prince) and Fernando Autori (Timur); the conductor was Vincenzo Bellezza, Charles Moor the producer, and the elaborate settings made in Italy were based upon Chini's designs for La Scala. The critics and audience were more impressed by the sumptuous staging than by the singing. After the first night Scacciati was replaced by Florence Easton, who had been singing the role in the United States during the Metropolitan's spring tour of 1927, and she sang the other three performances given in London that summer.

When *Turandot* returned to London in 1928, it was given six times between 5 June and 14 July, being strongly cast with Eva Turner in the title role, while Margherita Sheridan and Pampanini shared the part of Liù; Aroldo Lindi and Salvatore Baccaloni sang the roles of the Prince and Timur respectively, and once again the musical direction was in the hands of Vincenzo Bellezza. The English fondness for *Turandot* may be ascribed to the first assumption of the title role at Covent Garden by Eva Turner; her vocal ease, stamina, and straightforward projection were judged to be close to ideal for this daunting part. Turner returned the next season to sing Turandot three more times, but she was unavailable for the three performances given in 1931, the role of Turandot being shared by Nemeth and Odette de Foras in her absence. Turner returned to the role for the Coronation Season of 1937, when she was partnered by Martinelli's Prince, and Sir John Barbirolli conducted. Further performances, always with Turner, took place in 1939 and again during the 1947/48 season.

With its initial performance of 16 November 1926 the Metropolitan started out from strength, Gatti-Casazza obviously hoping to surpass the impact of the La Scala production of the previous April. In Jeritza and Lauri-Volpi he had the services of the two singers Puccini himself had envisioned for Turandot and the Prince; he added two debutantes to this cast: an experienced Czech bass, Pavel Ludikar, as Timur, and as Liù an unknown American, Martha Attwood.[25] In a lavish gesture, the role of Ping was assigned to Giuseppe de Luca. Tullio Serafin conducted; the production was directed by Wilhelm von Wymetal, with scenery designed by Joseph Urban, a compound of "bewildering vistas and Far East fantasy."[26] The critical reaction was more favorable to the production than to the score; a frequently sounded motif was that *Turandot* marked still another downward step in the erosion of Puccini's gifts, a phenomenon that some dated as starting after *La Bohème* and others after *Madama Butterfly*. (These were the same New York critics, it should be remembered, who failed to appreciate Verdi's *Don Carlo* and Janáček's *Jenůfa* when those works had lately been introduced at the Metropolitan.)

Turandot continued at the Metropolitan for the next three seasons, averaging six performances a year. During this time the company introduced the work to a number of other American cities, during its regular out-of-town subscription series and its annual spring tours: still in 1926, Philadelphia (1 December); in 1927, Baltimore (19 April), Atlanta (27 April), Cleveland (3 May); in 1928, Brooklyn (28 January). With the onset of the depression, and because Jeritza refused to continue in the title role, *Turandot* was given but once in the 1929/30 season and then dropped from the repertory. Thirty years would elapse before it returned to the Metropolitan.

The opposing trajectories of *Turandot* in London and New York in its first decades reveal how much the early success of the opera depended upon the singer in the title role. While Eva Turner went on from strength to strength, Jeritza was on the brink of vocal decline. Of Turner's Turandot there survive both her 1928 commercial recording of "In questa reggia" and in-house takes of her performance in the Enigma scene from the 1937 Coronation Season. Jeritza left no recordings of Turandot's music, a rather surprising omission as she was under contract to a leading American company at the time she sang the role. It is only fair to point out, however, that Jeritza's discs give few clues to the dramatic temperament often mentioned in reviews of her stage performances.

Jeritza was five years older than Turner, having made her stage debut in 1910, at twenty-three, while the English soprano did not begin to sing major roles until 1920, at twenty-eight. Jeritza pursued an exceptionally strenuous career, moreover, giving 350 performances with the Metropolitan during the decade that she was a member of that company, as well as making annual appearances in Vienna. Some insight into Jeritza's way of sing-ing the role of Turandot comes from two descriptions of her singing by the New York critic W. J. Henderson. After the New York première he complimented her on her "amazing prodigality" of tone, but when he came back to hear her in the third performance of that season, he decided that she was only a "screaming scold."[27] Today there can be little doubt that singing the role of Turandot contributed to the waning of Jeritza's powers. Turner, on the other hand, although she sang the heaviest dramatic so-prano roles, had a more leisurely career, on the whole, than Jeritza. She sang her first Turandots at Brescia and Trieste in 1926; a less willful singer than Jeritza, she was also fortunate in that the high tessitura of much of Turandot's music suited her bright resonant voice, which she produced without undue strain.

Two further quotations will place the contrast between these two fa-mous Turandots in a stronger light. The first concerns Jeritza and comes from Lauri-Volpi's *Voci parallele*, giving us the impression that she pro-duced upon her Calàf.

> But where Jeritza made her impact was in *Turandot*. This Oriental princess was not the usual Chinese woman of a low or medium height, but an idol, a creature of a divine race, descended to earth in deceptive guise to rule over the common people. With rapid, gigantic strides she burst upon the stage clad in an imperial cloak; she ascended the staircase and went to the top, having covered her face with a golden veil. From up there she launched her enigmas like bolts of lightning. At the foot of the steps the unknown Prince remained dazzled, taken aback, hoping to solve these enigmas that the arrogant Princess dis-closed to him with such defiant self-confidence and insolent security. Conquered, the cruel, capricious goddess did not want to surrender herself, and she reacted to the victorious boldness of Calàf with a shudder that ran all through her, and her eyes dilated with fear.[28]

The second quotation comes from Eva Turner herself. Among the notes she contributed to a reissue of some of her recordings, writing in 1960 or so, she demonstrates her view of the role as well as something of her own generosity of spirit.

> I feel that singers and critics alike tend to place too much emphasis upon Turandot's cruelty. To me her over-riding emotion is fear; a fear from which all her other qualities stem. In the great scene after Calàf has solved the riddles . . . her voice mounts and mounts in an ecstasy of fear. "Non guardarmi così!" This is not a cry of anger but of fear. She knows instinctively that she has met her match, a man for whom

she has a real affinity—and he for her—pre-ordained and inescapable.[29]

At La Scala *Turandot* was performed with about the same frequency as at Covent Garden, at least until the mid-1960s. After Rosa Raisa temporarily renounced the role at the close of its introductory round of eight performances in Milan, Bianca Scacciati, so little liked at the London *prima*, made the role her own at La Scala in three seasons' revivals. The next singer to dominate the role there was the French-born Gina Cigna, who after assuming it for the first time at La Scala in 1935 was soon in great demand to appear as Turandot all over Italy. In 1937 Cigna's assumption of the role took on a new dimension when she sang Turandot in the first complete recording of the score.[30] Particularly for those in the United States, where there was no chance to experience *Turandot* on stage after 1930 until its production in Chicago in the late 1940s, this record set, impressive for its period, allowed a new generation to learn to appreciate the opera's particular strengths. Besides the magisterial Turandot of Cigna, the well-balanced cast included the evocative Liù of Magda Olivero, a brilliant Calàf by Francesco Merli (who had sung the Roman première), and a capital trio of Ministers in Afro Poli, Gino del Signore and Adelio Zagonara, all given coherent momentum under the musical leadership of Franco Ghione. This recorded performance stemmed from a living context of stage experience and made a positive contribution to the future performance history of the opera. The implication for many of us was: if *Turandot* can be so exciting on disc, what an impact it must produce in the opera house!

Because of its spectacular elements *Turandot*, like *Aida*, has proved particularly adaptable to lavish mountings in the outdoor arenas that have become such a notable feature of Italian summer festivals. The oldest of these, in terms of twentieth century performances, is the Arena di Verona, but other such facilities were adapted later at the Terme di Caracalla in Rome, at the Arena Flegrea just north of Naples, and the Arena Sferisterio at Macerata. Some brief account of *Turandot* at the Arena di Verona can represent this phase of its performance history. Forzano himself produced *Turandot* at its debut there in July 1928, with Anne Roselle and Georges Thill heading the first cast, this production being given nine times.[31] Vittorio Gui conducted it at its next appearance in 1937, when the female roles were sustained by Cigna and Mafalda Favero. It did not reappear at the Arena di Verona until 1948, when Maria Callas sang Turandot five times and Antonino Votto conducted. It returned in 1954 and again in 1958, both times still under Votto's guidance; in the latter series of six performances Franco Corelli aroused *fanatismo* as the Prince. The next production at the Arena di Verona was not until 1969, when the reigning Turandot of that period, Birgit Nilsson, sang opposite Placido Domingo, with Molinari Pradelli on the podium.

Although Nilsson and Corelli did not appear at the same time at the Arena di Verona, they were together in one of the most notable post–World War II productions of *Turandot*. This was the revival on 24 February 1961 at the Metropolitan, when the work returned after a thirty-year hiatus.[32] This revival was originally to have been conducted by Dmitri Mitropoulos, but his death caused the Metropolitan to turn to Leopold Stokowski as his replacement. An evocative and eminently practicable staging by Cecil Beaton, with costumes and makeup designed by Yoshio Aoyama, contributed much to a critical and popular success. The new generation of New York critics no longer bemoaned Puccini's supposedly declining powers, but greeted the work as a welcome and worthily presented addition to the current repertory. Nilsson and Corelli were joined by Anna Moffo (Liù), Bonaldo Giaiotti (Timur), and Frank Guarrera (Ping). With the exception of the role of Liù—Moffo's extraordinary roster of alternates was Teresa Stratas, Leontyne Price, and Licia Albanese—casting remained relatively constant that first season. In the first four years of this revival—it was temporarily rotated out of the repertory in 1963/64—*Turandot* received thirty-two performances, eleven more than its original run at the Metropolitan had achieved in a roughly comparable space of time. It was duly repeated there in a number of subsequent seasons. The Beaton production was replaced in 1987 by one adapted by Franco Zeffirelli from his 1983 Milan production.

Turandot, a work that requires both its two principal singers and its mise-en-scène to be on a grand scale, survives handily in the repertory today. In 1977 the San Francisco Opera revived it with Montserrat Caballé and Pavarotti, with Riccardo Chailly conducting. This combination was supposed to perform it at the Metropolitan several seasons later, but a labor dispute forced the project's cancellation. Ghena Dimitrova demonstrated her vocal prowess as the Princess in Zeffirelli's 1983 La Scala *Turandot*, and that summer she sang the part again at the Arena di Verona; as we have noted, that staging owed much to Forzano's *disposizione scenica*, and is now available on videotape.[33] In 1984 Covent Garden sponsored a lavish new production with Gwyneth Jones and Placido Domingo in the leading parts, giving it first at Los Angeles in conjunction with the summer Olympic Games being held there, before bringing it home to London.

The possibilities for lavish spectacle that made *Turandot* a drawing card for the outdoor arenas in Italy are equally favorable to recent trends in production style, with their decorative irrelevancies in constant motion, designed to beguile an audience surfeited with familiarities, as well as those who watch opera in their homes on television screens. Although many who really want to hear as well as see an opera find this undue emphasis on visual elements in motion a distraction away from the focal points of opera—the singers and the musical action they embody—*Turandot* can survive superfluous extravagances better than more fragile works like *La traviata*. Its equally extravagant variety of orchestral and harmonic color can scarcely be ignored by the ear, no matter how glutted the eye, and the long-range interrelationships in the score endow it with a musical coherence that repays familiarity.

Turandot serves modern trends in performance in yet another way. Because more recent works are rarely profitable at the box office, and the financial risk in mounting a brand-new and untried score is forbidding, a vogue of mounting established operas in different musical editions has arisen. This trend, which has been responsible to the revival of such "novelties" as the 1789 *Le nozze di Figaro*—not to mention *Figaro* with "original" instruments—or the 1806 *Leonore* of Beethoven, or the La Scala 1904 *Madama Butterfly*, has now seen the disinterment of Franco Alfano's original ending to *Turandot*. Its first performance since the early German-language performances was at London's Barbican, in a concert performance promoted by Alan Sievewright and Denny Dayvies; since then it has been sung on stage at the New York City Opera and at Bonn. The experience of encountering it makes one more eager than ever to have a performing edition that conflates the longer "Del primo pianto" and slightly fuller concluding scene of Alfano I into Alfano II, which preserves Puccini's own material more faithfully, as we have suggested in Chapter V.

So far this sketchy summary of *Turandot*'s acceptance into the repertory of the world's leading opera houses has given little sense of the geographical spread of the opera's travels. In 1928 *Turandot* reached both Scandinavia (Stockholm) and Australia. In 1929 it was sung for the first time in English, in Halifax (Nova Scotia). It has thrived in Balkan opera houses, sung in a variety of local languages. More recently it has established its popularity with South African audiences. There are no signs that *Turandot* is likely to lose any of the ground it has gained in its first six decades.

Turandot occupies a special place in the Italian repertory, for it is indeed the end of the Great Tradition; it is aesthetically and culture-historically inconceivable that genuinely new works still mining that vein can be created. But if the operas in the Great Tradition are in one sense museum pieces, nonetheless they cannot be hung on walls; like other manifestations of the temporal arts, they must be produced. And as long as Italian opera in the Great Tradition lives on in production—and in the affections of the opera-going public the tradition shows no signs of coming to an end—*Turandot* will live.

APPENDIX

[rh with Roman numeral means "rehearsal number" in the respective act in any Ricordi score, + the number of measures after it, counting the measure at the rehearsal number as "1"]

APPENDIX

A. Sunset: awaiting the execution.
   1. The Mandarin's proclamation (rh I.0)
   2. Recognition (rh I.4)
   3. Interlude (rh I.7)
   4. Executioners' chorus (rh I.9)

B. Moonrise: the Prince of Persia; first entrance of Turandot
   1. Moonrise chorus (rh I.17)
   2. Children's chorus (rh I.19)
   3. Funeral cortège for the Prince of Persia (rh I.21)
   4. Interlude (rh I.25)

C. The three Ministers and the unknown Prince
   1. Entrance of the Ministers (rh I.28)
   2. Interludes (rh I.35)
      a) Chorus of Turandot's handmaidens
      b) Ministerial warnings
   3. The ghosts of Turandot's former suitors (rh I.38)
   4. Conclusion (rh I.39)
      a) The Ministers try again
      b) The severed head of the Prince of Persia

D. Finale
   1. Transition (rh I.41 + 3)
   2. Aria of Liù (rh I.42)
   3. Aria of the unknown Prince (rh I.43)
   4. *Concertato* (rh I.46)

A. Trio of the three Ministers
   0. *Scena* (rh II.0): Ping calls his confrères
   1. *Tempo d'attacco* (rh II.1): they are ready for any eventuality
   2. *Andantino* (rh II.9): their bucolic nostalgia
   3. *Tempo di mezzo* (rh II.13)
      a) They recall recent executions and ancient glories
      b) They hope this time to prepare a bridal chamber
   4. *Stretta* (rh II.21): their fantasy of love and peace

B. Change of set: the Court assembles
   1. Transition
   2. Processional (rh II.26)

C. The first confrontation
   1. The Emperor and the unknown Prince (rh II.34)
   2. Brief ceremonial conclusion (rh II.39)

D. Turandot
  1. Reprise of the Mandarin's proclamation (rh II.40)
  2. Reprise of the Children's chorus (rh II.42)
  3. *Aria di sortita* of Turandot (rh II.43)
E. The second confrontation: the Enigma scene
  1. The first enigma and response (rh II.50 + 2)
  2. The second enigma and response (rh II.54 + 3)
  3. The third enigma and response (rh II.59 + 2)
  4. Coda and concerted piece (rh II.63)
F. The third confrontation
  1. The Prince's enigma (rh II.65 + 9)
  2. The Emperor's reaction (rh II.67 + 3)
  3. Full ceremonial conclusion (rh II.68 + 3)

ACT III

A. The Prince alone
  1. Introduction and chorus of heralds offstage (rh III.0)
  2. *Romanza* of the unknown Prince (rh III.4)
  3. Entrance of the Ministers and populace (rh III.6 + 5)
B. The tempting of the Prince
  1. The first temptation (rh III.8 + 5)
  2. Two more temptations (rh III.9);
    entrance of Liù and Timur (rh III.15)
  3. Entrance of Turandot (rh III.16 + 5)
C. The slave-girl and the Princess
  1. *Tempo d'attacco* (rh III.20): torture of Liù
  2. Aria of Liù (rh III.24)
  3. *Tempo di mezzo* (rh III.25 + 6): further torture of Liù
  4. Suicide and funeral cortège of Liù; Timur's grief (rh III.27)
D. The thawing of the Princess
  1. The Prince's accusation and his wooing (rh III.35)
  2. The Princess weakens (rh III.39)
  3. Aria of Turandot (rh III.42).
  4. The Prince tells his name (rh III.46)
E. Change of set (as in Act II set 2): the final scene
  1. Fanfares: appearance of the Court (rh III.50)
  2. The Princess tells the Prince's name (rh III.53)
  3. The final chorus (rh III.54)

NOTES

❧

INTRODUCTION

1. William Weaver, *The Golden Century of Italian Opera: from Rossini to Puccini* (London and New York, 1980), 242. Weaver's account of the War of the Verdian Succession, where Puccini himself had been the "crown prince," is on his pp. 193–97.

2. Rubens Tedeschi, *Addio fiorito asil* (Milan, 1978), 95.

3. Lorenzo Bianconi and Thomas Walker, "Production, Consumption and Political Function of Seventeenth-Century Italian Opera," *Early Music History* 4 (1984), 235.

4. Idem, 248, 253.

5. Harold Powers, "*L'Erismena* travestita," *Studies in Music History: Essays for Oliver Strunk* (Princeton, 1968), 324.

6. Tedeschi, *Addio fiorito asil*, 97–98.

7. Unlike most other Italian composers of the early 20th century, Puccini never succumbed to the temptation to collaborate with D'Annunzio or set one of his verse plays: "Oh meraviglia delle meraviglie! D'Annunzio mio librettista! Ma neanche per tutto l'oro del mondo" (Oh wonder of wonders! D'Annunzio my librettist! But not for all the gold in the world), after Jürgen Maehder, "The Origins of Italian *Literaturoper*," in *Reading Opera*, ed. Arthur Groos and Roger Parker (Princeton, 1988), 92–128, the title quotation.

8. A particularly interesting instance is Des Grieux's aria "Donna non vidi mai" in Act I of *Manon Lescaut*, where an octave of mixed *versi imparisillabi* was fitted to music originally composed to a repeated quatrain of *versi ottonari* (by Felice Romani) during Puccini's conservatory days. See Michael Kaye, *The Unknown Puccini* (New York and Oxford, 1987), 35 (for the source) and 42–44 (for the original text and music).

9. See Maehder, "The Origins of Italian *Literaturoper*," especially pp. 92–97.

10. Robert Redfield, "The Social Organization of Tradition," in his *Peasant Society and Culture* (Chicago, 1956), 67–104; in revised form in *The Far Eastern Quarterly* 15 (1955), 13–21.

11. Milton Singer, "Search for a Great Tradition in Cultural Performances," in his *When a Great Tradition Modernizes* (New York, 1972), 71.

12. Bianconi and Walker, "Production, Consumption and Political Function," 259–60.

13. For an instance amusing as well as revealing, see Irving Kolodin's account of the origins of New York's Metropolitan Opera in his *The Metropolitan Opera 1883–1966: A Candid History* (New York, 1966), 4–6, built around the following (from Lilli Lehmann's *Memoires*): "As, on a particular evening, one of the millionairesses did not receive the box [at the Academy of Music on 14th Street] in which she intended to shine because another woman had anticipated her, the husband of the former took prompt action and caused the Metropolitan Opera House [at 39th and Broadway] to rise." The founder of the "old Met," and evidently the husband referred to in Lehmann's memoirs, according to Kolodin, was William H. Vanderbilt. The boxes at the Academy of Music were the preserve of "old New York"; the "old Met" was the answer to "old New York"

169

offered by the new, post–Civil War rich and powerful. The "new Met" at Lincoln Center in turn is liberally labeled with the names of its individual and corporate patrons.

14. Bianconi and Walker, "Production, Consumption and Political Function," 242.

CHAPTER I

1. For the most original and extreme exposition of this approach to the relationship between an opera and its libretto, see Gabriele Baldini, *Abitare la battaglia* (Milan, 1970), translated by Roger Parker as *The Story of Giuseppe Verdi* (Cambridge, 1980), especially Book III Chapter 5 on *Il trovatore*. Baldini characterized Salvadore Cammarano's libretto as "the perfect musical libretto, a text which fully allowed for the musical life of its characters and for that alone; essentially a phantom libretto, which became completely engulfed by the music and, once the opera was finished, disappeared as an individual entity" (Parker translation, p. 210).

2. Frits Noske, "Ritual scenes," Chapter 10 of his *The Signifier and the Signified: Studies in the Operas of Mozart and Verdi* (The Hague, 1977).

3. We have designated its four movements with the nineteenth-century terms now generally used by students of the Italian Romantic *melodramma*, though with another kind of appropriateness we might have regarded them as analogous to the conventional four movements of a symphony. In one of his letters to his librettist Giuseppe Adami, Puccini described this number as "a *morceau* outside of the action [*senza scena*] and thus an almost academic piece" (Adami, ed., *Epistolario Giacomo Puccini* [*EGP*], ltr 213, p. 286).

4. *EGP*, ltr 237, quoted in Chapter III, p. 88.

5. William Ashbrook, *The Operas of Puccini* (2d ed., Ithaca, 1985), 225. Regrettably, the videotape of the Arena di Verona production of 1983 shows that this was one of the productions where "Del primo pianto" was cut—doubly regrettable in that this may become the image of *Turandot* for many in the future (as was the great Cetra recording of 1937 for many of us in the past), and in that one does not know how Ghena Dimitrova—in our view a great interpreter of the role—might have rendered it.

CHAPTER II

1. For an account of the Oriental origins of the Turandot story, see Lynn Snook, "In Search of the Riddle Princess Turandot," *Esotismo e colore locale nell'opera di Puccini*: Atti del I° convegno internazionale sull'opera di Giacomo Puccini, Torre del Lago, 1983, ed. Jürgen Maehder (Pisa, 1985), 131–41.

2. The Prince's question, asking Turandot to discover his name and that of his father, appears in all the subsequent transformations of Gozzi's play. When the Prince poses his question in Act II of Puccini's opera he does not in fact mention his father, yet he reveals his identity in Act III as "Calàf, figlio di Timur."

3. The mythical Persian royal name Kaikobad, as in Firdausi's *Shahnama*, also belonged to several historical rulers, the most important of whom were a late 5th-early 6th-century Sassanid king of Persia, and a 13th-century Seljuk Turkish king. In Hugo von Hofmannsthal's libretto for Strauss's *Die Frau ohne Schatten*, Kaikobad—lord of the spirit world and father of the Empress, one of the two principal female roles—is the powerful Mage who drives the plot, though he

never appears except as an important motive attached to the syllables of his name.

4. The first of Gozzi's *fiabe*, *L'amore delle tre melarance* (1761), is almost entirely in *scenario* form. There is an echo of this old practice, where such a text was called a *copione della commedia a soggetto* (script for an improvised play), in the title of Pirandello's play *Questa sera si recita a soggetto*.

5. This episode eventually provided Puccini's librettists with the basic idea for the *fuori-scena* (Act II set 1) for Ping, Pang, and Pong.

6. Pantalone's lines are written out rather than summarized, but they are in prose, as opposed to the unrhymed *endecasillabi* (Italian blank verse) of the courtly characters; further, he speaks in the Venetian dialect, not the formal Italian of the others. Tartaglia's lines are also in prose, but not in Venetian.

7. The Prince has to remain incognito because of the risk of his enemies discovering him; thus he is risking his life in a double sense when he later asks Turandot to find out his name.

8. In his edition of Schiller's *Turandot*, Professor Güthke reports that the enigmas were regularly varied in productions subsequent to the Weimar *Uraufführung* (30 January 1802); he lists fourteen variants, to which Goethe contributed yet another (Friedrich Schiller, *Turandot*, with an afterword by Karl S. Güthke, Stuttgart, 1960, p. 92).

9. The list of works in this section is summarized from Chapters IV and V (pp. 66–262) of Kii-Ming Lo's 1988 Heidelberg dissertation *Turandot auf der Opern-bühne*, which contains much useful comparative analysis of libretti and settings as well as extensive documentation, excerpts from contempory criticism, and a complete account of the Chinese melody from Rousseau's *Dictionnaire* that was used in Weber's incidental music.

10. John Warrack, *Carl Maria von Weber* (Cambridge, 1976), 74–75.

11. This work was projected by Verdi for the first anniversary of Rossini's death and completed by the thirteen composers who took part, but in the end it was not performed on the occasion for which it was composed; as is well known, Verdi revised his own contribution, the concluding movement "Libera me," for his Manzoni Requiem. The composite "Messa per Rossini," following an equally composite edition prepared by the Istituto di studi verdiani, had its première in Stuttgart in the autumn of 1988, was repeated a few days later in Parma, and was heard in New York in the autumn of 1989. For an account of the "Messa per Rossini," see *Quaderni dell'istituto di studi verdiani* no. 5 (Parma and Milan, 1988).

12. Rafaello De Rensis, *Franco Faccio e Verdi: Carteggi e documenti inediti* (Milan, 1934), 63–64. Ricordi's opinion of Bazzini's opera may be to some degree colored by the fact that the rival publishing house of Lucca had the rights to the opera.

13. *Giornale di musica* (Milan) vol. 2 no. 17 (26 April 1868), as quoted in Kii-Ming Lo, *Turandot*, 228. A month before Filippi's comments on Bazzini's *Turanda* were published the original version of Boito's *Mefistofele* was produced, a work that would have sunk with little more trace than Bazzini's *Turanda*—if with rather more immediate ripples on the journalistic surface—had it not been later revised and brought into line with the "exigencies of the theater," in which form it triumphed and still survives. What might have happened to a revised *Turanda* by Bazzini had librettist Gazzoletti survived to do his part? It is difficult to tell from the surviving available music, three *pezzi staccati* published by Lucca in

1867 in piano-vocal score: from Act III, Adelma's *canzone* "L'usignuolo e la rosa" and Nadir's aria "Scendi soave immagine" from the banquet scene; from Act IV (the final scene), the Turanda-Nadir duet "Tu m'hai vinta." There is also a disordered and unpaginated mass of autograph pages in the library of the Brescia Conservatory, mostly in pencil and some of it unreadable, comprising both sketches and finished score, and even so, incomplete (Lo *Turandot*, 226–27).

14. Gazzoletti's setting of the action at the time and court of the Sassanid King Chosroes (Khusrau) II—who happens to have been the grandson of the historical Sassanid King Kaikobad (the name used for Adelma's father in Gozzi's play)—and his use of Persian names, with the Indian Nadir as the unknown Prince from abroad, appear to represent some sort of attempt at historical consistency of time and place.

15. Gazzoletti has adapted the details of Nadir's sleeping and involuntary revelation of his name to Adelma from Act IV of his source, putting them in a new setting.

16. Edward J. Dent, *Ferruccio Busoni* (Oxford, 1966), 155, 179.

17. Dent, *Busoni*, p. 199.

18. Busoni was his own librettist for *Arlecchino*—which he called *Ein theatralisches Capriccio*—as well as for *Turandot*.

19. In Puccini's *Turandot* the *maschere* always come on stage together, and are treated primarily as a trio ensemble, though the baritone Ping is always the leader, with a number of solo passages. Busoni, on the other hand, treated his Truffaldino (a tenor buffo) as an independent major character as well as one of the group of *maschere*, giving him a separate aria in each of the two acts; Pantalone and Tartaglia, to the contrary, are completely subordinate roles.

20. The Prince's reiterated words in this quartet are a slight modification of Schiller's text: "Tod oder Turandot. Es gibt kein Drittes" (Death or Turandot; there is no third way).

21. Busoni's *Turandot* was not performed in Italy during Puccini's lifetime. Before 1924, the year in which both Puccini and Busoni died, the work was given twice in Germany, in Frankfurt (1918) and in Berlin (1921), with Leo Blech conducting. The first Italian performances were over the radio, from Turin (1936) and Rome (1938). The first staged performance of Busoni's *Turandot* in Italy was in Florence at the Maggio fiorentino (19 May 1940), conducted by Ferdinando Previtali. The cast was headed by Maria Carbone (Turandot) and Alessandro Ziliani (Calàf). This Italian première formed the second half of a remarkable double-bill that opened with the world première of Dallapiccola's *Volo di notte*.

CHAPTER III

1. Simoni did have one link with the publishing house, in that his first libretto, *La secchia rapita*, had been set by Giulio Ricordi (1910).

2. The plot of *Sly* derives from the Induction to Shakespeare's *The Taming of the Shrew*, expanded, and with comic and tragic elements, the latter predominating at the end. Forzano's treatment was first produced as a play (Milan, 1920) and was later adapted as a libretto for Ermanno Wolf-Ferrari (La Scala, 1927).

3. Carlo Paladini, *Giacomo Puccini* (Florence, 1961), 153–54. Paladini was a journalist from Lucca, and a crony of Puccini's since childhood.

4. The "first draft of the plot" was surely an expansion of the scenario Puccini had responded to in his letter of 18 July 1920 [*EGP*, ltr 180]; but Adami (see *Il ro-*

manzo della vita di Giacomo Puccini—[RVGP]) was writing nearly twenty years after the event and may have been thinking of the scenario provided in May and July.

5. The Fassini music box was still in existence and functioning until relatively recently; for its rediscovery by William Weaver and more on the connection of its contents with the final version of Puccini's opera, see Chapter IV, pp. 94–96.

6. The letter to Schnabl of 3 March is in *Giacomo Puccini: lettere a Riccardo Schnabl*, ed. Simonetta Puccini (Milan, 1981), 131–32; on p. 133 there is a photograph of the first page of the proof copy of the original two-scene Act I libretto. We are very much indebted to Dr. Kii-Ming Lo for supplying us a copy of her photocopy of this crucially important document in advance of the completion of her dissertation. The full text of the 1921 libretto is included as Appendix II of her *Turandot auf der Opernbühne* (Heidelberg dissertation, 1988), aligned with the final text of the libretto and the actual text found in the score; it is discussed in her Chapter 7, "Die Entstehung des Librettos."

7. One can infer from his letter of 7 June 1921, quoted on p. 71, that Puccini had probably set all three of the ghosts' stanzas, though of course the second and third stanzas will have been cut later, before the orchestration, possibly even before the original long Act I was divided. (See the discussion on pp. 101–2 of Chapter IV and Example 8 in Chapter I.)

8. The lines for the chorus on the eight sages that Puccini was to request later that summer, on 17 July, are of course not there (see p. 72), nor is the choral comment noting the Ministers' arrival.

9. In the present Act II Liù has one brief, pathetically ironic phrase, "E per l'amore!," directed to be sung "with a sob" [*con un singhiozzo*], in which she joins the Emperor and the crowd in encouraging the Prince after the second enigma.

10. Letter dated "Sabato Santo" (Easter fell on 27 March).

11. Dalla Rizza had created Magda in *La rondine* (Monte Carlo, 1917), and sang Angelica and Lauretta in the European première of *Il trittico* (Rome, 1919). In March 1921 she had repeated these last two roles, as well as singing Minnie in *La fanciulla del West*, at Monte Carlo.

12. That is, Turandot does not sing in the opening set (now Act I), which Puccini would have been composing at the time of the letter.

13. In Lanfranco Rasponi, *The Last Prima Donnas* (New York, 1982), Dalla Rizza is reported to have said: "when Puccini was composing *Turandot* . . . he wanted me as Liù. But he ended up writing the role for a lyric, and my voice was too heavy by the time the opera received its world premiere" (p. 125). She did sing the role of Turandot once, at Monte Carlo in 1927, but there only because the theater is intimate in size.

14. In the original long Act I, these were the arias for the Prince and for Liù, in that order, as may be seen in the summary above. One wonders to what extent the settings of these arias in June 1921 resembled the ones we have now, particularly Liù's in its position after the Prince's and with the stoic tone reflected in its opening and closing lines.

15. The second set in Part III of Gazzoletti's libretto for Bazzini's *Turanda* is a banquet, an event that does not appear in Gozzi, Schiller, or Maffei. See Chapter II, p. 55.

16. In the first set of Part III of his libretto for Bazzini's *Turanda*, Gazzoletti had called for an elaborate magic scene, including apparitions of various sorts,

which was probably the model for this part of the eventually discarded Act II. See Chapter II, p. 55.

17. Puccini may have finished and signed the letter of 13 September 1921 in which he hoped to persuade Simoni to condense the libretto into "two large acts" (*CP*, ltr 816, pp. 514–15), and then, to make what he meant even clearer, jotted down his "plan" on a second undated sheet, which later became separated from its accompanying letter. Having sent off the letter and "plan" to Simoni, Puccini might then have decided to reconstruct his plan from memory for Adami, to make sure that both librettists had the same suggestions before them.

Illustration I in Chapter 7 ("Die Entstehung des Librettos") of Kii-Ming Lo's 1988 Heidelberg dissertation *Turandot auf die Opernbühne* is a photocopy of the scheme Puccini sent to Simoni; it is also transcribed, as letter 42, in her Appendix I. The layout on the two pages is significantly different from the way the scheme is printed as letter 777 of Gara's *Carteggi pucciniani*. The heading "here is a sort of guide to the second act" is squeezed into the upper lefthand corner of the first of two sheets of paper, and the summary instructions for the act as a whole that follow in letter 777 are in fact written down the left margin. To the extent possible in our composite outline, we have adjusted our layout to reflect the layout of the scheme sent to Simoni, as shown in Dr. Lo's dissertation.

18. This order of Turandot's is proclaimed by the heralds in the present Act III, not as here by Turandot herself.

19. "The three" must mean the Prince, Liù, and Turandot, judging from what follows.

20. This second of the three sets in Puccini's plan was intended to be played on the forepart of the stage while the opening set was changed to the concluding set behind a drop.

21. The word *Pegonie* does not appear to exist in Italian; could this be a variant spelling or misspelling of "peonie" (peonies)?

22. It should be remembered that in Puccini's plan for Act II—September 1921 the duet for Turandot and the Prince preceded Turandot's exit as well as subsequent efforts by Liù, in a new setting, to soften her, and all this before the final confrontation in the presence of the assembled Court.

23. Puccini's mention of a "third act" here may mean that he was already beginning to have doubts about his plan for "two large acts." This "third act" would have been the equivalent of the present Act III set 2.

24. The proposal to prepare this other libretto—an eighteenth-century Venetian subject—had a double purpose. If *Turandot* could be satisfactorily salvaged, it could serve as their next work; but if *Turandot* should founder, it could replace it. Promised for the end of November 1922, the scenario never materialized and was heard of no more.

25. Although this letter is dated only "Thursday," Adami published it between two others dated 30 October and 3 November 1922, respectively, presumably on the basis of his recollection. Other matters discussed in it make some such placement plausible.

26. The matter was soon rectified however, although it had been nearly a year in abeyance, for on 22 November 1922 Puccini notified his publisher that his son Tonio would bring the manuscript of Act I, now complete, to Milan.

27. A draft for the melody of "Tu che di gel sei cinta" was published in a La Scala program book in 1951 by Teodoro Celli and has been reprinted in *Quaderni pucciniani* 2 (1985), 50; it is a half-step higher than the final version, all in 2/4

instead of the present alternating 2/4 and 4/4 measures, with some differences in the melodic line after the first few measures.

28. Once before Puccini had contributed the text of a climactic aria that he felt intensely, Cavaradossi's "E lucevan le stelle" in Act III of *Tosca*.

29. The first page of the fair-copy autograph of the Ministers' *fuori-scena* in the Ricordi archives is annotated "10 dic 1923 / Viareggio." The orchestration of Act II went rapidly—much of it had already been completed while it still formed part of the original long Act I—and on 11 February 1924 Puccini was able to inform Adami that the instrumentation of Act II was "almost finished" (*EGP*, ltr 227).

30. The important moments for the bass xylophone are the Emperor scene and the onlookers' interlude after the second enigma; it also plays in the coda of the Executioners' chorus in Act I and at the very beginning of Act II.

31. See Maehder "Studien zum Fragmentcharakter" and/or "Puccini's *Turandot*," Example 6 for a reproduction of the draft at "O fiore mattutino," and Chapter IV below for the expression "continuity draft" applied to this part of the musical material left for the end of the opera at Puccini's death.

32. In this same letter Puccini reminded Valcarenghi that the Finale of Act I was to be transposed down a half-step (at measure 5 of I.D.1). See the relevant excerpt, the discussion, and Example 35, in Chapter IV, pp. 103–7.

33. The last phrase almost certainly refers to the *motivo* that we have called "the theme of the Prince's name," to which the words "Ma il mio mistero è chiuso in me / Il nome mio nessun saprà" are set in the *romanza* "Nessun dorma"; the melody appears on f.19ʳ of the fragmentary sketches for the end of the opera in the Ricordi archives.

34. The first version of *Madama Butterfly* premièred at La Scala, 17 February 1904, and was a complete fiasco.

35. The "nightmare" had been caused by Toscanini's exclusion of Puccini from the *prova generale* of Boito's *Nerone* at La Scala the previous April. Although Puccini had come to Milan expressly to hear Boito's posthumous work, he had judged the score in advance as a "bluff," and rumors of his attitude had appeared in the press; he was turned away at the door on Toscanini's orders. On 4 August 1924 Puccini sent a long letter to Toscanini in the hope of healing the rupture between them (*CP*, ltr 894, pp. 553–54).

<h2 style="text-align:center">CHAPTER IV</h2>

1. "Volontà di Turandot," cited after the excerpt in *Musica d'oggi* 8, no. 5 (May 1926), 149. The review is also excerpted in *CP* (*Carteggi pucciniani*, ed. Eugenio Gara, Milan, 1958), 564.

2. English National Opera Guide no. 27: *Turandot/Puccini* (London and New York, 1984), 22.

3. Michele Girardi, " 'Turandot': Il futuro interrotto del melodramma italiano," *Rivista italiana di musicologia* 17 (1982), 175: "Questo tema è legata da Puccini all'immagine di Turandot come crudele giustizeria dei suoi pretendenti, e introduce, come i tre accordi di Scarpia, lo spettatore in un clima di tensione fin dall'inizio." The unison orchestral *fortissimo* and the short-short-long-long-long rhythm is also strongly reminiscent of the principal subject of Iago's "Credo" in Verdi's *Otello*, as has been remarked by Mosco Carner (ENO Guide).

4. Girardi " 'Turandot,' " 176.

5. Our use of the name "Mo-li-hua" for this tune is for convenience of reference only; as noted later, there is no reason to suppose that Puccini knew the tune by that name. This is the only place, incidentally, where Puccini used the whole tune; at all returns later he used only the first two, four or eight measures.

6. Girardi " 'Turandot,' " 176.

7. Abramo Basevi, *Studio sulle opere di Giuseppe Verdi* (Florence, 1859), 114–15. The notion of *colorito* or *tinta* for Verdi extends from the obvious orientalisms in *Aida*, through the characteristic swing of Riccardo's "Di tu se fedele" in *Un ballo in maschera*—sailorly as opposed to huntsmanlike, as Verdi himself observed (A. Luzio, *Carteggi verdiani* I, Rome, 1935, 252)—to whatever Verdi meant by "tinta" in a well-known letter regarding Hugo's *Le roi s'amuse* as the subject for what became *Rigoletto*, in which he wrote "I set myself to studying and thinking deeply about it, and in my mind the *idea* [and] the *tinta musicale* have been found" (G. Cesari and A. Luzio, *I copialettere di Giuseppe Verdi*, Milan, 1913, 106–7, and cited many times since; see for instance Julian Budden, *The Operas of Verdi* I, London and New York, 1973, 478).

8. Most recently in English National Opera Guide no. 27, as Example 1-b, p. 19.

9. A different form of this tune, having nothing whatever to do with *Turandot*, may be seen on p. 19 of van Aalst's *Chinese Music*, under the name "Hsiēn Huā."

10. In his broadcast talk William Weaver described this melody as the "modern Imperial hymn . . . written in 1912," evidently following Mosco Carner's identification after the 5th edition of *Grove's Dictionary*, to be seen most recently in the ENO Guide no. 27, p. 21, Ex. 1-f. But after the first five notes there is no resemblance at all between the two melodies; Carner's source, incidentally, was completely in error in identifying the tune as a "national anthem" (see Lo, *Turandot*, 370–71).

11. The source Mosco Carner believed to have found for this tune, to be seen most recently in the ENO Guide no. 27, p. 19, Ex. 1-a, bears even less resemblance to Puccini's melody than his source for the "Ferma! che fai?" melody. Carner thought he saw this melody in the part for *èr-hù* (two-string fiddle) in Example 3 of the article "Chinese Music" in Willi Apel's *Harvard Dictionary of Music* (Cambridge, 1944). For his example in the *Harvard Dictionary*, in turn, Apel had arbitrarily taken mm. 101–9 from the middle of Example 9 in Erich Fischer's "Beiträge zur Erforschung der chinesischen Musik," *Sammelbände der internationale Musikgesellschaft* 12 (1910–11), a 226-measure extract transcribed from a recording "from the musical drama Che-fung-pa."

12. Most recently as Exs. 1-c, e, g, h, pp. 20–21 of the ENO Guide no. 27.

13. Lo, 349.

14. This is a modification that may well have been made later: erasures of flat signs before low D in the lower contrabass line in Puccini's fair-copy pencil autograph, and the curious notation of the pitches in the harp and upper contrabass part in the autograph and existing score, suggest that the present signature of five flats at rh II.66 might have been written in after the melody and essential accompanying parts for the "Guiding March," and for the first appearance of the "theme of the Prince's name" that precedes it, had been written down with no signature or a signature with sharps in it. In that case the "theme of the Prince's name" here would have made its first appearance a half step higher, that is, in the same D Major in which it reappears at the beginning and end of Act III.

15. ENO Guide no. 27, p. 21; van Aalst more correctly had called it a hymn "sung in honour of Confucius."

16. *EGP*, ltr 231. The text Puccini eventually received, interestingly enough, begins with what happens to be a translation of the words for the four-note opening in van Aalst: "dà zài kǒng zǔ" means "O gran Koung-tzè" ("O great Confucius!" or more literally "How great is Confucius!"). This is surely a not improbable coincidence, however, for the rest of the text has nothing in common with the Chinese text or with its use as reported by van Aalst.

    The four measures of the "Hymn to Confucius" will have been added to the cortège for the Prince of Persia after the initial composition of the number: on 22 May 1921 Puccini was "starting on the Moon and the Funeral march," on 7 June he was "at the phantoms" and had done the Prince's and Liù's arias (see the quotations from these letters in Chapter III), yet as of 21 June he had still to see the van Aalst booklet.

17. In Puccini's fair-copy pencil autograph, Turandot's questioning echo of Liù's "Amore" was added later, in black ink and in a hand not quite like Puccini's. As with so many small but often very meaningful alterations in autographs or proof sheets from the late 19th century on, this is as likely to be the result of a telephoned instruction as it is of an instruction in person or a written instruction now lost.

18. The parallel seventh chords in the accompaniment to the two appearances of the main f♯-minor melody of Turandot's aria are a different manifestation in that piece of the Dissonance *tinta* (rh II.44 + 2, rh II.46 + 2, and see Example 19 in Chapter I).

19. "Avverto il M° Zuccoli che bisogna trasportare un [1/2] tono sotto tutto il finale primo, perchè così com'è [è] troppo acuto. Ma non è una cosa difficile perchè da Mi [naturale] si porta a Mi bemolle."

20. For contrasted interpretations of another piece transposed a half-step down from draft to final form, see James Hepokoski, "Verdi's Composition of *Otello*: The Act II Quartet," in *Analyzing Opera*, ed. Carolyn Abbate and Roger Parker (Berkeley, 1989), 125–49, in which Hepokoski discusses a surviving B-major draft of the quartet and the final version in B♭ major. On pp. 145–49 Hepokoski points out first the purely practical reason for the transposition (the high b″ just before the end was not good in Pantaleoni's voice); then he suggests two very different and equally valid musico-dramatic sets of associations for the quartet in the large: one of the original B-major conception; the other of the transposed B♭-major version we actually have.

21. See Frits Noske, "The musical figure of death," Chapter 8 of his *The Signifier and the Signified* (The Hague, 1977), for a stimulating account of the evolution of the ominous funeral-march *topos*; his interpretations of occurrences of this *topos* in Verdi's operas, however, are literal-minded—according to him it must *always* signify death in some way—and some are thereby very far-fetched.

22. The dominant appears twice in succession at the very end of Liù's cortège, on the last count of the measure just before Example 37-B, and again just before the concluding anapaestic e♭-minor tonic triads; its other appearance is at the climax of Timur's first solo episode, at "L'anima offesa ti vendicherà" (rh III.31 + 8–9).

23. Puccini's similar avoidance of the dominant until the very end of Liù's "Tanto amore segreto" has been noted above; there, as in the cortèges of Acts I and III, it results in a pseudo-modal coloring, which contributes to the wistful tone of

Liù's major-mode "musichetta di sapore cinese" as it does to the mournful tone of the two minor-mode cortèges. Puccini's technique of avoiding dominant and emphasizing pre-dominant harmonies is put to a dramatic, as opposed to coloristic, use in the Enigma scene, as discussed in Chapter V below. For a brief discussion of Puccini's predilection for pre-dominant harmonies, with a somewhat different bias, see Roger Parker, "Analysis: Act I [of *Tosca*] in Perspective," Chapter 10 of Mosco Carner, ed., *Giacomo Puccini: Tosca* (Cambridge, 1985), 130.

24. In Puccini's fair-copy autograph in the Ricordi archives, moreover, no vocal response is indicated for either the crowd or the Prince after Liù's suicide, so that Timur's "Liù! Liù! Sorgi!" might well have been the first words heard after Liù's final "per non vederlo più."

CHAPTER V

1. The Grand Duet of the Italian Romantic *melodramma* may be regarded as the paradigmatic model—speaking not historically but synchronically and analytically—for the nineteenth-century aria scene and internal Finale as well. Aria scenes, however, seldom have a kinetic movement before the first static movement, and the preparatory music and action before the first kinetic movement of a medial Finale is often quite elaborate. For a full discussion, with references to earlier literature, see Harold Powers, " 'La solita forma' and 'The Uses of Convention,' " *Acta musicologica* 59 (1987), 65–90. The terms "kinetic" and "static" were first advanced by Philip Gossett in "The 'Candeur Virginale' of 'Tancredi,' " *The Musical Times* 112 (1971), 327.

2. The Rigoletto-Sparafucile duet in *Rigoletto* Act I would be an early instance of a completely free-standing "dialogue duet," where the other duets in *Rigoletto* are "ensemble duets." In a discussion of the Rigoletto-Sparafucile duet in Abramo Basevi, *Studio sulle opere di Giuseppe Verdi* (Florence, 1859), 119, the distinction between that duet and "la solita forma de' duetti"—the standard four-movement "ensemble duet"—is clearly drawn. There are many examples in Verdi's operas of manipulated "ensemble duets," as well as a certain number of "dialogue duets"; the two types reach their apotheoses in the Otello-Desdemona duets in Acts I and III, respectively, of *Otello*.

3. At the beginning of Act III of *Un ballo in maschera*, however, Amelia and Renato are alone on stage in the challenge-and-response sequence that prepares "Morrò, ma prima in grazia"—unusual in that a solo aria is prepared by a lyric movement—as are King Philip and his Queen in the similar confrontation over her jewel case in Act IV of the 1867 *Don Carlos*. The musical settings, however, are repetitions at sequentially shifted tonal levels in the typical challenge-and-response manner.

4. Puccini's letter of 7 June 1921 to Simoni (*CP*, ltr 799, p. 506) is quoted in Chapter III, p. 71.

5. The most obvious trace of interpolations in the fair-copy autograph is at this point, now the juncture between the Ministers' *fuori-scena* (II.A) and the Processional music (II.B). Ricordi had printed up some special staff paper for Puccini to use in scoring *Turandot*, in the form of elephant bifolios with instrumental staves already labeled plus seven unlabeled staves for vocal and choral parts. The Ministers' *fuori-scena* is scored on 18 bifolios plus a single (cut) sheet whose *verso* is only half filled; at that point mid-page, an "al segno" indicator is cued

over to the beginning of the next bifolio, which is right where the Processional music begins in the pit orchestra, at rh II.26.

6. Traces in the autograph orchestral score of the junctures where "In questa reggia" was grafted in are less obvious but more intriguing. The clearer instance is at the end. The Enigma theme at Turandot's "Straniero, ascolta!"—her first words in the original long Act I libretto that Puccini set in spring–summer of 1921—also begins a bifolio, and the music for the first few measures of the preparatory modulating transition (rh II.49), which connects into the Enigma scene from the preceding ensemble epilogue in A♭ Major on the "Mai nessun m'avrà" melody, is not the same in the autograph and the engraved score. Unfortunately no relevant external document is known—nothing comparable with Puccini's letter regarding the transposition of the Act I Finale (*CP*, ltr 884, p. 548)—to authenticate the version in the engraved score, or to confirm our belief that the differences in the two versions of the transition have to do with the compositional grafting in of "In questa reggia."

   Any speculation about the fair-copy autograph and the juncture for "In questa reggia" at its beginning is necessarily tied in with the question of whether the reprise of the Children's chorus—for which (as noted in Chapter III) there is text neither in the original nor the final libretto—was part of Puccini's composition of the long Act I. The autograph at that reprise, as at the reprise of the Mandarin's proclamation, has annotations and changes that show Puccini returning to the passages after they had been fully scored, and all those changes were incorporated into the engraved score.

   Further investigation of this (and several other such points) would require more time with the autograph than is normally possible under the combination of Ricordi's eminently reasonable security concerns and the monstrous size of the volumes.

7. Two other instances of reductive "liquidation of the motive" have been illustrated and discussed earlier: see Example 6 in Chapter I and p. 109, and Example 32 above and pp. 90–93.

8. The typical tenor's preference for the optional high c″ in this phrase is understandable but doubly deplorable in that, by canceling out the carefully prepared musical effect, it also obliterates the crucial dramatic point. One can hear this moment at its glorious best in the 1959 Nilsson-Bjoerling recording (RCA VLS 03970), as well as in the 1937 Cigna-Merli recording (Cetra CC 2066/2081, 78 rpm, remastered at 33 rpm as Cetra LPO 2028).

9. "(October 1921) I think the central nub [*nocciolo*] is the duet. And the duet as it is doesn't seem to me what is wanted. In the duet I think we can work up a high pitch of emotion. And to do that I think Calàf must *kiss* Turandot and reveal his great love to the icy Princess" (*EGP*, ltr 196).

   "(25 March 1924) . . . when the heart speaks, whether it be in China or Holland, the sense is all the same and the purpose [*finalità*] is that of all people" (*CP*, ltr 892).

10. Jürgen Maehder, "Studien zum Fragmentcharakter von Giacomo Puccinis *Turandot*," *Analecta musicologica* 22 (1984), 297–379; "Studi sul carattere di frammento della *Turandot* di Giacomo Puccini," *Quaderni pucciniani* 2 (1985), 79–163; "Puccini's *Turandot*: A Fragment," English National Opera Guide no. 27 (London and New York, 1984), 35–53.

11. See for example Mosco Carner's entry on Puccini in *The New Grove* 15 (1980),

436, or the reprint in *The New Grove Masters of Italian Opera* (New York and London, 1983), 337.

12. "Ho delle idee in cuore duetto. L'attacco non lo cambio se non mi si propone qualcosa di meglio" (*EGP*, ltr 234).

13. In Act II this conclusion is followed immediately at rh II.49 by the ten-measure transition to the Enigma scene.

14. Both of Alfano's passages of music for the kiss, composed without guidance of continuity drafts, are his own composition. In his initial composition, moreover, he used only part of Puccini's draft for the preparation of the kiss. He kept the three measures of the "Mai nessun m'avrà" music in C major from folio 10ᵛ for the beginning; he also kept the melodic *motivo* of "Gli enigmi sono tre, una è la vita" from 11ᵛ for the Prince's words "[Il] bacio tuo mi dà l'eternità" at the end of the preparation, but he followed neither Puccini's bass nor its implicit harmonization. The four measures remaining, in the middle of the preparation, are entirely his own, though they start from Puccini's E-major triad at "Non mi toccar, straniero."

In Alfano's first composition of the duet the instrumental music for the kiss itself comprises 8 measures of a highly dissonant development, transformation, and breakdown of the "Mai nessun m'avrà" music—they may be seen in Example 5 of Maehder, "Studien zum Fragmentcharakter" and/or "Studi sul carattere"—followed by a four-measure sustained extension founded on the c–g♭ diminished fifth. Alfano's approach to the kiss music is appropriate in choice of subject, but in its harmonic idiom it seems highly discordant with what appears to have been Puccini's intent for the treatment of that subject. In the very much shorter second version of the duet forced upon him by Toscanini and the Ricordi directors, Alfano took over the whole of Puccini's draft preparation for the kiss (rh III.38 to rh III.38 + 9); for the kiss music itself he kept only the first (still highly discordant) measure of his original treatment and followed it with two measures of *fortissimo* low E and a *Generalpause* to conclude. Of his original ten measures for Turandot's first verbal reaction to the Prince's kiss Alfano kept an adjusted version of the last five.

15. In Chapter I we have noted and deplored the occasional omission of this aria in performance, above all in the videotape of the 1983 Arena di Verona production.

16. Jürgen Maehder has proposed that Alfano's two compositions for the duet and final scene be conflated, preserving the second version, containing most of Puccini's continuity draft, up to the measure before the instrumental kiss music— rh III.38 + 10—and shifting over to the first version from there to the end (Maehder, "Studien zum Fragmentcharakter," 350). We share Maehder's view in principle, but would prefer to merge the versions a little differently, avoiding on the one hand Alfano's music for the kiss as being out of harmony with Puccini's evident idea of its harmonic idiom, and retaining on the other hand Puccini's music for the Prince's revelation of his name. Thus, we would begin with the second version and continue through to Turandot's "la mia gloria è finita," which is the same in both versions. From there we would make junctures at two existing deceptive cadences. We would turn to Alfano's first composition from "La mia glorie è finita" up to and on through the penultimate measure of "Del primo pianto" (just before rh III.46 in the suppressed piano-vocal score). For the last chord of "Del primo pianto" we would turn back to the second composition (one measure before rh III.46 in the current scores) and continue on through the Prince's revelation of his name up to just before his high b♭' on the

word "[Ca]-làf" (one measure after rh III.48 in the current scores). In the suppressed piano-vocal score this bb' is reached at the third measure before rh III.47; beginning from that measure we would continue with Alfano's first composition on through to the end of the opera.

CHAPTER VI

1. Stroppa made his debut at La Scala with his designs for the production of *Madama Butterfly* given on 29 November 1925, the first anniversary of Puccini's death. Astonishingly, this was only the second performance of this work at La Scala; following its resounding rejection at the *prima* of the first version on 17 February 1904, Puccini had refused to allow it to be given there again as long as he lived.

2. The meeting in Paris occurred when Puccini was there for the French première of *Gianni Schicchi* at the Opéra-Comique (6 November 1922).

3. The Italian "secessionist" painter Galileo Chini (1873–1956) taught decorative arts at the Accademia di Belle Arti in Florence; he had designed the setting for *Gianni Schicchi* at the European première (Rome, January 1919).

4. Franco Alfano (1876–1954) failed with his first opera, *Miranda* (1896). His reputation was established by *Risurrezione* (Turin, 1904). His other best-known works up to the time of his participation in *Turandot* were *L'ombra di Don Giovanni* (1914) and especially *La leggenda di Sakùntala* (1921).

5. Maehder: "Fragmentcharakter," 328–37; "Studi sul carattere,"107–15; summarized in ENO Guide, 46–48.

6. There are a few recordings of *Turandot* sung by members of the original cast. Neither Raisa nor Fleta left any souvenirs of their Turandot and Calàf, but Maria Zamboni (1895–1976) recorded Liù's aria "Signore, ascolta!" and suicide "Tu che di gel sei cinta" (on English Columbia D-1572, recorded c. 1927). The original Pong (Giuseppe Nessi, 1887–1961) and Pang (Emilio Venturini, 1878–1952) are joined by Aristide Baracchi (1885–1964) as Ping—Baracchi had sung the Mandarin in the first-night cast—in two records that between them give a complete performance (with one short customary cut) of the *fuori-scena* of the Ministers (the opening section is found on both records). A 10″ disc (issued in England as Columbia D-1663) contains the first two sections, while a 12″ disc (issued as Parlophone R-20056) gives the opening and then jumps to the concluding portion of the scene.

7. Letter in the archives of the Metropolitan Opera House, Lincoln Center, New York.

8. A modern edition of the surviving *Disposizioni sceniche* for the Verdi operas is under way at Ricordi, under the general editorship of Francesco Degrada. James Hepokoski's edition of the last surviving of these, for *Otello*, is imminently expected; the first one was for *Un ballo in maschera*, to be edited by David Rosen. (The first production book actually published by Ricordi was for *Giovanna da Guzman*, but that was simply a translation from the Paris production book for *Les vêpres siciliennes* from which Verdi got the idea that Ricordi should also provide production books.)

9. The typescript of Forzano's *disposizione scenica* for *Turandot* is in the Ricordi archives; we are grateful to them for permission to translate from it. A note at the beginning of the document points out that "left" and "right" are from the point of view of the spectator, not of the character on stage.

10. Before the entrance of the Ministers, Forzano had Timur place himself between his son and the gong so as to keep the Prince away from it.

11. Forzano directed that the lights should come up for the final tableau at rh III.51.

12. See William Ashbrook, "*Turandot* and Its Posthumous *prima*," *The Opera Quarterly* 2, no. 3 (Autumn, 1984), 126–31, for further discussion of Forzano's *disposizione scenica*.

13. The 1983 production of *Turandot* at the Arena di Verona—now available on videotape—remained reasonably faithful to the directions of Forzano's production book. The vast stage space available at the Arena helped avoid the impression of overcrowding in the two scenes at the Emperor's court.

14. See Jürgen Maehder, "Puccini's *Turandot*: A Fragment," in ENO Guide no. 27; pp. 42–43 and 48.

15. Puccini's experience with La Scala replicated Verdi's of six decades earlier: between 1845 (*Giovanna d'Arco*) and 1869 (the revised *La forza del destino*) Verdi allowed no premières at the house that, he repeatedly complained, skimped on casting, rehearsal, mise-en-scène, and everything else he deemed essential to the successful launching of a new opera.

16. Della Corte's "The will of Turandot" is of course the motive we have called the Execution motive, heard in the first three measures of the opera.

17. Portions of Della Corte's review are quoted in *CP*, pp. 564–65; some of these excerpts as well as some others are quoted in *Musica d'oggi* 8, no. 5 (May 1926); our translations from this and other reviews are after these two secondary sources.

18. Loewenberg's *Annals of Opera* gives the Dresden date as 4 July 1926, but German sources give the correct date of 6 September 1926. The delay was caused by the late arrival of Brüggemann's translation at Ricordi for its inclusion in the Italian-German vocal scores.

19. The March 1926 date can be inferred from the Library of Congress copy of the edition containing Alfano I, marked "Received, 7 April 1926." Since this was before the days of transatlantic airmail, a mailing date in March is probable.

20. Roselle's "Die ersten Tränen" ("Del primo pianto") was recorded in 1928 on Grammophon 66744 (matrix 880bm), and is included on Preiser LV-77, an LP anthology of Roselle recordings. Lehmann's version dates from February 1927, with an orchestra conducted by Fritz Zweig; it originally appeared on Odeon 0-8720 (matrix xxB 7610), later reissued on an EMI LP entitled: *Lotte Lehmann 2: Die Lyriken der Gesangkunst*. This information was first brought out a number of years ago by Gordon Smith, who eventually discussed his findings in "Alfano and 'Turandot,' " *Opera*, 1973.

21. Cecil Hopkinson, *Bibliography of the Works of Giacomo Puccini* (New York, 1968), p. 53. Much of the following discussion of the possible performance of the two Alfano endings is based upon this work. See particularly pp. 52–54 (the bibliographical description of the *Turandot* scores); p. 68 (Appendix C—Number of Performances at Leading Opera Houses); and pp. 69–70 (Appendix D—Dates of Plate Numbers for Puccini Scores).

22. Hopkinson seems to contradict himself, for he says on p. 53 that this edition "did not appear until about June 1930," yet the May 1926 date on the Library of Congress copy of the edition is given, also on p. 53. This edition is identified as 12 B (*b*).

23. Hopkinson, p. 53.

NOTES TO PAGES 158–63

24. The copy of *Turandot* in the Hochschule für Musik with an accession date of June 1930 contains 384 pages, a sure sign of Alfano II.
25. Attwood's career at the Metropolitan never lived up to the opportunity afforded her at her debut. The following season her place as Liù was taken by Nanette Guilford.
26. From Olin Downes's review of the première, reprinted in Seltsam, *Metropolitan Opera Annals* (New York, 1947), 466–67.
27. Henderson's phrases are quoted in Irving Kolodin's *The Metropolitan Opera 1883–1966* (New York, 1966), 335.
28. Giacomo Lauri-Volpi, *Voci parallele* (Rome, 1955), 79.
29. These comments appear on p. 10 of the booklet accompanying *Eva Turner: Arias from Italian Opera*, Angel COLC 114, part of the "Great Recordings of the Century" series.
30. Cetra CC 2066–2081; technical reconstruction reissued on LP as Cetra LPO 2028.
31. Anne Roselle having been the first German Turandot and Georges Thill the first Paris Calàf, the juxtaposition of these two singers in an early Italian production nicely illustrates the international thrust of this score from the very outset.
32. In the interim New York had seen some performances of *Turandot* in a well-conceived if necessarily somewhat undernourished production by the New York City Center Opera.
33. We have also noted with sorrow that Turandot's final aria "Del primo pianto" does not appear on that videotape.

REFERENCES

❧

A: PUCCINI'S *TURANDOT*

1: Libretto

Adami, Giuseppe, and Renato Simoni: *Turandot: Dramma lirica in tre atti e cinque quadri* (Milan, 1926).

2: Scores

Puccini, Giacomo: *Turandot*, orchestral study score, Ricordi pl. no. P.R. 117.
———: *Turandot*, piano-vocal score, Ricordi pl. no. 121329 (with Alfano II).
———: *Turandot*, piano-vocal score, Ricordi pl. no. 119772 (with Alfano I).

3: Early Recordings

Puccini, Giacomo: *Turandot*, Cetra CC 2066–2081 (recorded in 1937): Gina Cigna (Turandot), Francesco Merli (the unknown Prince), Magda Olivero (Liù), Afro Poli (Ping), etc., conducted by Franco Ghione; reissued on LP as Cetra LPO 2028.
"Signore, ascolta!" / "Tu che di gel sei cinta" sung by Maria Zamboni (1895–1976), English Columbia D-1572, recorded c. 1927.
"Olà Pang! Olà Pong!" (II.A, *fuori-scena* of the Ministers), sung by Aristide Baracchi, Giuseppe Nessi, and Emilio Venturini: English Columbia D-1663 (10"; opening *scena*, II.A.1 and 2) and Parlophone R-20056 (12"; opening *scena* II.A.3 and 4).
"Die ersten Tränen" ("Del primo pianto"), sung by Anne Roselle (soprano), Grammophon 66744 (matrix 880bm recorded in 1928), reissued on Preiser LV-77 (LP anthology of Roselle recordings).
———: sung by Lotte Lehmann (soprano), Odeon o–8720 (matrix xxB 7610 recorded February 1927), reissued on *Lotte Lehmann 2: Die Lyriken der Gesangkunst* (EMI LP anthology).

4: Reviews, Letters, Biography

Adami, Giuseppe, ed.: *Epistolario Giacomo Puccini* (Milan, 1928; 2d ed. Milan, 1958; 3d ed. Milan, 1982) [*EGP*].
———: *Il romanzo della vita di Giacomo Puccini* (Milan, 1942) [*RVGP*].
Gara, Eugenio, ed.: *Carteggi pucciniani* (Milan, 1958) [*CP*].
Musica d'oggi 8, no. 5 (May, 1926).
Paladini, Carlo: *Giacomo Puccini* (Florence, 1961).
Puccini, Simonetta, ed.: *Giacomo Puccini: Lettere a Riccardo Schnabl* (Milan, 1981) [*LRS*].
Seligman, Vincent: *Puccini Among Friends* (New York, 1938) [*PAF*].

5: Secondary Literature

Ashbrook, William: "*Turandot* and Its Posthumous *prima*," *The Opera Quarterly* 2, no. 3, (Autumn, 1984).

Carner, Mosco: "The Score," in *Turandot/Puccini*, English National Opera Guide no. 27 (London and New York, 1984), 19–34.

Celli, Teodoro: "Gli abbozzi per 'Turandot,' " *Quaderni pucciniani* 2 (1985), 43–65 (updated reprint from 1951 La Scala program book).

Girardi, Michele: " 'Turandot': Il futuro interrotto del melodramma italiano," *Rivista italiana di musicologia* 17 (1982), 155–79.

———: "Puccini verso l'opera incompiuta: Osservazioni sulla partitura di *Turandot* e sul teatro musicale del suo tempo," in the *Programma di Sala* of the *Gran teatro La Fenice*, season of 1987–88, 7–28.

Lo, Kii-Ming: *Turandot auf der Opernbühne* (Heidelberg dissertation, 1988).

Maehder, Jürgen: "Studien zum Fragmentcharakter von Giacomo Puccinis *Turandot*," *Analecta musicologica* 22 (1984), 297–379; abridged as "Puccini's *Turandot*: A Fragment," English National Opera Guide no. 27 (London and New York, 1984), 35–53; in Italian as "Studi sul carattere di frammento della *Turandot* di Giacomo Puccini," *Quaderni pucciniani* 2 (1985), 79–163. [A preliminary version appears as "La trasformazione interrotta della Principessa: Studi sul contributo di Franco Alfano alla partitura di 'Turandot,' " *Esotismo e colore locale nell'opera di Puccini*: Atti del I° convegno internazionale sull'opera di Giacomo Puccini, Torre del Lago, 1983, ed. Jürgen Maehder (Pisa, 1985), 143–70.]

Smith, Gordon: "Alfano and 'Turandot,' " *Opera* (1973).

Snook, Lynn: "In Search of the Riddle Princess Turandot," *Esotismo e colore locale nell'opera di Puccini*: Atti del I° convegno internazionale sull'opera di Giacomo Puccini, Torre del Lago, 1983, ed. Jürgen Maehder (Pisa, 1985), 131–41.

B: *TURANDOT* BEFORE PUCCINI

1: Sources

Busoni, Ferruccio: *Turandot* (Leipzig, 1918 and Wiesbaden, 1946).

Gazzoletti, A[ntonio]: *Turanda: Azione fantastica in quattro parti . . . musica di A[ntonio] Bazzini (Milan, 1867)*.

Gozzi, Carlo: *Fiabe* (Venice, 1805).

Schiller, Friedrich: *Turandot*, ed. Karl S. Güthke (Stuttgart, 1960).

2: Secondary Literature

Dent, Edward J.: *Ferruccio Busoni* (London, 1933; 2d ed. 1966).

Warrack, John: *Carl Maria von Weber* (Cambridge, 1976).

C: PUCCINI IN GENERAL

Ashbrook, William: *The Operas of Puccini* (New York, 1968; 2d ed., Ithaca, 1985).

Carner, Mosco: "Puccini (5)," *The New Grove Dictionary of Music and Musicians* 15 (1980), 431–40.

Girardi, Michele: *Puccini: La vita e l'opera* (Rome, 1989).

Hopkinson, Cecil: *Bibliography of the Works of Giacomo Puccini* (New York, 1968).

Kaye, Michael: *The Unknown Puccini* (New York and Oxford, 1987).

REFERENCES

Parker, Roger: "Analysis: Act I [of *Tosca*] in Perspective," Chapter 10 *Giacomo Puccini: Tosca*, ed. Mosco Carner (Cambridge, 1985).

D: Italian Opera

1: General

Maehder, Jürgen: "The Origins of Italian *Literaturoper*," in *Reading Opera*, ed. Arthur Groos and Roger Parker (Princeton, 1988), 92–128.
Tedeschi, Rubens: *Addio fiorito asil* (Milan, 1978).
Weaver, William: *The Golden Century of Italian Opera: From Rossini to Puccini* (London and New York, 1980).

2: Beginnings

Bianconi, Lorenzo, and Thomas Walker: "Production, Consumption and Political Function of Seventeenth-Century Italian Opera," *Early Music History* 4 (1984), 209–96.
Powers, Harold: *"L'Erismena* travestita," *Studies in Music History: Essays for Oliver Strunk* (Princeton, 1968), 259–324.

3: Rossini

Gossett, Philip: "The 'Candeur Virginale' of 'Tancredi,' " *The Musical Times* 112 (1971), 326–29.

4: Verdi

Baldini, Gabriele: *Abitare la battaglia* (Milan, 1970), translated by Roger Parker as *The Story of Giuseppe Verdi* (Cambridge, 1980).
Basevi, Abramo: *Studio sulle opere di Giuseppe Verdi* (Florence, 1859).
Budden, Julian: *The Operas of Verdi* 1 (London and New York, 1973).
Cesari, G., and A. Luzio: *I copialettere di Giuseppe Verdi* (Milan, 1913).
Hepokoski, James: "Verdi's Composition of *Otello*: The Act II Quartet," in *Analyzing Opera*, ed. Carolyn Abbate and Roger Parker (Berkeley, 1989), 125–49.
Luzio, A.: *Carteggi verdiani* 1 (Rome, 1935).
Noske, Frits: *The Signifier and the Signified: Studies in the Operas of Mozart and Verdi* (The Hague, 1977).
Powers, Harold: " 'La solita forma' and 'The Uses of Convention,' " *Acta musicologica* 59 (1987), 65–90.

5: Anecdotal

De Rensis, Rafaello: *Franco Faccio e Verdi: Carteggi e documenti inediti* (Milan, 1934).
Lauri-Volpi, Giacomo: *Voci parallele* (Rome, 1955).
Rasponi, Lanfranco: *The Last Prima Donnas* (New York, 1982).
Turner, Eva: [liner notes for] *Arias from Italian Opera*, Angel COLC 114.

6: Reference

Kolodin, Irving: *The Metropolitan Opera 1883–1966: A Candid History* (New York, 1966).
Loewenberg, Alfred: *Annals of Opera* (3d ed. 1978).
Seltsam, William H.: *Metropolitan Opera Annals* (New York, 1947).

E: Miscellaneous

Redfield, Robert: "The Social Organization of Tradition," in his *Peasant Society and Culture* (Chicago, 1956), 67–104; revised in *The Far Eastern Quarterly* 15 (1955), 13–21.
Singer, Milton: "Search for a Great Tradition in Cultural Performances," in his *When a Great Tradition Modernizes* (New York, 1972), 67–80.

INDEX

❖

(Titles of works are listed under their composers or authors)